DOING BETTER
THE NEXT REVOLUTION IN ETHICS

DOING BETTER

THE NEXT REVOLUTION IN ETHICS

BY

TAD DUNNE

MARQUETTE
UNIVERSITY
PRESS

MARQUETTE STUDIES IN PHILOSOPHY
NO. 68
ANDREW TALLON, SERIES EDITOR

LIBRARY OF CONGRESS CATALOGING-IN-PUBLICATION DATA
Dunne, Tad, 1938-
Doing better : the next revolution in ethics / Tad Dunne.
p. cm. — (Marquette studies in philosophy ; no. 68)
Includes bibliographical references and index.
ISBN-13: 978-0-87462-766-4 (pbk. : alk. paper)
ISBN-10: 0-87462-766-4 (pbk. : alk. paper)
1. Ethics. 2. Lonergan, Bernard J. F. I. Title.
BJ1012.D86 2010
170—dc22
2010000578

©2010 Marquette University Press
Milwaukee, Wisconsin 53201-3141
All rights reserved.
www.marquette.edu/mupress/

FOUNDED 1916

♾ The paper used in this publication meets the minimum requirements of the American National Standard for Information Sciences— Permanence of Paper for Printed Library Materials, ANSI Z39.48-1992.

Association of American University Presses

MARQUETTE UNIVERSITY PRESS
MILWAUKEE

The Association of Jesuit University Presses

CONTENTS

PREFACE

Why is there so much disagreement on how to do better? A fundamental reason is that our methods of moral reflection are deficient. This is true of our everyday decisions as well as the ethical reflections of experts. In the present work, I invite you to discover for yourself the basic norms that affect all moral reflection as well as the several ways we disobey these norms. This invitation follows the generalized empirical method of Bernard Lonergan, in which the empirical methods of modern science are generalized to incorporate the data of consciousness. The discovery in your own consciousness of what happens when you make moral judgments will provide a foundation on which to build comprehensive models of morality, of key ethical categories, and of collaboration among ethicists. We will close with some implications for human studies, international relations, and education. An appendix gives 31 ethical categories defined in the style of a generalized empirical method.

My abiding gratitude goes out to many people who helped me understand method in ethics and write about it. But here I want to mention especially Joseph Wulftange, SJ, who introduced me to Lonergan's *Insight*; to Bernard Lonergan, SJ, who patiently listened to my questions and lovingly encouraged me to trust them; to Frederick Crowe, SJ, who directed my doctoral dissertation on Lonergan's social theory; to Colin Maloney, whose questions helped me understand how to integrate faith and learning; to Richard Wroblewski, whose persistent inquiries into the progress of this book was an encouragement all along the way; to Henry Toenjes, whose proofreading helped me shorten and simplify the manuscript; and to the gem of my heart, my wife, Dorothy Seebaldt, for her proofreading, her encouragement, and, above all, her heart.

1. INTRODUCTION

METHOD IN ETHICS

A mong ethicists today, there are many conflicting opinions about what is better and what is worse. Where these differences seem unresolvable, the conflicts can usually be traced to different approaches or, to be exact, to conflicting methods in ethics.

Can these conflicts about method be overcome? The natural sciences—physics, chemistry, biology—owe their fantastic success largely to a method that everyone accepts and whose results keep on coming. Can ethics do the same? Might we some day converge on a method that is significantly more effective in making our lives better? If we can, it will certainly require a revolution in human studies[1] as comprehensive as the revolution in the natural sciences and far more important for the quality of our lives.

Of course, there is a huge difference between the "nature" studied in the natural sciences and the "humanity" studied in the human studies. In nature, things are predictable; surprises are rare. But humanity is continually surprising. We are creative. We come up with unprecedented ideas about living well together. We develop sciences, laws, societies, technologies, and economies that make living far more efficient for millions of people. Our creativity is also moral. Through the arts, judicial systems, humanities education, philosophy, and religion, we provide moral guidelines to individuals and to our social institutions. It is a distinguishing characteristic of our species that we are driven by a creative desire to do better.

On the other hand, we also violate our creativity. We can suppress our own ingenuity when it comes to benefiting others more than ourselves. We can deliberately act against what we know is better. With every change in laws, politics, technology, or the economy, we tend to exploit new opportunities to benefit ourselves at others' expense. Nor do the arts, the judiciary, the humanities, philosophy or religion easily maintain high moral standards. These voices of culture are no less susceptible to the temptations of money, praise, and power.

This combination of high moral desire and low moral achievement sets the field of ethics above the field of the natural sciences. If an ethics is going to be effective, its method ought to clarify what the ultimate creative sources of our moral opinions really are and clarify exactly how we violate those sources. The more clearly ethicists uncover our basic moral sources and the dysfunctions to which they are prone, the better the chances for discerning between the really better and the really worse in human affairs—both what we know about our past and in what we propose for our future. These clarifications would not be abstract; they would regard concrete situations. Nor would they be solitary pursuits; they would be conducted in an open forum, where the roots of high moral desire and low moral achievement will be laid bare for the examination of ethicists working together. In two words, an effective method in ethics must be both *critical* and *collaborative.*

While the critical feature of method makes ethics unlike anything in the natural sciences, methods in the natural sciences have two features that an ethics needs to take into account. One is that a framework for understanding moral process must *account for moral development.* Just as the natural sciences rely on evolution to explain the emergence of new species, so ethics needs a way to explain both moral progress and moral decline, not only in the life of the individual but also in the histories of communities of any size, from friendships to neighborhoods to religions to civilizations. A second requirement is that moral assessments disclose the full experimental data on which these assessments are based. Just as empirical verification is the ground of any consensus about the processes of nature, so too is it the ground of any moral consensus.

To establish a critical method in ethics that accounts for development and collectively verifies its findings in data, we need to push theoretical understanding beyond its familiar territory bounded by what we can see, hear, smell, taste or touch. To understand morality, we need to explore the inner data on our processes of moral reflection. Specifically, we need to examine our direct experiences of feeling, imagining, noticing, symbol-making, language-forming, questioning, understanding, conceptualizing, formulating positions, weighing evidence, verifying, asserting, weighing options, making decisions, making commitments, and falling in love. Experiences like these belong to the data of consciousness—the locale where moral events occur in raw form—but their verification relies on the collaboration of many.

GENERALIZED EMPIRICAL METHOD

Because this approach generalizes the notion of data to include the data of consciousness, it has been named a "generalized empirical method"[2] by its chief proponent, Bernard Lonergan (d. 1984). In a major work, *Insight: A Study of Human Understanding*, Lonergan leads the reader to discover, first-hand, what actually happens when he or she learns anything. Lonergan distinguishes the different modes of learning proper to common sense, to aesthetics, to mathematics, to the natural sciences, to the human sciences, to hermeneutics, to historical scholarship, to metaphysics, to philosophy, and to theology. He helps the reader identify quite exactly what kind of knowledge each mode of learning can and cannot provide.

Throughout his works, Lonergan consistently sets his analyses of human studies in the context of an evolutionary view of the universe. For him, what is good is not an abstract quality of things or events. It is an appearance in history of some thing or event that actual people deem good. This appearance of a subjectively recognized objective good is neither predetermined nor purely random. It occurs under certain probabilities which may be heightened or diminished. Such an evolutionary perspective can provide ethics with a framework for tracking the moral progress or decline of an individual or a culture.

Over the past half-century, many people relied on this generalized empirical method in their respective disciplines. Hundreds of books and doctoral dissertations dealing directly with this approach appeared since Lonergan first published *Insight* in 1957. As of this writing, the University of Toronto Press has published over half of Lonergan's works in a projected 21-volume collection.

Under Lonergan's guidance, I became convinced that ethics must be considered a dimension of all human studies. It should hold a central place in psychology, sociology, cultural anthropology, and economics, to say nothing of its traditional home in philosophy and theology. Likewise ethical concerns should be evident in scholarly studies such as biography, textual interpretation, and history, as well as in the applied disciplines of counseling, social work, and pastoral care. I believe a revolution of this scope will occur only when ethicists overcome—primarily in themselves—certain fundamental ambiguities that impede genuine moral progress.

So what I will present here is not a new theory of ethics, let alone any personal opinion on specific moral issues. Nor will I directly engage other views on how ethics ought to be conducted. As I hope to make clear, the basis for any justification or criticism of any method lies ultimately in a personal exploration of what happens when we say X is better than Y. So I aim to present a guidebook for you, the reader, to explore the methods you actually use when you develop ethical theories and make moral judgments. No doubt, you already understand a great deal about morality. I aim to lay out a model—for you to verify—that incorporates in a single perspective both the origins and pitfalls of moral judgments.

At the end of this book, I will propose practical ways to hasten the revolution in ethics that looms on the horizon. On the assumption that others can make the same discoveries in themselves of what makes the difference between a good and a bad decision, I will sketch out a framework for collaboration. As you will see, this collaboration will incorporate a verification and ongoing correction of personal discoveries about inner, conscious events.

My primary purpose, then, is to rely on generalized empirical method to propose a method in ethics. My secondary purpose is to test the validity of a generalized empirical method itself by seeing how effectively it illuminates the moral realm. Partly to test the effectiveness of this approach, throughout this work I will draw on analyses of human systems worked out principally by Lonergan. In the endnotes you will find textual sources in Lonergan, but the sources of what I have to say here are not just texts; they are also my personal experiences. Not to give myself more credit than I deserve, I should clarify that I am referring to discoveries I made when I followed Lonergan's invitations in *his* texts, as well as to my integration of these discoveries in what I believe is a coherent, verifiable model of the moral realm. My own contribution is in large part pedagogical—relying on Lonergan's generalized empirical method to clarify what is needed for an effective method in ethics.

I also extend certain basic materials worked out by Lonergan. As Lonergan in *Insight* proposes exercises for noticing what we do when we understand, so I propose further exercises that reveal moral demands at all levels of consciousness. I also extend the classical notion of a static "good" into the dynamic notion of "better." I define the technical term "exigence" to account for human morality within an evolutionary perspective of world process. In the appendix, I define a few dozen technical categories related to ethics. I propose a comprehensive account of the role symbols play in moral reflection. I fill out the affective and moral aspects of the dialectical engagement Lonergan outlined for intellectual positions and counterpositions. I clarify how historical narratives complement the moral standards expressed in principles. And I draw out a number of practical implications of a revolution in ethics for human studies, for international relations, and for education.

If you want to explore more deeply some of Lonergan's analytical frameworks and invitations on which this book is based, notice that the endnotes begin with the key terms that relate to these frameworks and invitations, and are followed by references to Lonergan's more prominent treatments of these terms.

THE LENS OF BETTER

Our startup question is simple: What is moral progress?

The answer is not so simple. We want to explain moral progress in a way that all ethicists can agree on. Currently, the best framework we have for understanding any progress is the scientific idea of evolution. So let us start with an image. This image will set ethics in the scientific context of evolution by describing how our notion of "better" emerged.

Imagine a 1,000-page book on your lap. It is 3 inches thick, and there are 50 lines to a page. If the first character of the first word on the first page represents the Big Bang, and today represents the end of the book, on what page does Homo sapiens appear?

It takes an astoundingly long time. Although stars appear around page 60, earth, our home, is not formed until page 700. A few pages later, as if invited by a friendly atmosphere, prokaryotes emerge, the earliest form of life we know of. Now life takes off. Dinosaurs show up on page 985 and suddenly vanish on page 996.

Bipedal apes will be found on the very last page, halfway down at line 25. Seventeen lines later, their descendants make tools out of stone. At the first word on the bottom line, a mitochondrial Eve is born, the genetic mother of us all. It is in the middle of that last line, on that last page, that we place Homo sapiens. This is the first evidence we have of spoken words, funerals, and a northward migration out of Africa. At the ninth last character, someone painted a bison on a cave wall at Lascaux, France. At the fourth last character, dogs are domesticated, and people plant crops as an alternative to pitching spears at animals. At the second last character, spoken words are represented by written figures. Finally, within the .016-inch span of the final period, Abram leaves Ur, Plato writes *The Republic*, Jesus preaches God's loving forgiveness, Mohammed walks to Mecca, an apple falls on Newton's head, Neil Armstrong lays foot on the moon, and you and I showed up for our brief, forgettable scene.

The forces of evolution work by a process of trial and error in which there are innumerable trials and very nearly as many errors. And in that gap of *very nearly*, a success occasionally emerges, ordering otherwise random events into a higher system. Randomly emerging higher systems, in turn, mingle and churn until even higher systems of these systems emerge. In this way, despite the highly unlikely appearance of us, appear we did.

We might not have appeared, at least not yet. But here we are, the only beings we know of that can marvel over their own improbability. And given how quickly we are now learning about the universe, surely we would be rash to assume that there is nothing left to learn about ethics. We think of our arrival as a summit of a long, slow process of the universe improving. Evolutionary theorists believe their mission is to explain not just how things *change* but particularly how things *improve*. They acknowledge dead-ends, but without tears. They regard them as the random variations required by the natural selection process that ruthlessly terminates entities least fit for survival and successively produces higher systems out of otherwise unrelated lower systems. They dispassionately explain these higher systems as more complex and, at the same time, more effective in organizing their subordinate systems. And although many scientists are paranoid about moral judgments creeping into their investigations, universally, in their hearts, they believe that these higher systems are worth paying more attention to. Another term for this higher worth is *better*.

We can barely avoid the notion of *better*. It permeates our consciousness. Every day we say things like, "You better take Woodward Avenue. And you better bring your lunch." In quiet moments, when we contemplate our situation, we think of ourselves as fortunate, lucky and blessed—or unfortunate, unlucky and cursed. In any case, we see all of life, indeed everything in the universe, through a lens of better.

In ethics too, we do well to incorporate this evolutionary perspective. In an evolving universe, what we call *good* is either an improvement or an alternative to *worse*. The "good" suggests a static quality, while the "better" incorporates the dynamic processes by which anything we call "good" actually appears.

REVOLUTIONS IN ETHICS

Among the many better things that evolved, one most relevant to ethics is our ability to reflect on our choices. This ability appeared on our planet not in a sudden jump but with the gradual evolution of Homo sapiens along its several paths, including the many dead ends of earlier hominids. There have been real advances, as people with similar views set up the laws, the civic standards, and the alliances that improved their living together. But there have been horrendous dead-ends too. Hatred and retributions debilitated societies longer than anyone can remember. When everyone recognizes the better *when* it happens, they disagree on *how* and *why*. Moral philosophies galore lie comatose in history books. We have yet to develop a consistent and recognizably effective ethics. Some say it cannot be done; they give up trying. Others say it already has been done; but they convince very few. What is needed is a revolution in ethics, one as commonly accepted and even more practically effective as the Copernican revolution in astronomy.

Realms of Moral Reflection

To set the context for this revolution in ethics, we should first look at the different ways that people currently reflect on morality. Four distinct ways stand out. I do not mean that there are four distinct types of ethicists but rather that there seem to be four distinct *questions* that ethicists rely on, where each type of question carries distinct criteria for making moral judgments. We may identify each question as defining a unique realm³ of meaning related to moral reflection, keeping in mind that ethicists may reflect in one, some, or all all of these realms.

A first realm is directly concerned about action. "What should we do now?" "Should we fight or flee?" "Which path is better?" Where the actions of all other animals are unreflective *reactions*, we are the first animals to experience *questions* that occur between our perceiving and our acting. We question our options, our resources and our duties. These questions do not appear out of the blue; they are prompted by our symbolic representation of the sort of people we are and the sort of world we live in. Our images of our person, or family, or clan, or nation lay strong taboos and strong demands on our behavior. For the supernatural-minded, images of Heaven and Hell, angels and demons, ancient spirits and chthonic forces represent the perils of life in this world and the sacred rites necessary to protect ourselves. We can characterize this primeval realm of moral reflection by the appearance of *should* as in the question, "How should we act?"

A second realm is concerned about principles. In the fourth century BCE, Greek philosophers asked whether *should* is just a social convention that varies from culture to culture, or is a moral standard common to humans everywhere. Going with the common moral standard idea, they developed concepts of *natural right, justice, order, right/wrong,* and *virtue.* They proposed principles by which medicine should be administered and republics should be organized. This second realm may be characterized by the question, "What general *principles* best represent how *anyone* should act?"

A third realm is concerned about a culture's historical inheritance. A culture has always had power over a people's moral sense, but it was not until the last 50 years that the idea of culture underwent a profound transformation, from "culture" as the values that only civilized people have, to "culture" as whatever values any community has. So comments like, "She is such a cultured lady" are heard far less often than "She grew up in an oriental culture." Today, cultural anthropologists and historians study the unique attitudes of a society toward marriage, family, work, wealth, recreation, foreigners, and death. These attitudes are maintained chiefly through the symbols of ceremony, dress, architecture, and stories that strangers find strange. Anyone exposed to people of other cultures begins to wonder about the validity of his or her own views. This kind of reflection may be characterized by the question, "What specific values guide how people *in this culture* are expected to act?"

A fourth realm is about method. The power of principles to guide action goes only so far. Just as lawyers anticipate flexibility in civil laws regarding particular circumstances, so ethicists anticipate flexibility in universal moral principles to handle real situations. The power of historical analysis also leaves unanswered questions. There are limits imposed by available data; and there are challenges that historians themselves experience insofar as learning about the moral priorities of another culture raises new questions about their own. This helps explain why many contemporary philosophers suspend the project of promoting standard values for all cultures. It appears to them that each community must find its own way toward moral conviction. Both of these issues—the ineffectiveness of moral principles, and the relativism of morals based on social convention—raise the question of how to resolve differences in moral views. The answer to that question will be about method: an account of how anyone develops moral views. So the question that characterizes this fourth type of reflection is, "How do we create these symbols, principles, and cultural standards about how anyone should act, and by what criteria do we discern between a truly better and a truly worse?"

True, there are many communities whose members agree on explicit moral standards. But not all—perhaps very few—reach the deeper understanding of how their moral symbols, principles, and traditions were developed. Most lack the intellectual resources to refine their moral heritage to meet new circumstances. When new technologies or new hatreds arise (and when will they not?) and communities have no common understanding of how their principles were forged, things are more likely to get decided by the few who wield power than by the few who understand how their revered traditions originated and how prone they may be to corruption.

Stages of Ethics

The differences among these four realms of moral reflection define three revolutionary transformations[4] in ethics that can be dated within a century or so.

Revolution 1: Universal Moral Standards.

Early humans apparently lived in the realm of symbolic images about actions alone. I say "apparently" because all we have are descriptions of what heroes and villains did; there is no evidence of universally applicable standards like justice and honesty. In the absence of such general moral standards, it seems plausible that disputes between two individuals were usually settled by appeal to shared taboos, sanctions, and the standards represented by group heroes. But when disputes broke out between two groups that have different taboos, sanctions, and heroes, the brute force of war would be a strongly tempting solution.

At some point in each group's history, no doubt, the horrors of war prompted ideas about what should be done *before* one does it. To overcome enmities between groups, guidelines had to be accepted by all groups. This may be how there emerged the notion of *moral principles* that applied to all moral action, in whatever cultural setting. It marks a first revolutionary achievement in ethics. By setting up standards that made sense across group boundaries, it likely helped move human groups from isolated clans to inter-group cooperation, from defensive enmities to cooperative alliances, from constant apprehensions about survival to cooperative attention to civilized living. We can see written evidence of this emergence by comparing Homer (ninth century BCE) to Socrates (fifth century BCE). Homer depicted Greeks whose moral standards were based on the laws of their community, without any higher standards, even among the fickle gods, by which to say that one community's laws are better than another's. Socrates, in contrast, proposed that moral standards and civil laws should be based on a human nature, which is the same in communities everywhere. Here is where the notion of an "objective moral obligation" appears as a universal standard, higher than the de facto priorities of any specific culture. This move to theoretical analysis of everyday problems changed forever how we deal with moral questions. It introduced a tension between what people *feel* is better for their group and what reflection suggests actually *is* better.

We also have vivid evidence of the emergence of universal moral standards in the history of Judaism. As Hebrews made their shift from henotheism to monotheism, the idea of wisdom enlarged from being a desirable human virtue to a divine characteristic. If God reigns over all creation, then the wisdom and will of God is the universal moral standard. So where the Greeks expressed a moral universalism as abstract principles of human nature, the Hebrews (and their Christian and Muslim progeny) expressed it in concrete commandments and moral disciplines dictated by God, who created the universe.

Revolution 2: Experimental Moral Guidelines.

Still, these relatively independent breakthroughs to universal moral standards have their problems: not everyone agrees on what these universal standards ought to be. It is obvious from history that logic is incapable of resolving differences among ethical theories. Nor do the great monotheistic religions speak with a common voice about God's view of an optimal social order or specific moral issues such as war, the equality of women, suicide, and the economy.

To complicate matters, the very ideal of objective moral standards fell apart. We may roughly assign the beginning of its collapse to Immanuel Kant's *Critique of Pure Reason* (1787), which raised the question among philosophers whether the human mind can have any objectivity at all. At the same time, among the growing number of people who learned modern science, there was a shift of attention away from moral moral *certitude* about human nature toward moral *probability* about concrete events. One trigger for this shift can be traced to Isaac Newton (d. 1727). When he defined concepts in physics based strictly on their explanatory usefulness rather than their "objective truth," he established the empirical method that governs all the natural sciences. When empirical scientists developed new concepts such as *mass* and *valences*, they demonstrated that concepts are simply products of the mind trying to manage nature. So theorists in physics, chemistry, and biology enjoy immense success today because they embrace, not "truth" but, more modestly and realistically, the "best available explanation."

Meanwhile, when moral standards are taught as objective laws about life without any connection to the originating moral wisdom that emerged from a people's experience, they can appear as just the arbitrary decisions of authorities. To meet these shortcomings, ethicists turned to historical-critical methods to uncover the actual moral problems to which these standards were proposed as solutions. They came to regard all so-called universal standards not as fixed, eternal ideas but as lessons in morality that history itself teaches. The underlying assumption was radical: if our present standards are sediments from past historical situations, then future standards will be sediments from how well we deal with our present situations.

This second major revolution in ethics, then, is the discovery that most moral opinions are provisional. Certainly, some moral opinions are unrevisable. It is undoubtedly better to face the truth rather than live in illusion, or to pay attention to what might harm us or benefit us. But today, for example, opinions about the sanctity of life raise questions about the lives of the unborn, of enemies in battle, and of people in a permanent vegetative state. Indeed, in most of our everyday choices, we seldom believe that our opinions about better and worse are unquestionable. This provisional character of morality aligns well with the "best available opinion" goal of modern science. It also aligns well with modern scholarship, where a rich historical narrative is presented not as the final word on the subject but as the latest in a stream of views.

Revolution 3: Method in Ethics

However, with this discovery of the provisional nature of moral views and of the historical origins of moral standards, moral conventionalism returned with a vengeance: If all moral standards are subject to testing among real people, then huge ranges of moral questions will remain unsettled. If standards about life, property,

and the social order are the products of specific historical communities, there seems to be no higher standard by which to criticize
anyone's views about them. The counter reasoning to this points to
conscience: If we all have a common nature, and if it is our nature to
discern between better and worse, then we at least must share the
same inner moral criteria, which we call the conscience. But just
exactly how the conscience contains criteria, particularly criteria
that are essential to everyone's human nature is quite another
question. Thus the need for reflection on *method* in ethics emerged.
It lifts our attention above specific actions, above specific principles, above historical exemplars, above the dictates of conscience,
to the methodological criteria by which we, "in good conscience,"
say anything is better or worse than anything else.

The higher viewpoint we seek requires a third revolution in
ethics—the revolution that this book is all about. It has begun, but
barely out of the gate. Currently, the exploration of method in
ethics is going on along three main branches:

A "positivist" branch applies the methods of the natural sciences
to human studies. It does not take into account the enormous
difference between blind processes of nature and the creative yet
devious processes of humans making history. Because it relies
exclusively on externally observable data, it excludes the data of
consciousness, where human moral process occurs. Sociological
studies of public opinion just show the differences without saying
how each affects the quality of life. Courses in "Values Clarification" identify values as incontrovertible facts, but the "facts" of
humans making history are highly controvertible, owing to the
biases and willfulness that are beyond the field of the natural
sciences. No significant ethics has blossomed from this branch.

A "suspicious" branch extended Newton's dethroning of "objective truth" by attacking the very idea of unassailable concepts
everywhere. Kant (d. 1804) blasted the notion of a "pure reason" and
raised questions about the limits of practical and moral reasoning.
Darwin (d. 1882) proposed that a study of natural history will
clarify the origins of higher human faculties in subhuman life.
Engels (d. 1895) denounced a "false consciousness" that the bour-
geoisie perpetuated among the proletariat. Nietzsche (d. 1900)
mocked the exclusion of affectivity in sound thinking and asserted

that in human affairs there can be no final answers, only 'perspectives." Freud (d. 1939) exposed how unconscious motivations and phobias slant how anyone thinks about anything. Today, philosophers referred to as "postmodern" reject all philosophical systems and religious narratives that propose to explain all human phenomena within a single view. Instead they dedicate themselves to studies of the languages and cultural commitments of local communities. This branch has succeeded in exposing the shortcomings of traditional philosophies, particularly the erroneous assumptions behind many moral pronouncements, but it has not achieved agreement on a constructive ethics that can guide genuine developments, particularly any process or principles aimed at overcoming differences between local communities.

A "constructive" branch takes seriously the findings of the suspicious branch, but also uncovers the fundamental ways that humans construct meanings and seek values. Friedrich Schleiermacher (d. 1843) pioneered the exploration of hermeneutics; Wilhelm Dilthey (d. 1911) advanced historical-critical methods; Ernst Cassirer (d. 1945) revealed how powerfully symbolic forms affect any culture; Bernard Lonergan (d. 1984) proposed that an analysis of what occurs when we think, choose, feel, and love can not only support a claim to objectivity but also can generate verifiable models for use by any scientist or scholar; Eric Voegelin (d. 1985) led his readers to validate major political ideas in history by attending to their own inner experiences of the pulls and counter-pulls of a consciousness seeking order. By identifying how people actually understand and prioritize their lives, this branch appears strongly promising for developing a common and effective method in ethics.

Ethics and Human Studies

This brief sketch depicts three major revolutions in ethics. These are revolutions in the scientific sense, where past achievements are secured on more solid footing and future achievements become more likely. We may depict these revolutions as higher systems emerging upon a stack of lower systems already in place. In this stacked-systems view, the emerging higher system has certain key characteristics:[5] It is not just a further development of existing functions in the lower. It does not abolish but rather incorporates lower systems of functions. It more effectively controls living and improves the probability of survival as a system.

Yet, while these *revolutions* in ethics have the same emergent structure as biological *evolution*, there is one radical difference. Biology aims to explain the evolution of species and biological functions. When an event comes up that does not fit expectations, the biologist reexamines those expectations. The idea that any biological specimen might not act according to its nature is simply out of the question. But human studies aim to explain the emergence of human ideas and decisions, and when these do not fit expectations, it is not just the expectations of the investigator that may be deficient. The humans whom the investigator investigates are free and subject to bias. When their freedom is not biased, they create some unprecedented "better." When it is biased, they act against their own thoughtful and responsible nature; they make things "worse."

Human studies move along two paths: the scientific and the scholarly. Scientific studies aim to clarify the *general systems* that underlie psychological, social, linguistic and economic functions that shape human living. Scholarly studies aim to clarify the *unique priorities*, commitments, and moral standards of specific individuals and cultural groups. Unfortunately, the practices of both science and scholarship are hardly uniform when it comes to moral issues. In the sciences, psychologists disagree on whether to accept people's behaviors as just "dysfunctional" or to charge them as being morally regressive. Some sociologists stick strictly to reporting how societies function, while others attempt to compare the moral advantage of one social structure over another. Economists disagree on whether economic principles should support only monetary efficiencies like trade and budget balances, or should also support the ongoing improvement of a standard of living for all. In scholarship, many exegetes and historians focus on establishing what meanings and trends characterize a culture without inserting their view on whether the culture is doing better or worse. Others go on to name certain meanings or trends as either a corruption or a refinement of a tradition. Even then, scientists and scholars themselves disagree on what corrupts and what refines. More to our concern, all practitioners in human studies lack a common method for reaching consensus. Where the natural sciences vastly expanded our knowledge of how *things* work and what *can* be done, human studies have a long way to go in expanding our knowledge of how *humans* work and what *should* be done.

Still, we made beginnings. We developed a healthy suspicion of explanations in practically every area of life. Yet even the healthiest skepticism does nothing more than clear the deck. We have yet to agree even on what moral criteria we should use to justify out choices: Consequences? Ideals? Promises? Authority? Roles? Conscience? The problem is that among these different kinds of explanations we often find reasons both for and against the same option. True, we overcame cultural differences by listening to people with wider perspectives than our own. Likewise, while the young are typically narrow-minded about what sort of explanations should count, as their respect for elders grows and their experience broadens, their understanding develops. However, some differences are more fundamental and less amenable to resolution. No evidence is more obvious about this than our inability to get along with one another, even among people who live in the same culture and attain the same level of development. Nor can these differences be resolved by appealing to moral principles, when it is precisely the principles that we disagree about. There must be some more fundamental moral criteria. But what are they? By what criteria do we develop principles, grow intellectually, and enrich our cultures? These questions present a challenge. How we meet the challenge will determine whether or not we can revolutionize ethics in ways that significantly improve the ability of human studies to improve life.

THE REVOLUTIONARY CHALLENGE

This revolutionary challenge occurs one person at a time. I make the leap by identifying the criteria I actually use to judge that doing A is better than doing B. It involves understanding both how I make and how I reject moral judgments. If I find your moral judgment suspicious, and I conclude that your criteria are insufficient for saying what is really better, you may well conclude the same about mine. Sometimes both of us are building moral judgments on sand.

So we need to understand how errors in moral judgments arise in the first place. And we need to see this principally in ourselves.

This challenge is complicated by a fundamental confusion about what it means to understand anything at all. As a result, we can think we understand a moral issue even when we do not. We fall into that unhappy state of being both certain and wrong. To clear up this confusion and to understand how moral reflection occurs, we first need to notice a radical difference between understanding the nature of things in themselves and understanding how things affect us in our everyday practical affairs.

Common Sense and Theory

Since this is an extremely important point, let me rephrase it: To *understand* how moral reflection occurs, we need to personally grasp *what kind of understanding* we are after, since human understanding occurs in quite different manners.[6] In fact, the differences are so significant that I dare say the single greatest obstacle to reaching consensus about methods in all human studies is the failure to understand these differences in how we understand.

As a first step in understanding our different ways of understanding, notice the difference between commonsense curiosity and theoretical curiosity. In both we seek to understand our world. In both we ask *how* and *how likely* and *why* and *what for*. In both, we wonder about certain kinds of relationships. But here's the difference: In the commonsense mode of understanding, we understand the relationships between things and ourselves. Our concerns are practical, or interpersonal, or social. We want to understand *how to act*, or *why we act* in a specific situation or *what may be the consequences* of our actions. Then, in the theoretical mode of understanding, we understand the relationships between some things and other things. Our concerns are about *the nature of things*. We want insight into *how* cells differentiate, or *how likely* tornados will be in certain weather conditions, or *why* a neurosis is so resistant to therapy, or *what may be the consequences* of a steady rise in wages anywhere.

Each mode of understanding has its proper criteria, although not everyone reputed to have either common sense or theoretical acumen can say what these criteria are. One key difference lies in how each mode of understanding deals with images. In the commonsense mode, we have vivid images of how our actions affect our environments and ourselves. They are so vivid, in fact, that we *imagine* that thinking is like *imagining*, seeing in our mind's eye what is really out there. By contrast, in the theoretical mode, we play with images of the things we want to understand, but we are more aware that what we hope for is not another image, but the occurrence of the event called understanding. In this mode, we *understand* that thinking involves *understanding*. Thinking is an act of our intellects, not our imagination.

In the theoretical disciplines, scientists and philosophers aim to understand the nature of things, not to imagine how they really look. They require making correlations among data, not full-color pictures about how this should appear. But far too many experts in human studies work under the misguided assumption that theoretical understanding must deliver clear images of things. Quietly but thoroughly, this confusion about understanding infects every discipline. It never occurs to many experts that they may not know what they are doing when they "do" theoretical analysis. Consider these examples:

Puzzle lovers who are unaware of this duality cannot solve the old conundrum about the tree falling in the forest: If there is no one around to hear it, does it make a sound? If we *imagine* the tree falling, we see no reason why it does not make a sound, regardless of whether anyone is within earshot. But if we *define* sound scientifically as the impact of air pressure waves on an eardrum, then there certainly is no sound. The conundrum works because the answer is Yes with commonsense understanding and No with theoretic understanding, and not everyone understands the difference.

Mathematicians who blur understanding with imagining will find it difficult to *imagine* how 0.999... can be exactly 1.000.... They *imagine* the number with 9s running on and on as getting ever closer to 1.000..., but never actually arriving dead on 1.000.... Now most adults understand that $1/3 = 0.333...$, and that when you triple both sides of this equation, you get exactly 1.000... and 0.999.... In other words, 1.000... *is* 0.999...! But only those who *understand* that an insight is not an act of imagining but an act of understanding will be comfortable with this explanation. Among them are the physicists who understand what Einstein and Heisenberg discovered about subatomic particles and macro astronomical events: it is not by picturing that we know how they function but by understanding the data.

Scriptural exegetes who confuse the two ways of understanding are not happy with textual interpretations until they have a rich visual picture of what a religious figure was actually doing. Those exegetes who do understand are happy if they can explain what the authors had in mind when they scribed these particular marks for others to read.

Even when we do understand the difference between common-sense and theoretical understanding, it is no easy trick to keep a theoretical perspective. As you read further in this book, you may find yourself losing this focus. You may wonder, "How might I apply this in my personal life?" or "How can I introduce this material in my course?" That is, you can slip into a commonsense mode of understanding how *you* might apply this material to *your* practical concerns. It is quite difficult to remain in a theoretical mode of understanding that seeks to grasp why things-in-themselves are as they are. Mind you, I have nothing against common sense. We cannot survive without it. What we need is the ability to move between common sense and theoretical modes of thinking without confusing their respective scopes and criteria.

A Theoretical Understanding of Moral Reflection

What will a "theoretical" understanding of moral reflection give us? Already, the term "theoretical" can throw some people off. It does *not* mean "irrelevant," as in "Oh, that's just theoretical." The reason many people dismiss a theory is that theories are provisional. Theories are ways of coherently understanding data, but may be superseded by later theories that understand wider ranges of data and more coherently. So, for example, Aristotle's theory of a universal moral order is incorporated into Aquinas' theory of a divine ordering of creation. Hobbes' theory of a social contract did not account for human nobility, while Locke's did. The advance of both science and philosophy takes place precisely through theoretical reflection that aims at the best available opinion.

It should be no surprise to discover that the same confusion about understanding infects ethics. Those who imagine human rights as "out there inside people" will gloss over the historical origins of this or that right, insulating it from understanding and criticism. Those who imagine other people or nations as "objectively evil" mistake this vivid image for a genuine explanation of moral danger; worse, they appeal to this image to justify high-minded horrors to rid the world of them. Theoretical understanding seeks first of all to grasp the *nature* of such things as rights, moral objectivity, and evil. Although this approach is not as immediately forceful as high-minded condemnation, it is more realistic in understanding moral reflection in general and ultimately more effective in making better decisions about what to do.

The challenge is not to promote new moral standards for practical living. Nor is it even to develop a new ethical theory. It is a third and prior task of understanding what we do when we develop ethical theories and moral guidelines in the first place. This requires a personal intellectual conversion. It means focusing on understanding the data of our experiences of learning, choosing, and loving. Most fundamentally, it means discovering for oneself that there are moral norms inherent in the dynamics of consciousness itself. Most fundamental indeed: As I hope you will attest for yourself further on, there simply are no more fundamental norms than those that structure our very consciousness.

Although the challenge is personal, it changes how we work with others. This is because, as we draw more explicitly on our personal knowledge of how our own learning, choosing and loving work, we can more clearly express to others our criteria for testing the validity of all ethical theories. If enough of us agree on what makes ethical theories valid, a new kind of moral dialog will emerge. We will express our moral opinions in theoretical concepts drawn from personal verifications of how moral reflection works. We will assume that if shared moral norms arise from norms inherent in the common dynamics of consciousness, then we will appeal to these normative criteria to ground our views. We will expose to each other the historicity of our moral imagination and the moral concepts that structure our thinking. We will humbly admit that we may be biased. By opening the kimono to reveal how we actually reached our moral views, we will more likely refine and implement any ethical theory that survives our tests for validity. Of course many people do this already, but two things are usually missing. One is a theory and conceptual language for speaking about inner events. The other is a critical mass of conversation partners in each discipline to engage in productive collaboration at this level of method.

In chapters 3 and 4, you will find experiments designed to validate the normative dimensions in how you think, make choices, and engage others. I will encourage you to verify these insights in your personal experience. It is only by verification that you can claim a comprehensive viewpoint on morality. It is only by verification that you will know how to elicit the productive collaboration of others that moves the revolution in ethical method forward.

DEFINITIONS

I have already used some commonsense terms with theoretical meanings. So to sharpen our focus on a theoretical understanding of moral processes, let me give some definitions of terms you will find throughout this book.

Morality, Ethics, Method

To refer specifically to the realm ordinary actions, I will use the terms *morals* and *morality*. Moreover, I will use these terms empirically. For example, if I refer to people's *morals* or *morality*, I mean the values inherent in their actions, whether noble or mean. So I may say "His morals need improvement," but I will avoid normative expressions like "He has no morals." Thus: *Morality is the field of reflection about the value of specific actions.*

To refer to the realm of moral guidelines, I will use the term ethics. Thus: *Ethics is the field of reflection on moral ideals, principles, and standards.*

So in what follows, "ethics" will refer to the field of general assertions about right and wrong, better and worse. Here too I will avoid normative expressions ("She has no ethics") in favor of empirical expressions ("Her ethics are based on Kant").

To refer to realm of reflection on the workings of the mind and heart that underlie ethics, I will use the expression *method in ethics*— or just *method*. (*Metaethics* refers to the same approach.) By this I will mean reflection on the inner sources of the ideals, principles, and standards on which ethics reflects. Thus: *Method in ethics is the field of inner resources on which ethicists depend in order to reflect on morality.*

Keep in mind that these "resources" are neither other ethicists nor revered moral texts. They are the inner resources of mind and heart in ethicists. Also, this definition of method in ethics is of a more fundamental order than a method of collaboration *among* ethicists. All collaboration is a collaboration of people with inner resources. And it is their inner resources—their assumptions, moral inheritances, intelligence, wisdom, and commitments, as well as dysfunctions in these resources—that shape how any collaboration plays out. The next several chapters will identify these inner resources and their various dysfunctions. Then, in chapter 9, we will turn our attention to a method of collaboration.

Ethicists

To speak of women and men who reflect on the ideals, principles, and standards relevant to morality, I will use the term "ethicists." But right away, let me insist that many ethicists are not called ethicists. Ethicists include not only experts in philosophy and theology but anyone who questions the conventions, standards, ideals, language, ideas, policies, and juridical procedures that shape life in society. However, I am *not* speaking of people who, while they may be deeply concerned about specific moral choices, are unfamiliar with the critical questions about moral standards.

2. WE LIVE IN A MORAL UNIVERSE

MORALITY: A UNIVERSAL PHENOMENON

We considered human morality as a special case of evolution. And because we think of evolution as a universal phenomenon, we may begin by considering that the universe itself is deeply moral. If this can be demonstrated, we will have set up a framework for understanding ethics which is, in theory at least, compatible with anything modern science and scholarship comes up with. Let us look at the data.

Astronomers gaze up, between the stars, wondering if carbon, hydrogen, and oxygen combined in ways like our own. A question occurs. Are planets out there inhabited by creatures we call living, perhaps conscious, possibly even intelligent and moral? Awe arises about the immensity and the age of the physical universe, as well as about how little anyone knows about anything beyond our tiny neighborhood. Even the little we do know has one insurmountable limitation: Since the light from nearly every star we see was shot toward us long before we were born, whatever we learn about these stars will always be knowledge of very ancient history.

Still, these wonderments about the starry panoply overhead reveal dynamics that work everywhere and always. Newton's great contribution to physics was to demonstrate that our experience of gravity here is evidence of a law that holds throughout space and time. That bold extrapolation has been verified by thousands of experiments and ever more comprehensive theories; hardly anyone disputes the idea of universal laws of physical forces. Following these leads, then, we can consider whether our experience of moral concern here is evidence of universal forces that can produce moral creatures. Indeed, this is the assumption of every fancy about intelligent life elsewhere. The forces of the universe are potentialities, searching, we might imagine, for increasingly more orderly arrangements. To state an obvious but persistently astounding fact, these potentialities culminated in us—beings that appreciate, deliberate, and prioritize. With a freedom unlike anything we know as yet, we make choices that not only affect our surroundings but also color our self-awareness, sometimes with satisfaction and sometimes with regret.

The appearance of events of appreciating, deliberating, prioritizing, and choosing raises a fundamental question about what is really *in* the universe. Most of us were taught that this evolution of consciousness is an evolution of intelligence: scientists seek *intelligent* life elsewhere in the universe. One particularly stubborn result of giving priority to intelligence is a black-and-white universe. In such a universe, intelligence works on the principle that any X either exists or does not exist. So our statements must be either true or false. What you see is either really out there or you are imagining things. Nothing can qualify statements like these. Logically, there seems to be no third possibility.

But there is a third, even a fourth possibility. No doubt, intelligence can clarify moral options, but even our earliest hominid forebears who applied their intelligence to their circumstances saw value in doing so. Today, we often say to ourselves, "I'll have to think about that." This "have to" about thinking is a moral activity. Moral concern is the reveille of intelligence. Both primitive hominids and modern scientists use their intelligence to understand their worlds, but they *want* to know because of a conviction that knowing is preferable to ignorance. Knowing is *better.* It is something we *ought* to do. It is *ought* questions that prompt our *is* questions.

We are part of the universe. Indeed, hustling around on our glowing little blue globe, we sometimes value ourselves as the most wondrous thing that ever happened in a wondrous universe, not just because we are *smart* but also because we are *concerned.* Our very performance reveals that the universe of everything knowable is not black-and-white. We not only assume that there is a real difference between what *is* and what *is not,* we also assume there is also a difference between really better and really worse. Knowledge is really better than ignorance, and some events are really better than others. So in an evolutionary view of realty, besides an A that exists and a B that does not, there can be a C that exists but *ought not* because it worsens some sector of the universe, just as there can be a D that does not exist but *ought to* because it would improve some sector of the universe. The universe is a moral place.

THE EXIGENCES OF THE UNIVERSE

To think theoretically about this *ought* in the universe, we need a concept that applies all along the evolutionary time line from the Big Bang to today, and from today to any possible future open to us.[7] This would establish a base for ethics in the universally recognized scientific method and perhaps avoid both heavy-handed moral dogmatism on the far right and culture-bound moral conventionalism on the far left.

What might this unifying concept be? Consider the data. At the Big Bang, an original chaos did not remain chaotic. Atoms emerged when random particles partnered into stable orbits. Molecules emerged when random atoms happened to group. Life emerged when random molecules hit upon cellular arrangements that can replicate themselves. Consciousness emerged when randomly-associated neural systems in cellular masses formed psychic images of threats and opportunities. Intelligence and morality emerged when loosely-associated psychic systems in conscious beings hit upon the ability to form images at will, enabling us both to picture and to prioritize actions we might take. As a result, we humans are able not only to adapt our habits to our surroundings, but also to point our conscious systems in directions we think are better.

The possibilities inherent in universal matter and energy are not abstractions, eternally frozen in mere possibility. Nor are they automatically destined to become realities by some universal pre-coded program. Rather there is a process in the universe by which some possibilities become realities and others do not. We recognize not only abstract capabilities for higher systems but also concrete movements toward them. Higher systems emerge under the laws of probability, not necessity.[8] This movement represents a potential in otherwise unrelated events or things—a fertile incompleteness, a directionality among a plurality, a dynamic orientation of lower levels to higher levels of functioning.[9]

The unifying concept we will use to represent this forward-moving dynamic is an exigence: *An exigence is a functioning relationship between a set of events or things and a more comprehensive system to which they may contribute.*

Our choice of *exigence* as a unifying concept may be justified by its very generality. From a lean mathematical perspective, an exigence is simply a probability that some X will emerge with a power to organize otherwise unrelated elements or events. But from an enriched scientific perspective, an exigence is a demand function that is evident not only the universal dynamism that produces higher species but also the explicitly moral dynamism that produces higher levels of human living. Moral consciousness was a possibility in the Big Bang. By whatever name, this notion of an exigence lies at the heart of the theory of evolution and its extension into theories of social and scientific revolutions. We acknowledge that while the universe is full of haphazard and random elements, evolution itself is not just haphazard. It is a dynamic process that includes rising probabilities that the better may emerge, though without any guarantee of success.

THE INTENDING EXIGENCE

To trace how these exigences of the universe show up in humans, we should first consider what may be called an *intending* exigence. It emerged in a tremendous leap from the level of merely biological systems, where cells differentiated and multiplied, to the psychic level, where an animal's activities are organized into a conscious purposefulness. We will speak of this conscious purposefulness as "intending." Animals have it, but plants do not. This intending is an *exigence* insofar as it appears as a functioning relationship between the vast field of things perceivable and the actual perceptions and attitudes toward them which, when they occur in the animal, are organized into a seamless world of experience. Intentionality is the world whose demand function is apparent on any spring morning as the birds chatter away and the bees buzz about the flowers, driven by what appears to be a felt need, a psychic impulse, a conscious purposefulness.

Within this conscious purposefulness of intending, we can distinguish three important types of awareness. First, and most obvious, is an animal's *perceptions of objects*. A beaver sees trees, water, the sky, and other animals. This is an "intending" in the minimal sense of "noticing."

Second, a little less obvious, our beaver is aware of *affects* or *attitudes* regarding these perceptions. Affects may be desire-based, as the sight of a tree invites munching down, or fear-based, as the sight of a wolf plunges the beaver into the safety of its hutch. In either case, an animal's affects are ingrained behavioral responses that function to preserve its livelihood. These affects constitute the "intending" in the larger sense of "intending to act."

Third, very often overlooked, is the beaver's awareness of *self*. This self-awareness is quite unlike the awareness of outer sensory perceptions and inner affective leanings. When the beaver sleeps, this self-awareness is minimal, but when the beaver awakes, it spontaneously organizes *in relation to itself*, the otherwise random perceptions and affects that it notices. While the percepts and affects are transient, the self continues. With every event where perception and affect combine, the beaver's self-awareness is poised for action. This self-awareness unifies the beaver's consciousness by orienting its attention toward specific perceptions with specific affects.[10] It is the self-awareness of the one who experiences the intending exigence by doing the "intending."

This intending is a functioning system of a triple awareness—of perceptions, affects, and self. It is fueled by perceptions and affects and is driven by a conscious experience of an intending exigence to deal with them. Perceptions are what conscious beings perceive, and affects are the feelings that move them. In bugs, they appear as blind responses to perceptions while in humans they appear as initial impulses subject to the higher controls of reflection. In any case, this intending exigence unites otherwise disparate and transient perceptions and affects into actions of animals conscious of their own continuing selves.

It seems tautological to say that the intending exigence occurs in conscious things and does not occur in nonconscious things. But the important point is that this intending is precisely what makes anything conscious, for when animals experience neither perceptions nor affects, they are quite unconscious. Simply put, consciousness is the self-awareness that is intrinsic to any animal's intending. And it is this intending exigence that organizes otherwise random perceptions and affects into a conscious movement of an animal toward opportunities and away from threats.

THE SYMBOLIZING EXIGENCE

There is yet a higher level—tremendously higher—in the functioning of exigences. Besides the leap from non-intentional systems to intentional systems, there is a further leap within intentional systems. Where animals order otherwise random perceptions and affects within a self-awareness, the human species can freely imagine what is not immediately perceived—an ability apparently present in us but absent in apes.[11] We can imagine things that are far away, people who have long since died, and events that never happened. With each of these freely-formed images, we still feel some sort of affect, some attraction or repulsion. By this combination of freely-formed images linked to feelings of attraction or repulsion we can consider alternative ways to act, as well as the kind of selves we want to be. We will call these affect-laden images *symbols*.[12] And we will define this *exigence to represent freely-chosen attitudes through feelings "the symbolizing exigence."*

We can only speculate how the symbolizing exigence evolved, but a few developments must have occurred along the line. One is the emergence among four-limbed animals that walked on the back two, leaving the front limbs free to gesture – a facility greatly expanding their ability to express distinct perceptions and their corresponding affects. Eventually, the animal we call Homo sapiens appeared, among whose later branches anthropologists trace the two distinct branches of the Neanderthals and anatomically modern humans. Neanderthals made tools; they buried their dead. Presumably they experienced affective movements both toward fruit-laden trees and away from tigers on the prowl. If they taught their young how to eat and hunt and socialize, they likely did so by example, not by explanations. They certainly had an ability to symbolize things. Besides using gestures, they likely knew words to draw one another's attention to particular things they wanted or feared. However, based on current evidence, their ability to symbolize seems limited to their "here" and their "now." To date, nothing that archeologists have unearthed indicates ceremony or ritual surrounding burials, which would focus affects on images of non-visible forces of fate, destiny and divinity. Nor do we have any evidence of Neanderthal art—images that stimulate affective responses to things not-here and not-now.

Along what appears to be our own ancestral line, there occurred a Big Bang of Imagination to cover absolutely everything in the universe. What our ancient forebears realized, and what we now take for granted, was that the range of what can be imagined has no limits. We can imagine anything we please. We picture the not-here, the not-now. We even imagine ourselves imagining, thinking, and feeling about anything. In about half the time Neanderthals spent on our planet, we learned to count, which requires imagining a number scale, against which to compare perceptions of physical objects. Counting allowed us to speak quite exactly about the relative worth of sheep and goats, weapons and food, precious metals and gems. Having learned about remembering and forgetting, some of our ancestors became teachers, imparting to the absorbent imaginations of the young the noble exemplars of old.

Today, we can identify at least four highly fruitful ways that free imagination began to function: Free images can be *mimetic*, in the sense that we freely conjure up a picture or sound or smell of something familiar—a horse, a whinny, manure. The mimetic images we conjure up can also be *conjectural*, in the sense that we imagine new arrangements of familiar elements—like a flying red horse and any invention, like the first wheel. As the mother of invention, conjectural images vastly expand the scope of alternative actions by considering them first in the mind, rather than by lengthy and dangerous trials and errors. Images can also be *abstract*, in the sense that we imagine a single feature common to many instances, like "large" or "small," "hurrying" or "lagging." Abstract images have immediate moral implications: A large tiger is more dangerous than a small one; and when a large one is chasing you, hurrying is better than lagging. Again, images can be *conventional* when they represent objects not by visual resemblance but by social agreement. In languages, most words are conventional images, except for onomatopoetic words like "snort" and "tinkle." The shape of alphabet letters are conventions which, when strung together in sentences like this one, can record meanings far beyond the range of the mimetic pictograms they replaced.

These images are not pictures projected on some mental screen. In the first instance, they are recognizable patterns in consciousness with recognizable associations to sight, sound, smell, texture, or movement, as well as emotional states such as joy and anxiety. (This technical definition of "images" as simply patterns of consciousness—not "pictures"—is particularly evident in the blind.) Then, in second and higher iterations, images are recognizable patterns in consciousness with recognizable associations even to abstractions such as *mass* in physics and the *coda* in music.

We were able to create schools because we could entertain an abstract image of a single lesson drawn from many experiences. So instructors teaching civics and math and history rely on abstract images of cities, numbers, and timelines. We could create money by the conventional image of lightweight tokens for the exchange of heavy goods. An acre of land may sell for 20 horses, but 20 gold coins do the trick expeditiously. Politics requires the combination of mimetic images of specific persons and conventional images of promises they made, which is the basis for exchanging goods for services, for establishing contracts, and for assigning all the social roles that make cities possible.

This proliferation of free images releases a corresponding proliferation of distinguishable affects. The mental images our forebears used for counting and pricing goods also tailored their affects of hope for gains and regret over losses. The images they presented to one another to collaborate on some plan were tied to sharing emotional commitments to the plan. Today, teachers use images to lead their students to insights, but unless their students experienced the prior affects of trust (or fear!), and some expectation of a subsequent affective satisfaction, not much insight will occur.

We watch children recapitulate this multi-millennial evolution in just a dozen years. Infants feel moved by undifferentiated desires and fears. Youngsters play make-believe—valuable exercises for their emerging free imagination. Later they make affective distinctions as they notice differences between feeling frustrated and feeling apprehensive, between jealousy and envy. Each affective difference they notice is secured by a distinct conventional name for a distinct emotion provided by their heritage.

These affect-laden images are the elementary carriers of human morality. As images, they can represent known situations or proposed plans, but as affectively colored, they also stir feelings that affect choices. The variety of possible feelings is enormous—far more than the total number of names we have for them, as anyone can verify by listening to good music. Each feeling moves us regarding a distinct perception of an image (remember: not a picture but a pattern of consciousness). The movement does not automatically trigger action, but we experience an inner movement toward or away from what the corresponding image represents to us. Ordinarily we call these preliminary movements *urges, impulses, dispositions,* or *attitudes.* But from our theoretical perspective, these preliminary movements are a unique exigence, an inner demand, to distinguish better and worse. They play a dominant role in securing each person's morality. We maintain our personal priorities by a unique set of linked images and affects. Many a mother has told her child, "Sweetheart, that's *dirty!*" She does not explain that dirt is bad. With her tone of voice alone, she imprints upon her child's mind an internal symbol in which the image of dirt is tied to an affect of repulsion.

The child's consciousness of self (the unity moving forward via transient images and affects) is itself symbolic. Consider, for example, the powerful symbolic effect of hearing your own name. Cup your left hand around the back of your left ear, and cup your right hand across your mouth so that your right-hand fingers touch the baby finger side of your left hand—making an acoustic tunnel. Then whisper four first names, pausing a little between each, with the soft urgency of trying to wake someone up. Make your name the fourth. You immediately experience an affect about your name quite different from your affects about the first three. This is because your name is the internal symbol that works without your reflection to protect your life, to boost your reputation, and to respond to the attention others pay you.

Internal symbols perform another essential function in human life. Besides being the media that enable us to respond quickly to everyday opportunities, they are also the media by which we reach beyond what we know and love. When we welcome the pure innocence of a newborn child, the image of this one child also stands for a purity and innocence of every child. It is the vocation of religious artists and architects to create the external symbols of divine reality which they hope will excite the internal symbols of worshipers' awe and reverence—the internal symbols that already shape the artists' and architects' own consciousness of self.

Symbols also represent the entire moral field to each person. Ethicists divide up this field in many ways, but prior to these distinctions, each person begins from symbols that blend, in compact fashion, what the world is all about and how he or she ought to behave in it. What is important for ethicists to notice is that these prior, protean symbols can be remarkably different from one another. A man suffering from neurotic obsessions sees the field as almost completely populated by demands and threats, save the one small psychic area carved out for his personal security. A self-absorbed woman divides the field in two sections: "What can I get for myself, and what can't I get?" Similarly, people whose identity depends completely on belonging to a specific group see these two sections as "What can *we* get for *ourselves* and what can't *we* get?" Others see the field in terms that apply commonly to everyone on the globe: "What can *we* do for our *entire human family?*" Still others see the field in universal, religious terms: "What do *you* want for *your* human family, almighty God?"

While these symbols of the moral field differ from one another, it does not follow that each person necessarily relies on one to the exclusion of any others. To some extent, everyone feels the demands of several different symbols pulling in their different directions. Indeed, is it not true that when we struggle with any personal moral question, we also struggle with how we imagine life itself? Is life essentially about psychic security, or self-gain, or a common good, or ever the greater good, or surrender to divine forces?

In summary, then, the symbolic exigence is an experienced demand to represent our freely-chosen moral attitudes in images laced with affects. Since this symbolic exigence plays an irreplaceable role in any choice, an effective method in ethics must include it among the methods that are innate to moral consciousness everywhere.

EXIGENCES FOR LEARNING, CHOOSING, AND LOVING

Still higher than the intending and symbolizing exigences are exigences for learning, for choosing, and for loving. In chapter 7, we will examine each of these exigences in detail. For now, it is important to see how these three functions distinguish us from other animals.

About learning, the originating event is, again, the experience of an exigence. Our experience of ignorance demands facts. Our experience of confusion demands an explanation. Our experience of chaos demands a plan. This inner demand to know comes prior to a decision to investigate. It moves us to formulate a question, but we experience the demand before we formulate our question. We become aware of the possibility of meaning before we know much about what that meaning may be. This is why, in the middle of a discussion, we say, "Wait a minute!" and then grope for the connections we suspect are missing and the words to formulate a question about what bothers us.

About choosing, we experience an exigence to improve our lives. We are not satisfied with learning; we learn in order to make good choices. We want to make a difference. Over a wide range of matters—the thousand everyday choices, the far fewer strategic choices, the singular choice to be a different kind of person—we want to improve life. Usually, we first experience this demand as feelings. Our feelings withdraw us from risks and draw us toward opportunities, often prior to any thought. And, just as with learning, where we experience concern about the possibility of meaning before we formulate a question, through feelings we experience concern about the possibility of better or worse before we ask ourselves what we ought to do.

About loving, we experience an exigence to bond with others. Despite our youthful efforts to escape the expectations others have of us, we look for companions in the struggles of life. True, most animals socialize; it protects them from enemies, gives them food, and ensures the continuance of the species. What makes human social nature unique is that we appreciate the value of one another simply for being. Waves of gratitude rush upon us for other human beings whose value lies not just in what they do, but more fundamentally in who they are. We also experience a spontaneous attraction to them, not only for who they are, but also for what we together might become by sharing our lives.

THE OPENNESS OF HUMANITY

However, learning, choosing and loving do not completely satisfy us. We are not content with what we know; we want to know more. We do not rest with the good we have done; we want to do better. We are not entirely happy with what we have made of ourselves; we want to become better persons. Unsatisfied with our cluster of immediate friends, we become parents of children, participants in society, and critics of cultures that degrade people's well-being. When a loved one dies, our love for them lives on.

This ever going beyond is what drives our desire to know more, do better, and engage one another in love. It is the open-endedness of being human, the restlessness of being mortal. It is not a passive openness to random sensory inputs but rather an active, thirsty, searching openness to whatever may be real and good and engaging of our entire selves. It is an elemental being in love—a most strange yet most familiar love. Strange, because we love what we do not fully know. So we use abstractions, saying that we love justice or goodness. We use religious symbols of God or gods to represent the multi-faceted, alluring, divine beyond. But this love is also totally familiar. It is the *experience* of wanting to learn, of wanting to do better, of wanting to have character, of wanting to both deepen and widen our personal relationships, of wanting perhaps to be holy. We name the beyond of our open-ended desire to know, *wisdom* and *philosophy*. We name the beyond of our open-ended desire for the better, *benevolence* and *goodness*. We name the beyond of our open-ended desire for community as *friendship* and *philanthropy* and *holiness in God*.

Definition: Transcending Exigence

We are citizens in a worldwide, history-long dynasty of longing, aching for what no one will ever completely embrace in life. This is our human condition. So to develop an ethics that integrates all the exigences that make us who we are, we need to give this primordial, universal exigence a theoretical definition. We will speak of it as a "transcending exigence:"[13] *The transcending exigence is the pull on consciousness to the more complete truth, the ever better, and the fuller personal engagements.*

Note that the exigence is defined not by concepts but by events. And not by events described in history books but by events that occur in you. You experience these events as a "pull" or as a "demand" to enlarge yourself beyond yourself. Obviously, "pull" and "demand" have ordinary meanings, but we use theoretic meanings—those inner movements that raise questions in us about the truth, the better, the personally engaged. And as we reach answers, we experience corresponding satisfactions—an intellectual satisfaction at learning the truth, a moral satisfaction at choosing the better, and an affective satisfaction at engaging others in love.

We think about this transcending enlargement in ways that evolve as we grow up. For youngsters, the "beyond" amounts to what is "out there"—the things they want, the roles of their friends, and the games they play. As they blossom into teenagers, their emerging intelligence notices the shocking difference between the "out there" and an "in here." Beneath their complaints about mixed messages from their parents "out there," they are disturbed about mixed messages hatching within their private thoughts "in here." Their spontaneous childhood friendliness becomes tentative and complicated. Eventually it dawns on most teenagers that the "objective" world of their childhoods has been colored by highly "subjective" assumptions all along. And while they typically find this disturbing, by and large the truth of it carries them beyond wishful thinking and into the world as it really is—a reality whose meaning is made by people whose hidden subjective efforts make objective differences plain for all to see.

Eventually, many adults experience a contemplative moment when they realize that everybody, everywhere, is drawn like this. Imagining themselves as observing the universe from the outside, they see the entire cosmic process as an unfolding drama in which they are bit players. Images like these trigger realizations about the truth of things. A 65-year-old woman watches her husband reading the paper, sipping his coffee, and it occurs to her, like a thought she never thought before: *This* is the man in *this* my life. Burt Bacharach's character sings, "What's it all about, Alfie? Is it just for the moment we live?" In his Myth of the Cave, Plato describes this movement as one where we are gradually forced out of our fixation with visible things and turning toward a light in which the sense and coherence of everything is refracted, while the light itself still blinds.

It is a distinguishing mark of humanity to experience this transcending movement. I say *experience* because experiencing it is not at all the same as imagining it or understanding it or accepting the existence of an order of reality that transcends the human, let alone surrendering wholeheartedly to this mysterious pull and acting accordingly. Primitive humans worshipped trees, rivers, the sun, the stars. The ancient Greeks imagined fickle gods seducing and attracting, tricking and killing the humble the proud alike. The ancient Hebrews worshipped one God. And although philosophies and religions understand our human condition in quite different ways, at least we can say that the *experience* of the transcending exigence is common and, as common, it is the starting point for reaching the common images, insights and truths about our human condition and about a divine beyond that can give us a ground for collaboration in ethics.

The transcending pull functions as a topmost exigence in a world-system of ascending exigences. Physical systems are open to chemical integration. Chemical systems are open to biological integrations. And so on up the ladder until we get to human systems. Human systems climb the further rungs of the patterned, then the coherent, then the real, then the better, and ultimately the shared. But no matter how successfully human systems give birth to happy families and social progress, they remain open to yet higher integrations shrouded in the mysteries contemplated by sages and embraced by worshippers.

The experience of this transcending exigence enlarges the intending and the symbolizing exigences by opening our awareness of objects, affects, and ourselves to an unlimited horizon. From above, as it were, it raises our efforts to learn, to do better, and to live in love. We realize that we will never know everything, but we keep on wondering. We accept the fact that our moral habits will never completely jibe with what is truly better, but we keep on trying. We resign ourselves to the puzzle that we are to ourselves, but we accept the drive to become better selves and yield to the paradoxical self-sacrifices that mutual love demands. We wonder about the meaning of everything, the ultimate worth of anything, and the mystery of why there is anything at all. We obey, more or less, what seems like not only a mysterious desire within us but also a mysterious pull from beyond us.

Beauty and Symbols of Transcendence

It is the persistent longing and open-endedness of the transcending pull that drives progress on every level of life. Despite our inability to fully know what pries us open, we use our imagination to represent both the transcendent beyond and our desires to move us toward it. This is why beauty is so central to moral living. Beauty is a symbol of transcendence. It simultaneously represents the beyond and draws us toward it. Prior to thinking about what may be better and worse, beauty captures us; we feel stunned—by the Pacific Ocean crashing on a rocky shore, a towering sequoia, a mother cradling her infant. Even the ordinary: You are walking in your neighborhood, preoccupied by some problem when, suddenly, you hear a Haydn largo on a nearby radio, and your problem falls away while you absorb the magnificent, and you feel something like a promise.

We express ourselves through beauty in many ways. We primp, embodying what we hope others will find beautiful in us. We weave our senses in different combinations through art, music, sculpture, architecture, landscape, dance, and perfume. What is common to all these expressions is some order, some pattern standing beyond us in a gesture of invitation: Come forward; there is always more. Artists of works that endure trim away incidental sights and sounds to allow the nameless essence of reality to capture us. Beauty is an experience largely overlooked by ethicists. This is strange, given how immediately nature and the arts tap our experience of moving toward the better. By the same token, ethics is a discipline largely overlooked by art critics, which is strange in its own way, given how often they talk about the *value* of works of art.

Definitions in the Realm of Method

There are many definitions of beauty, but hardly any stick to the mind. When we make definitions, we usually define things as types of something else. A hat is a type of covering for the head; red is a type of color. These kinds of definitions use terms that need further definitions. (What is a head? What is a color?) Eventually we reach the point where we must set the entire stack of definitions on some recognizable "ground" experience. This is true of all definitions, of course, but when we investigate human issues, the ground experiences are events of our minds and hearts. Beauty is such a ground experience. It is not a type of anything. However, what we can do—must do, really—is define it in terms of other ground experiences. So what is beauty? *Beauty is a pattern of sense experiences that prompts transcendent desire.*

Like our definition of *transcendence*, this one points ultimately to events, not to concepts. We understand something essential about beauty when we see the connection between certain visual, aural, olfactory, kinesthetic, or tactile experiences and a desire to go beyond ourselves. There may be better definitions of beauty in this style, but the point here is to notice the style itself. It secures the meaning of a term by an invitation to consult our experience—particularly those fundamental events in human learning, choosing, and loving. As a result, familiar terms like *understand, pull, learn, love, judge,* and *symbol* are used in technical senses whose meaning requires experiments that verify their meanings in one's personal experience. This is an important issue to keep in mind as we go forward. In particular, the next chapter will lead you through experiments to secure the meanings of five "ground" experiences—being *attentive, intelligent, reasonable, responsible,* and in *love.*

MORALITY: A UNIVERSAL EXIGENCE

We considered how the universe is appropriately called a moral place. This is important because a single and universal model for ethics that explains the emergence of anything we deem better avoids the many partial and often incompatible models that are based chiefly on only certain features of morality—such as duty, consequence, virtue, utility, natural law, and so on. Why then do we focus on evolution as a framework for this single and universal model? Mainly because it is currently the best available explanation of how anything we consider better appears. Still, as it will be increasingly evident, the theory of evolution as it is ordinarily understood in the natural sciences needs to be complemented by

introducing the data of consciousness as highly relevant to understanding morality.

In summary, then, we can say that the phenomena of a universe
evolving may be understood as driven by a universal, all-
encompassing exigence. As all-encompassing, it includes the many
specific exigences proper to levels of evolution, including many
differentiations within human consciousness. Between what is
guaranteed by the nature of things and what is pure random
chance, there is an evolutionary process that favors the survival of
higher, more orderly systems. We find the evidence all around us in
nature, but we find it pre-eminently *within* ourselves in the irrepres-
sible experience of transcendent inner drives toward further
learning, better choices, and richer interpersonal relationships.

On Kant's tombstone, we find, in German and Prussian, a passage
from the end of his *Critique of Practical Reason:* "Two things fill the
mind with ever new and increasing admiration and awe, the more
often and steadily we reflect upon them: the starry heavens above
me and the moral law within me." What we are saying is that the
starry heavens above and the moral law within are ultimately parts
of the same thing.

3. OUR NORMATIVE SOURCES ARE WITHIN

HOW DO WE CHANGE OUR PRIORITIES?

As physicists and astronomers study the exigences that release higher material forms and spin more stable arrangements, their very intelligence and dedication give us the evidence of just how far the exigences of the universe have gone toward becoming better. Their wonder and concern will not reach answers to all their questions, but the questions themselves have no inherent restrictions.

We do not clearly see the beyond toward which our questions impel us. Ultimate beyonds are more properly the realm of religion and theology. Yet, by considering our questions as a personally experienced drive toward learning the fuller truth, choosing the better, and loving more deeply, we can identify in ourselves the source of any moral priorities we happen to have. So now we need to ask precisely how these exigences work to establish our moral priorities. By understanding how we personally set and change our priorities, we can seek a common understanding with others regarding the broad outlines of how anyone, anywhere, develops moral opinions. What is more, by understanding morality within the larger perspective of our experience of the pull of transcendence, we encompass not only all moral claims based on logic, and on insight into human nature and historicity, but also those based on love, including the love between friends, heartfelt devotion to social harmony, and religious commitment to a divine source and destiny of human living.

To actually change our priorities we have to allow the transcending exigence to open us to change in the first place. But what does it mean to be "open"? For human animals, being open is not at all like an open camera lens, letting in all images within its field of vision and all affects from the depths of consciousness. Being humanly open requires letting the transcending pulls focus our attentions. We consider new experiences. We entertain alternate explanations. We realize truths previously unknown. And as we deepen or lessen our appreciation of the people and things around us, we shift our loyalties and loves.

But how do we know which experiences, explanations, truths, values, and people *should* elicit a change in us? We change our priorities all the time, but *how* do we change them? How does the transcending exigence to conduct ourselves in ever better ways focus our intention in ever better directions?

EXERCISES FOR NOTICING OUR NORMATIVE DRIVES

To answer these questions, we need to notice that the transcending pull "differentiates" along five quite distinct, but functionally related acts of consciousness. We feel pulls to pay attention, to understand, to verify our ideas, to make good decisions, and to relate to one another. With each distinct pull, we also know when the pulling stops. Regarding any particular situation, we generally know when we paid attention enough, understood enough, verified enough, decided enough, cared enough. Each different inner pull has its own criteria for when it has been satisfied. In other words, these processes are *normative*.

These processes are also exigences—in the technical sense that they are concrete, functioning relationships between existing questions and possible answers. Because our questions *demand* answers, we also called these processes *drives*. So, to distinguish these exigences from the layers upon layers of subhuman and nonhuman exigences in the evolving universe, let us call these uniquely human exigences *normative drives*.

These normative drives operate in the consciousness of any person.[14] Certainly, ethicists derive many normative guidelines from principles based on an analysis of human nature and history. They express these guidelines in the verbalized standards we also call *norms*. But these explicit, verbalized standards emerge from prior normative drives that are the implicit, but operative, promptings of our nature. Of course, these drives do not work infallibly. We can be wrong about what is truly better and, to our shame, we can know the better but do the worse. Still, the normative drives are what prompt us to discover our error and to change. The normative pressures may appear as regret or shame or guilt. If we harden our hearts against doing better for others, we have to fight against our natural proclivity to be friendly. In any case, our consciousness is disturbed, and our consciousness would not be disturbed were it not for its inner drives toward the better.

Here we come to a fundamental conclusion about ethics. These elemental normative drives in our experience are the ground of any and all moral norms, standards, and guidelines that we formulate in an ethics. In other words, here, in the experienced normative drives of human consciousness, are the moral criteria that belong to our nature, on which all historically-conditioned moral reflection depends. So, to move forward in our understanding of method in ethics, we need to understand, each one for oneself, just what these drives are.

So I invite you to identify in yourself five distinct differentiations of the transcending exigence:[15]

- Normativity of Experience: The exigence to pay attention.
- Normativity of Understanding: The exigence to get insight into what, or why, or how, or how likely, or what for.
- Normativity of Reason: The exigence to sift reality from illusion, truth from falsehood, sound from unsound explanations.
- Normativity of Responsibility: The exigence to know the better and do it.
- Normativity of Love: The exigence to share one's life with others.

In the following sections, notice each of these drives in yourself; aim to understand how each one entails a normative function; and verify that your consciousness really works like this. Be forewarned, however. What you notice will not be anything that feels new or dramatic. The goal here is first to identify differences among the various drives that you experience all the time but perhaps have yet to notice, then to notice especially the *normative character* of each drive, and then to gain insight into the connection between these experiences and your moral opinions within a theoretical framework applicable to ethics anywhere.

THE NORMATIVITY OF EXPERIENCE

Can anyone who is conscious not notice anything at all? Impossible, is it not? You can close your eyes, block your ears and pinch your nose; you might even drug your body into insensitivity; but you still wonder, still imagine. Even when we wake from a deep sleep, we recall fragmentary images. The point is that being conscious and noticing are the same thing. Being conscious means being attentive to something specific. This is our experience of an elemental normative function of consciousness. In sleep, it produces dreams in patterns. It wakes us up in the morning. Throughout the day it alerts us to threats and presents us with opportunities, as it does in all other animals.

It may seem that our noticing is passive, as if our attention is entirely determined by what we experience as input from our five senses or from spontaneous inner images or feelings. But a little reflection will show how, without our thinking much about it, an exigence quite actively channels our attention in several different pre-patterned ways: Take a few moments to let yourself notice anything at all. You might let your consciousness just float, or you might go back to what you were aware of before you started reading. In any case, turn away from this text now and, without closing your eyes, take about 20 seconds just "experiencing."

Now consider what you experienced. You will find that your experience occurs in patterns: You may have noticed that you are uncomfortable in your chair, or that you are hungry. In this case, your experience is *biologically* patterned. Or you may have noticed an untied shoelace or an odd-looking switch on a wall. Now your experience is *practically* patterned. Perhaps some person came to mind; you found yourself curious about someone's appearance or who someone's friends are. You may have wondered about your appearance or about your feelings toward someone. Here your experience is *dramatically* patterned. It may happen that you focused on the colors, textures and arrangements of trees outside or remembered a song that makes you smile. This is an experience that is *aesthetically* patterned. Maybe your mind kept working on the ideas and concepts being presented here. In this case, your experience is *intellectually* patterned. Or even if your attention drifted without direction, consider that you mainly noticed either sights or sounds or tastes or smells or textures or movements, despite the fact that they affected all your sensory organs.

The point is that noticing, paying attention, "experiencing," is not at all like running a mental camera. Noticing is not completely determined by sensory events in our eyeballs or on our eardrums. If consciousness is a stream, it runs through a labyrinth of moving dams and sluices. It is quite selective. Much of our selective noticing depends on our interests. Even if you skipped over the 20 seconds of your time that I requested, it is because you were *interested* in something else. Politicians see voters where lawyers see clients.

This selective noticing also depends on what is already patterned. We do not notice the sound of traffic because nothing stands out from the roar, but we do notice pictures on a wall and the pecking of a distant woodpecker. We especially notice beauty, and the feeling of enticement it conveys. As we mentioned earlier, beauty represents to us, in symbolic form, the order, the goodness, and the love we feel impelled to embrace. Experiencing, then, has a normative function that is interested in patterns and relationships and overlooks what appears unrelated to anything else.

THE NORMATIVITY OF UNDERSTANDING

Besides being selective in our experiencing, we also seek to understand. We spontaneously ask *what* or *why* or *how* or *how often* or *what for*. The answer we hope for is an explanation. It may be an explanation of what stock futures are, or why we behaved badly, or of how the basement became flooded, or how often to rotate our tires, or what the star button on the phone is for.

Between asking a question for explanation and arriving at an answer, there is the act of insight. It is quite important to identify the experience of an insight for ourselves because it is easily confused with just looking or just memorizing.

To catch an insight in the act, consider this example: I bought a maple sapling from a nursery. The salesman encouraged me to plant flowers at its base. But why should I plant flowers at the base of a tree I bought?

You will find an explanation further down, but for now, it is more important to notice the push of your curiosity and its dissatisfaction with half-baked ideas. This push is evidence of a drive, and this dissatisfaction is evidence of its normativity—something is incomplete.

Notice how images function in curiosity. You probably imagined a sapling and some flowers at its base. Perhaps your image included the nursery and the salesman. You did not work at conjuring up this image; it was spontaneously crafted by a normativity inherent in your drive to understand. In *On the Soul*, Aristotle pointed out that when we understand anything we make connections among elements in an image (III, 7, 431 a 16). Images can help us get insight into how to organize a bookshelf or why there is a rainbow after a rain. Just as the experience of confusion is represented to us by mental images, so too the exigence to understand drives us to play with these images in ways that move us to find an explanation. Yet these images function in ways quite different from the symbolic exigence. For besides our ability to link up images with affects, understanding requires the ability to *unlink* them so that we can play with images to trigger insight in ways quite independent of the pull of affects.

However—and this is the key point—notice that your mental image is not yet an explanation. These pictures do not answer "why" it is good to plant flowers at the base of a new tree. Children and artists imagine trees and flowers all the time without looking for explanations. An explanation is the result of an insight, and an insight grasps an answer to a question. To reach an explanation of why anyone should plant flowers at the base of a sapling, you need an insight into the data represented by the image.

What exactly is an insight? When we look for explanations, we search for "sense" or "cogency" or "coherence" among the elements in the situation we are trying to understand. An insight is a grasp of the intelligibility that is inherent in the data. It is what Aristotle called "form" and what modern scientists call "the nature of" or "the likelihood of."

Maybe you thought of several explanations: That saplings are happier with the pleasant company of flowers. Or that the salesman was trying to add flowers to my purchases so his profit would be higher. Or that some chemical in flowers is good for maples. Maybe you thought of all these explanations but are still not satisfied.

Something does not measure up. Being intellectually dissatisfied is prime evidence that your consciousness has inner norms for understanding.

As it happened, I asked the salesman "Why are the flowers important?" He told me that most people automatically water their flowers, but not their trees. But young trees need plenty of water. So, plant some flowers around the sapling, and it gets the water it needs.

Aha! I got it! The explanation made sense. I notice a distinct change in my mind between entertaining various images and grasping a "why" that made the most sense. This change, this grasp, is an act of understanding. An insight.

This pairing of understanding with the understood is a wonderful phenomenon. When I understood why I should plant flowers around my sapling, a singular part of evolving reality in the universe—my particular consciousness seeking to understand—grasped what can be understood in some other part of reality. The universe is so structured that some things in the universe (we) can "grasp" or "contain" the inner dynamic governing the functioning of other things in the universe. Because of the normative functions of understanding in human consciousness, the *intelligibility* of reality is searched out by the *intelligence* of reality. It happens every time anyone asks why, or how, or how often, or what for.

THE NORMATIVITY OF REASON

This act of understanding brings an intellectual satisfaction. However, no matter how coherent our understanding may be, we can still miss the mark. There may be better explanations. So, besides being intelligent, we are also reasonable. We are reasonable when we try to distinguish between adequate and inadequate explanations, between correct and incorrect conclusions, between reality and illusion. So satisfaction on the level of understanding can lead to dissatisfaction on the level of reason. On this level, we ask quite different kinds of questions.

- We may ask about actual occurrences—whether or not it is raining outside.

- Or we may ask about logical conclusions—whether it is valid to conclude from, "All humans are created equal," that therefore "All humans deserve health care."
- Or we may ask about the plausibility of an explanation— whether the reason maple saplings thrive when surrounded by flowers is really because of the additional water they get.
- Or we may ask about the truth of a proposition— whether Mary is the daughter of Judith.

It is important to notice the big difference between the normative drive to understand and the normative drive to make reasonable affirmations. Despite the fact that the difference is remarkable, many an astute philosopher has failed to notice it. When we do understand something and express what we understand, it usually takes a few sentences because explanations connect a number of elements in a specific way. Then, by our reason, we use the answers of understanding as our starting point for asking *whether, really, no kidding, is that correct?* We seek to verify what understanding proposes. This is because reason only affirms or denies propositions. Where understanding expects an explanation in many words, reason expects just a yes or no, probably or not.

For example, I assume it made sense to you that planting flowers around saplings assures that they will get watered. But is it true? Has anyone tested the survival rates of saplings with and without the circle of flowers? If these questions occurred to you, then you experienced the normative drive to be reasonable.

Here is a more thorough exercise for noticing the normativity of reason in your consciousness. Imagine the kind of spool used for electrical wire. It has 4-inch diameter wheels and a 1-inch axle. And imagine a few feet of string wrapped around the axle, with the end emerging underneath the axle toward you. If you pull the string toward you, will the spool roll toward you?

If you have experience with spools—from sewing, for example—you may be satisfied that you know what the spool will do. But can you convince anyone else? Or, if you are not sure, can you find the answer?

Prompted by the normative drive to *understand*, you may play with various explanations of *why* you think the spool will—or will not—roll toward you. Whatever explanation you come up with, it is *up to your reason* that you come with your explanation. It is like the attorney who comes up to a jury with an explanation for a hoped-for yes or no—a verdict of guilty or not. Maybe you think the answer is *no* because you figure that pulling the string from *beneath* the axle must revolve the spool *away* from you. Or maybe you think the answer is *yes* because you figured that pulling the string from a point *above* the ground must tip the spool *toward* you.

But sooner or later, your *reason* moves you to run a test. Here, notice how the drive of reason sets certain conditions that must be met by experience before saying your yes or no. In the case of our spool, you set up this simple condition for reason:

> The question is, will the spool roll toward me when I pull the string? If the spool rolls away, the answer is no. If the spool rolls toward me, the answer is yes.

Of course, it is not these words that set the conditions; you, by your reason, set the conditions. It is your reason that moves you to consider the data of experience to see whether or not the conditions have been met. So test it out. Get a spool, wrap string around its axle, and pull.

At this point if you are wondering what the spool will actually do, then you are experiencing the normative drive of reason. This normative drive in us is alert for experiences that may not fit. We experience the same norms whenever we say things like, "Really?" and "Nonsense!" and "I was *so* mistaken!" When I conduct this experiment in a classroom with an actual spool, it is not long before the normativity reason is too much for students to bear. "Well, pull the string!"

Notice how different this feels compared to the normative drive of understanding. Questions for understanding—what, what for, how, how often, why—aim for internal consistency, pattern, cogency, and logic. Our minds play around with various explanations. But once we settle on one explanation over all others, our minds come home and get serious. We move on to ask the *whether* question—whether this or that explanation satisfies us. This difference between understanding and reason corresponds to John Henry Newman's distinction between a notional assent on the level of understanding ("It makes sense") and a real assent on the level of reason ("It's really so!").

By testing assertions against experience, the normative drive of reason protects us from both overcertainty and undercertainty. We are overcertain when our strongly held opinions do not square with experience. This happens when we ignore certain experiences that are relevant. We are undercertain when we withhold judgment long after we have run out of good questions. This happens when we raise further questions about experiences that are not relevant to the matter at hand. At each extreme, the normative drive of reason disturbs us because the relevant experiences have not been given their due.

While overcertainty ignores certain relevant experiences and undercertainty entertains non-relevant questions, we can also experience *probable* certainty. This happens when no further relevant questions occur to us except this one: Have all the relevant questions occurred to me? The broader our experience, the less likely there are relevant questions that we have not considered. In things we experience firsthand, we can be absolutely certain about many things: your shoes are brown; the weather is stormy. When it comes to believing others, the question of their trustworthiness will be relevant. What we hear from less trustworthy sources, we say, "It might be true" or "It is probably true;" what we hear from more trustworthy sources we say, "It's very likely true" or "It's practically certain." The *probability* of a statement being true is simply the probability that further relevant questions may exist.

There are several processes that come into play under the normative drives of reason, and we need to define them with technical terms. One is the act of judging. By *judging*, we will mean our act of verifying some idea, of affirming or denying some proposition. Our act of judgment does not issue in an explanation (as the act of understanding does) but rather in a yes of affirmation or a no of negation. Likewise, by *reflecting* we will mean not just any kind of thought process but the kind that reflects on the ideas presented by understanding for the purpose of coming to a judgment. In the chapters that follow, we will use the terms *judging/judgment* and *reflecting/reflection* in these defined senses.

Before moving on, would you like to know if the spool will roll toward you? (If you do not, then the experiment has failed on you.) The answer is yes. It rolls *up*, against your pull. One cogent explanation for this is that at any single instant, the pivot point is where the spool touches the ground, and you are pulling toward you from a point above the pivot. If this surprises you, perhaps you mistakenly imagined the pivot point to be through the center of the axle. In any case, if you feel an urge to test this out, then you are feeling the normative drives of reason.

THE NORMATIVITY OF RESPONSIBILITY

Being reasonable is making sure our thinking corresponds to reality. But besides thinking about reality, we often aim to change it. Interest in action is what distinguishes animals from plants. Interest in *appropriate* action is what distinguishes humans from the rest of the animals. In short, being responsible is being interested in appropriate action. And because, unlike the rest of animals, we can create any image we please, we have the ability to ask ourselves what we *might* do, before deciding what we *will* do. Specifically, we feel impelled to ask questions like *Should I? Ought we? Is it better or worse? Is it worth our while?* These questions are clearly normative.

They represent the most fundamental and central moral drive to live in a responsible way.

The normative drive of responsibility is different from the normative drive of reason. When, being reasonable, we focus on knowing the truth, we put aside our feelings. We think with cool heads. But when, being responsible, we focus on action, our consciousness is flooded by feelings. We deliberate with warm hearts.

For example: Someday you will die. No one doubts this. But suppose your doctor diagnoses you with pancreatic cancer and tells you to get your affairs in order because you have six weeks to live. Now the exigence to act is upon you. Your feelings rush in. The relevance of your entire life comes to the fore. Long-neglected questions appear—how you ought to have lived, how your family will deal with your loss, and what, if anything, remains of *you*.

For an exercise to notice the normative function of being responsible, read the form below.

Advance Medical Directive for the End of Life

If I lose the ability to recognize family and friends, and my sense of humor, and my appetite; and if these conditions are independently determined to be irreversible by two physicians, then do not force food or antibiotics on me, nor any water except to keep my mouth moist and comfortable.

___This statement represents my wishes.
___This statement does not represent my wishes.

Name: _____   Date:_____

To gain the most from this exercise, please write down one of the two "statement" testimonies on a piece of paper along with your signature and the date.

No doubt you have a few concerns about starving yourself to death. Maybe you feel annoyed that medical forms like this are foisted on the elderly. Perhaps you feel apprehensive about severing the ties to your loved ones like this. Or maybe, feeling indecisive, you did not sign it. Perhaps you feel dismissive about this little exercise here—in a book you had intended to read to learn something about ethics.

Whatever you did, notice how different your consciousness is. Did you notice that suddenly your feelings play a central role? This is because our self-*image* is deeply tied to our self-*affects*. Our self-image is always a unity—the identity we call "me,"—that continues under every change. At the same time, our self-affects indicate which image of ourselves may be better or worse. In any decision we experience the symbolizing exigence. It links affects with images to give normative direction to our question, What is better for me to do?

But after experiencing your feelings about signing this, notice that you moved to "deliberate" or weigh the relative values of the two options. This is the experience the exigence to be responsible for the self you want to be. To notice this demand is to notice the fundamental "should" that underlies all our decisions.

This exercise is about a life-and-death decision. But we experience the normativity of responsibility anytime the *should* question occurs to us. It occurs not because we make it occur but because human consciousness is naturally an active, normative process that moves us toward the better.

THE NORMATIVITY OF LOVE

When you considered signing the advance medical directive, did it occur to you that you would not make this decision alone? To whom would you go for advice? In your mind, name the people you would probably ask. Also, name the people who are deceased whom you wish you could ask.

I doubt that you selected people because of their counseling skills or medical knowledge or expertise in ethics. Probably you did not *select* them at all. More likely, they are people who are already a part of you. This is because when we speak of *self*-consciousness, our *self* is always a connected self. We are each a child of parents and a companion to companions. Where we cherish these relationships, and even where we abhor or simply lack them, we experience the exigence to share our lives with others. Few people imagine themselves as peering out upon the world from the little wagon of their egos asking others for a helpful push now and then. Most of us imagine ourselves as walking arm in arm with companions in the same direction. We experience ourselves as radically social every time we do something with others—sing a duet, play tennis, contribute money, work on a production line, and even cast a ballot in the privacy of a voting booth. When we see a little girl stumble, we spontaneously reach out to save her from scraping her knees. Our "personalities" emerge from a prior "interpersonality" that is so immediate we seldom think about it. We carry this prior interpersonality and our express mutual commitments with the abiding questions, *Who is with me? With whom do I share my life?*

We experience the normativity of love in this awareness of ourselves as part of a "we." When we relish being alive, we simultaneously relish our relationships. As part of taking good care of ourselves, we commit ourselves to nourishing our close friendships and strengthening our broad loyalties to our countries. We live in a gravitational field in which human masses are drawn toward one another. People in love do not feel like themselves when their beloved is away, nor does their beloved. Without discounting the value of solitude, every religion and philosophy recognizes that it is not good to be completely alone.

The normative drives of love push us toward moral wisdom. Certainly, when we successfully bond with others, we gain a higher perspective on what really is better because we complement our viewpoints with theirs. But more than that, we welcome invitations to join in common enterprises and to share outcomes, subordinating our personal hopes and risks to the enrichment of the life we share with others.

Still, being in love is more than being moral. Not everyone who upholds high moral standards yields to this exigence to share his or her spirit. In that wonderful biblical story of the prodigal son (Luke 15: 11-24), Jesus described three people—an errant son, a dutiful son, and a loving father. The errant son runs off and squanders his inheritance. He returns years later to find his father rushing out open-armed to welcome him, while the dutiful son stands arms-folded in resentment. It illustrates the rather common phenomenon by which highly responsible people can still be blind to what is really better. The dutiful son lives mainly by the obligations he knows. He keenly feels the norms of responsibility—so keenly, in fact, that he is fixated on duty but blind to love. His bitter homage to obligation has blocked the normative drives of love in his heart, norms that would draw forth compassion for his brother and drive out resentment toward his father.

What we notice here is how love can reveal values beyond our sense of individual responsibility. Our personal sense of responsibility often tells us only what seems better from our personal perspective, even when we are personally committed to objective moral principles. In contrast, love—the assumption of connectedness—can reveal what is better from the perspective of enriching that connectedness. The truly better is realized when that love becomes mutual, and a higher "we" emerges.

Finally, where the four normative demands to be attentive, intelligent, reasonable, and responsible prompt us through specific questions about our situations, the demand to be in love is experienced differently. It comes as an inner demand to *be* a new kind of person—being myself, not by myself, or for myself, but in relation to others. At the same time it comes as an outer invitation from those who love me and want to be in relation to me. To be *in* love is to rely on the "we" of love as a new principle for all our imagination, thoughts, feelings, and decisions.

THE VALUE OF THE EXERCISES

What do these exercises accomplish? They should give you firsthand evidence of the inner criteria you rely on whenever you change your priorities. So, to reflect on method in ethics, it is essential that we become familiar with these normative drives, to notice the differences among them, and to understand what each of the five accomplishes. Here, by verifying how all moral opinions originate in the same normative drives of consciousness, we lay the foundation on which to build a commonly accepted method in ethics.

These exercises also define a basic language for a unified method in ethics. Key terms are experience and attentiveness, insight and understanding, reason and judgment, responsibility and decision, shared living and love. In later chapters more definitions will be added, but before going any further, it is important to recall *how* these terms are defined. Earlier we remarked how a definition of "beauty" is best done by relating it to what we called a "ground experience" of being moved by some sight or sound. Beauty is one experience, among others, of self-transcendence. In the same manner, the above terms refer to ground experiences. This is why their definitions require exercises to define for ourselves what they mean.

4. OUR NORMATIVE DRIVES ARE ORDERED

AN INTEGRATING SPIRAL

Each of the five exigences of our consciousness not only makes its particular demand; it also measures its own success. It will continue to disturb us as long as its demand has not been met and will rest satisfied when it has. These drives do not work automatically. Like any other system in the evolutionary process, their emergence largely depends on whatever prior developments we have undergone, what opportunities we currently have at hand, and what forces may impede our efforts to be open-minded, caring, and connected to others. Then there is that awful wound in our moral nature whereby we can deliberately refuse to follow their demands.

Integrated Levels of Our Normative Drives

But when they emerge, the drives display a beautiful, spiraling self-organization. Just as biological systems leave open possibilities for organization at the neurological level and neurological systems leave open possibilities for organization at the subconscious level, so each level of normative functions in our consciousness leaves open possibilities for organization at the next higher level. And when that organization occurs, the higher level integrates the functioning of all the levels below it, directing them toward ends proper to that higher level.

Our subconscious arranges our experience of situations into patterns at the level of conscious awareness. That is, the normativity of experience allows into awareness what is patterned and what appears capable of being patterned. It moves past what presents no possibility of being patterned.

When we pay attention to these patterned experiences, whether in the symbolic forms welling up from our subconscious, in our imagination, in our memories, or in what we perceive through our five senses, we feel the drive to understand what we experience. The normativity of intelligence has taken over, directing our consciousness to raise questions looking for explanations.

Then, at the level of being reasonable, once we have some understanding, we experience the normative drives of reason to verify that we did not *mis*understand. We do this by checking to verify that our understanding of a situation really accounts for the relevant experiences of that situation.

Having reasoned that X is what is really going on, or is the best available explanation of a situation, we rise to the level of responsibility. Here we deliberate and eventually decide what, if anything, we ought to do about X, and we act on our decision.

Love—the highest level—functions not strictly within anyone's individual consciousness but essentially in a common consciousness of those who share a world. Our "personal" decisions are largely shaped by values inherited from forebears and motivated by love for our contemporaries. At the same time, others seek in us a willingness to improve life together.

To the degree that we obeyed the prompting of these normative drives of our consciousness, we savor a deepening sense of being our true selves. Had we been bluffing ourselves or others, our actions usually make things worse. Then, because of our ever-ready normative drives, we again feel the urge to pay attention to experiences we may have overlooked, to understand these further experiences, to correct our prior oversights and to consider how to do even better. So besides the five distinct exigences to transcend ourselves, the overall transcending exigence requires that all the normative functions of consciousness work together. Being moral, in other words, is not restricted to "doing the right thing." Nor is it restricted to "making the best value judgments." Being moral requires the full collaboration of all five of the normative drives of consciousness.

Believing Others

So far, we focused on the normative drives we experience as individuals, but I do not want to leave the impression that being moral is a strictly individual matter. These experiments to discover the normative drives of consciousness give evidence of the moral character of the universe which, when it appears in humans, represents the workings of a cosmic exigence that drives all of us to do better together. We all are moved by the same sorts of drives to improve ourselves and our situations.

So from a fully theoretical perspective, morality is not restricted to operations of the individual's consciousness toward doing better. The full scope of the moral order encompasses an exigence shared by all humans to mount through and combine with one another all the inner normative drives to struggle toward improving our shared life over time. This functioning of the moral exigence of the universe between persons is evident when we consider how extensively we rely on believing what others discovered firsthand.[16] I have never verified that the world is round or that my uncle died young. Nor have I independently become convinced that democracy is better than monarchy and that Gandhi was a profoundly good person. I was led to these convictions because of the overwhelming convergence of the moral opinions of people I trust.

And why do I trust them? Again, I trust because the normative drives of all levels of consciousness urge me this way. The drives of love bind me to others, so that I share knowledge and values long before I scrutinize them. The drives of responsibility press me to maintain the bonds of love not only by telling others what I learned firsthand but also by listening to what others learned firsthand. The drives of reason move me to test these inherited beliefs against my personal experiences. The drives of intelligence urge me to integrate new beliefs into my current worldviews, making adjustments where logic and my personal insights dictate. The drives of experience impel me to widen my perception to take in the new vistas that open when I integrate the horizons of others with my own. Everything we take to be true and everything we honor as valuable originates in someone, somewhere, making these personal discoveries. In only a few instances have you or I been the original learner.

Affectivity and Creativity in History

Our shared normative drives form a system—a self-organizing, evolutionary process by which we humans actually do better together. As self-organizing, improvements in any one of the five drives realign the functioning of the other four. As self-organizing, the system of normative functions is also self-repairing. No part begins to fail without increasing the demands in the other four parts for correction, sometimes initiated personally and sometimes under correction from others.

With the emergence of humans on this planet, then, there seem to be two simultaneous movements toward doing better. In one movement, all first-hand learning represents our creative movements in history, rising upward from experience to understanding to reason to responsibility to love. In the other, all interpersonal trust and inherited beliefs represent our affective movements in history, merging downward from love to responsibility to reason to understanding to experience.[17] Doing better is the result of both movements occurring simultaneously.

Affective Movement
↓
Doing Better
↑
Creative Movement

These two movements marvelously complement each other. From above downward, the affective movement makes our selves "engaged" selves. Besides the reality of our persons, there are the wider realities of friendships, communities, and universal solidarity. It includes all the ways we believe others. Our love for one another, along with our love for transcendent reality, reveals values beyond what mere creative reasoning can see. The affective movement tells us what is worth investigating. It tells us who is worthy of our trust. The affective dimensions of these value questions occur not only in families working out everyday practical problems but also in lawyers, politicians, doctors, scientists, artists and scholars. It would be difficult to conceive of any genuine intellectual and aesthetic development that is not strongly influenced by affective bonds among collaborators.

At the same time, going from below upward, the creative movement includes all the ways anyone reaches factual or moral knowledge firsthand. Something bothers you about a situation. You seek to understand the situation correctly. When you learn what is really going on, you ask what you ought to do and whom you can trust to work with you. Where you rely on inherited worldviews that are valid, your creativity enriches your heritage. Where you scrutinize your heritage for myths and misplaced priorities, your creativity purifies that heritage. Even when your personal insights lead you to conclusions that your parents have been telling you all along, your learning becomes a more deeply effective part of your life, and you more authoritatively pass it on to your children. In all these cases, you contribute to the betterment of your world.

Morality, then, is both affective and creative. It is a harmony between our interpersonal commitments and our insightful successes. Speaking analogically, these two movements together constitute a kind of experiment, conducted by historical process, in the enriching morality of the universe. Still, although both movements have always functioned in the evolution of our species, it appears that some periods were dominated by the ideal of affectively bonded communities while other periods were dominated by the ideal of intelligent, creative changes. These two ideals—with Community and Stability on the one side and Progress and Change on the other—are related dialectically: as one brightens the other tends to fade. Platonic and Aristotelian philosophers promoted the stable society, glued by virtue; change aroused suspicion. The Enlightenment and modern science promoted progress, incited by insight; Individual Reason was the rising star, while community and mutual care fell into the shadows.

We aim for an ongoing engagement of both. By trying to integrate reason and feeling in practice, we move toward a resolution in our personal lives the contrary philosophic ideals of rationalism and romanticism. Mind you, the ideal is not to establish an ideal standpoint but rather to maintain a moving, empirical viewpoint on what happens anytime we try to do better. Our viewpoints will keep on moving as long as we remain open to developments in our understanding of ourselves, be they scientific, scholarly, aesthetic, mystical or philosophical.

Verifying

So much for an account of how our affectivity and creativity are intertwined. Does it pan out in your experience? By way of a personal experiment, consider this:

Jeff, a 55-year-old patient in the cancer ward, recently completed his third round of chemotherapy. He learned that because his lung cancer has spread to his liver and lymph glands, the cancer will soon end his life. With his wife, Dianne, he decides to forgo any further chemotherapy. His doctor advises them that he has only two options. One is to let the cancer take its course, until he dies in about three months. Painkillers can numb the pain, but they will numb in his mind as well. The other is to forgo food and water, except for keeping his mouth moist, in which case he will die in about three weeks, while the body's natural analgesics will gradually reduce his pain and with less numbing of his mind.

Jeff immediately answers that the second option is out of the question, since he believes suicide is morally wrong. Dianne is alarmed. "Sweetheart," she says, "I can't bear the thought of you suffering needlessly. How about if we talk about this for a few days?"

You recognize the moral dilemma: Is it better to "let nature take its course" or to hasten an inevitable death with far less pain? What matters for us, however, is not what Jeff and Dianne should do. Our interest is in the consideration you just gave to the case. What just happened to you?

If you ever lost a beloved to terminal illness, the case probably engages you. If so, then, certainly, as you read the words, you made sure you understood the situation. You pictured Jeff, Dianne, the doctor, and the hospital room. You felt the emotional stress. You also felt some intellectual stress stemming from certain moral principles you hold. You made at least an initial judgment about what should be done. Further questions sprung to mind to help you make a final judgment. Now all this happens so quickly that the different levels of your consciousness seem to blend into one. Our interest, though, is to catch the method of moral reflections in the act. Since there are quite distinct acts involved, it will help us distinguish and interconnect them if we notice how the acts at each level might be frustrated.

When just paying attention to this case, notice that you spontaneously shut out any distractions as you read. If something distracted you, then you either ignored the distraction or "bookmarked" where you were reading. Here, you might name any distractions that might have occurred while you read the case.

You paid attention not simply for any pleasure of seeing words on paper but *in order to* understand. That is, your intelligence was directing your attention. Here, recall what efforts you made to focus your mind on *understanding*, particularly as distinct from just *imagining* the scene.

Maybe you backed up to make sure you correctly understood the facts of the case. Maybe you wondered about further possibly relevant facts, such as whether Jeff *really* had only two options, or whether starving to death *really* triggers natural pain-reducers in the body. In any case, you sought to understand not just for the pleasure of understanding but *in order to* verify that what you understood is correct. Here, notice the point where you said, in effect, "I got it." That is, you correctly understood everything presented in the case description.

You likely felt Jeff's and Dianne's moral urgency. I say "felt" because feelings are our initial responses to the possible presence of values and their absence. In moral situations, we feel *in order to* make a value judgment. Here, name the feelings you have for Jeff; name those you feel for Dianne.

This may be as far as you went. You *feel* the moral issue without yet making your own judgment about what they ought to do. You may not want to make this judgment. Perhaps you reached a conviction about what Jeff should do. So here, say to yourself either, "I am convinced that I should not make a judgment about what Jeff should do" or "I am convinced that Jeff should ...." and finish the sentence.

If this case engaged you, these different levels of self-transcendence all worked together. In a real life situation like this, you would pay attention to understand, understand to verify reality, verify reality to respond morally to a real situation, initially in feelings and finally in a moral judgment. In the above case, what you experienced, first-hand, is the creative movement from which all moral progress ultimately springs.

At the same time, there were powerful affective and historical factors shaping your moral horizon. It is important to notice them, to name them, to claim them as shaping not only all moral judgments you personally make but also any moral judgment made by anyone, anywhere. So let me ask you some further relevant questions:

When you considered Jeff and Dianne, did some particular person in your own life come to mind? Perhaps it was a terminally ill friend who faced a similar decision. Maybe you found yourself thinking something like, "If Leo made this choice, then it cannot be a bad choice." If so, then you can understand how powerfully our affective links shape our moral views.

Here's another question: What is your last name? (If it was changed through marriage, what was the last name of the family you were born into?) What does this name mean to you? For example, if your family name is, or was, "Richards," then you know what it means to "act like a Richards." The name symbolizes a host of values that makes the Richards clan proud. So, what about it? Name those particular values and priorities that you inherited along with your surname.

The same is true of the moral heritage you happen to accept from a larger community. Whether this means being an Italian or a Methodist or a Democrat, your values are overwhelmingly shaped by your heritage. Your contribution may improve it or degrade it, but no one person can eliminate a heritage from the face of the earth. What is more, while traditional values are usually formulated as moral principles, all values are originally "incarnate"—the value of certain noble persons and exemplary communities about whom stories reveal, in the flesh, values that cannot be named. Indeed, how do we name these values? Do we not first recall a story, a narrative, a history? We drop our conceptual buckets into the deep well of a story to haul up some abstraction which, though valuable for teaching, still leaves unfathomable depths of values that our buckets cannot reach.

So why have you accepted these values? Why have you left unquestioned so many of them? Is it not because you love and are loved? Are not most people, like you, born into an affective web of values?

Again, these affective links to our fellows and forebears integrate the several levels of our consciousness into a unity. From above downward, they shape our moral concerns, which in turn shape what we know of reality, which shapes our understanding of reality, which shapes what we notice in our everyday lives. So my hopes are mainly our hopes. My successes are mainly our successes. My self-consciousness is simultaneously a "we" consciousness.

Of course, our affectivity and our creativity do not work quite so smoothly. Later on, we will explore how these movements can fail. But first we need to finish our account of how the normative drives of consciousness function in an ordered manner. In particular, we need to realize how absolutely fundamental the normative drives of consciousness are to any moral claim that X is better than Y. You can see where this is going. If we can verify, by personal experiments, what the ultimate sources of any moral view may be, we will have common grounds for explaining, promoting, criticizing, and revising any moral views whatsoever.

THE PRIMACY OF THE NORMATIVE DRIVES

Certainly you experience the drives that move you to pay attention, to understand things, to verify that what you think is true, to be responsible for doing better, and to be in love. Certainly they affect you during your every conscious moment. But experiencing them is not the same thing as noticing them. Nor is noticing them the same thing as understanding them. Nor is understanding them the same thing as verifying that your understanding is correct. Nor is the knowledge that you are correct the same thing as acting responsibly on this knowledge. Nor is acting responsibly the same thing as being a person affectively linked to others in love. These drives work behind the scenes. What we have done is slipped backstage and given names to the workings of the drives, images, affects, thoughts and choices going on back there.

In contrast, most of the moral norms ethicists talk about are on-stage, and we are the ones who brought them under the spotlight. Driven by our inner normative questions, we select some standards over others—"The Ten Commandments are basic for me" or "My philosophy is 'Be good to yourself.'" Or we select some exemplars over others—"I am a follower of Dorothy Day," or "I am a loyal Muslim." The normative functions of our consciousness lead us to consider these standards and exemplars as the sources of the moral values we honor in our everyday decisions.

What we are trying to make clear is that long before we honor any such moral standards or exemplars, we first honor the normative drives in our consciousness. Our inner normative criteria work before we know they are working. But because they work prior to all formulations, they are the source of all formulated norms, principles, standards, commandments, rules, and guidelines. They are the criteria by which we decide to emulate this exemplar rather than that, to honor one book above others, and to be loyal to one community over others. They are the *norma non normata* of ethical reflection—the norms not "normed" by anything else.

Although we use words for these inner normative drives, the words here are not ideas to put into practice. "Be intelligent" is not a rule to consider and embrace. It is the prior drive that already moves you to consider and embrace whatever rules make sense to you. These words are just an invitation to discover in yourself the working of your innate exigence to be intelligent.

The disturbing, but ultimately liberating, fact is this: All explicit moral norms selected by humans at any time and place in history originate in these implicit normative drives to be attentive, intelligent, reasonable, responsible, and in love. The test for this hypothesis lies in a standing invitation: Suppose you think that some other moral source—a rule or guide or person or book or heritage—may be more primary than these inner normative drives. How might it you have accepted it except on the word of persons being attentive, intelligent, reasonable, responsible and loving, in the manners that you have verified by the experiments in chapter 3?

I say this realization is disturbing because it raises questions about the validity of the teachings in revered writings and the examples of virtuous men and women. But that is the point: It *should* raise questions. All moral teachings and noble exemplars mean something only to human minds. While everyone experiences these five exigences, everyone also is vulnerable to their opposites—being myopic, narrow-minded, irrational, self-absorbed, and hateful. So the teachings and stories by which our moral standards have been passed down to us may be distorted by human minds in all sorts of ways. Were we to assume otherwise, we would mindlessly teach and publicly embody distorted moral standards.

This is why I also say that this realization is also liberating. By recognizing the workings of the normative functions of consciousness in ourselves, we will have sharpened the personal tools to ask the right questions about how the teachings and stories in our moral inheritance were first developed. Like moral threshers, we can winnow the husks of what made things worse from the kernels of what made things better.

DEFINITIONS

If, then, these inner normative functions are the absolute base of any moral advance, we need a shorthand way of talking about them.

Authenticity

Let us say that the more we yield ourselves to these inner normative demands, the more *authentic* we become. To be authentic does not mean being perfect or never wrong. It means nothing more or less than relying on these normative drives for our living. So: *Authenticity is obedience to the exigences to be attentive, be intelligent, be reasonable, be responsible, and be in love.* [18]

Being authentic, then, is being guided by the compound norma-tive drives we experience in our consciousness. We usually talk about it as "being my true self" or "being real," or "being centered." But not everyone notices how being our best selves means being obedient to five distinct drivers toward the better, and still fewer recognize how these drivers combine to pull us out of our self-absorption and throw us, ruthlessly at times, into the real world. So we come to the paradox of human life: Being one's true self means being self-transcending. Being a real person means being part of a higher reality of an "us." Being a centered self means being fully engaged beyond one's self.

Should

With this definition of authenticity in mind, we can now define, within a theoretical context, the meaning of *should*—that nucleus around which all moral questions revolve.

This real world, of which we are a part, is a moving, moral reality. Haltingly, experimentally, but relentlessly, it leans toward the better. Compared to nonhuman animals, we search out the better less by chance and more by consciously experienced normative drives. So the primary meaning of our word *should* is found in our experience of the exigence to be authentic. We *should* be attentive. We *should* be intelligent. We *should* be reasonable. We *should* be responsible. We *should* work to be in love.

The meaning of each of these shoulds will not be found in a dictionary. Nor is it enough to understand the meaning I am offering here. As is probably evident by now, *should* is a ground experience. What counts is noticing the exigences in your experience, understanding the differences among them, and verifying that they indeed underlie all your everyday shoulds—to work hard, to be kind to others, to obey the law, and so on. It is this constant *should* to be authentic that produces the variable shoulds about particular options in our lives.

So we can give a definition of the fundamental meaning of should: *Should is the experience of the exigences to be authentic.*

While this theoretical definition belongs to the discipline of ethics, it is nearly incomprehensible in ordinary moral deliberations. When people sit down to talk about what to do next, they use *should* in different senses, some of which are legitimate and others illegitimate. Of course, people justify illegitimate shoulds by all kinds of rationalizations. Dictators—whether the big-minded autocrat in the capitol or the small-minded tyrant in the den— think *should* means whatever they tell others to do, no matter how irrational. Literalists think everyone *should* accept their naïve interpretations of documents or rules or definitions or grammars. Cowards think they *should* put security above freedom and compliance above challenge. The reason we call these people irrational, naïve, or cowardly is that we assume that their authenticity is not well developed and, as a result, that their *shoulds* are not legitimate.

But essentially, legitimate shoulds can be justified only by a single test. Any claim that X *should* be done, or not done, must ultimately find its justification in the authenticity of its proponent. The laws, customs, historical exemplars, and ethical principles that tell people what they should or should not do are only as legitimate as the authenticity of the people who first proposed them and the people who modified them to meet new challenges.

Conscience

Closely associated with the notion of *should* is the notion of *conscience.* To define *conscience,* we need to approach it from our wider understanding of *consciousness.* We saw that the normative processes of consciousness are not just processes *within* consciousness; they *constitute* consciousness. Not to experience any inner normative drive is to be *unconscious.* Moreover, we are not simply conscious or unconscious. Our consciousness rises in distinguishable stages. Our exercises for noticing these normative drives revealed five distinct levels:

> Anyone who is not unconscious is at least selectively noticing—a self often wishing and craving, and as often dreading and resenting, even in dreamy sleep.
>
> At times, being conscious is being intelligently conscious—a self feeling perplexed over what makes no sense and toying with possible explanations.
>
> At times it is being reasonably conscious—a self setting aside wishful thinking and simplistic explanations to figure out what really is so.
>
> At times it is being responsibly conscious—a self alert to what should not be and pushing for what should.
>
> All the while, as a *basso continuo* under the more salient themes, being conscious is also being affectively conscious—a shared consciousness of the "we" that one is with others.

The first three normative drives—to pay attention, to understand, to reason—have knowledge as their objective. By themselves, they do not produce any action; prior to action, we can change our minds. But when we swing into action, a new set of events occurs. Here, driven by the normative drive of responsibility, we make commitments that change both our surroundings and our individual selves. We cannot take it back. We normally refer to the deliberations of responsibility as "conscience." And it seems worthwhile to retain this term within the theoretical discipline of ethics. To do so, we need to connect the notion of conscience to the innate, natural normative functions of consciousness. This will give a definition of conscience that is precise and capable of being understood by anyone who has discovered these normative drives.[19] What particular language anyone speaks will make no difference because the definition will appeal to commonly available data internal to us all. So: *Conscience is responsible consciousness.*

Whenever we deliberate, whenever we weigh options, whenever we wonder about what to do, we experience our conscience, which is the same as experiencing ourselves as alert to what should and should not be—an experience of ourselves as responsibly conscious. While popular views think of conscience as a moral police department, conscience itself is essentially creative. It is about seizing opportunities to do better and avoid worse. The reputation of conscience as just an inner nagging voice likely stems from the primitive fear of scolding and abandonment that dominates the consciousness of children. For most adults, better and worse are not about rewards and punishments but about objective values and disvalues.

The voice of conscience speaks to us from several different angles simultaneously: our knowledge of a situation, our spontaneous feelings about it, our habitual values, the expectations of others, guidance from the wise, promises we made, the duties involved in our social roles, and what we think will result from our actions. The voices of many philosophers restrict the normativity of moral consciousness to a single element: to virtue, or ideals, or obedience, or promises, or obligations, or consequences. But each of these aspects of moral deliberation, valid by itself, draws its full validity from being combined in an actual person dealing authentically with his or her compound moral disturbance.

5. OUR NORMATIVE DRIVES ARE WOUNDED

FROM NORMATIVE DRIVES TO DOING BETTER

If everyone experiences the same inner normative drives as the source of all improvements in life, why do we often disagree on what is the better thing to do? A simple answer is that we bring different experiences to bear on our shared situations. We have not all learned the same things, and even where our upbringings are similar, we are not equally concerned about what we learned. But then why do we not learn from each other's experiences and priorities? Should not different perspectives widen our viewpoints? Should not the exigence for authenticity working in each of us eventually converge on concerns and priorities shared by all of us?

Somewhere between the inner normative drives and the outer action, the exigence to do better is blocked. We know that people can be mean, and people can be stupid. Unhappily, some people are both. But to get beyond name-calling, we first need to understand the various forces that come into play as our inner drives press for outer action, and what sort of obstacles block their natural progress. There are three dynamics that deserve particular attention. They each involve the combination of the creative movements that initiate moral progress and the affective movements that bequeath moral traditions.

1. **The Interplay of Authenticity and Heritage.** Our inner normative drives can tell us one thing and our heritages can tell us another. Sometimes these inner drives challenge our heritage, and sometimes our heritage focuses our attention on these inner drives. So, from a historical point of view, the creative movement and the affective movement can conflict.

2. **Blind Spots.** There are areas where we do not see well. We ignore certain questions about our obsessions, our self-image, our heritage, and about any problem that demands diligent, thoroughgoing analysis. These subjective limitations block both the creativity that would solve new problems and the affectivity that would prompt people to reconcile their differences with others.

3. **Willfulness.** We see what we ought to do, but we do not do it. Or we see what we should not do, and we go ahead and do it

anyway. So even when different parties verbally agree on some plan of action, the actions actually taken by some can undermine and even reverse the actions taken by others. Unlike the subjective blind spots that narrow the scope of questions we will ask, to act against our better judgment is to refuse to make decisions on reliable answers springing either from our creativity or from affection we have for others.

Each of these dynamics has a distinct way of preventing the functioning of the normative drives of our consciousness, which leads to contradictory standards and actions, and ultimately of preventing us from doing better. The more deeply we investigate how each one functions, the easier it will be to understand how to resolve them. So, postponing to the next chapter the discussion of how these contradictions may be resolved, let us understand exactly how these dynamics impede moral progress.

THE INTERPLAY OF AUTHENTICITY AND HERITAGE

We saw how doing better happens in two simultaneous move-ments—a rising, creative movement by which individuals discover better ways of living, and a descending, affective movement by which a culture bequeaths values to its members. For the sake of speaking about conflicts between these movements, let us say the creative movement is carried by the individual's *authenticity* and the affective movement is carried by a culture's *heritage*.

Let us first be clear about what a heritage is *not*. A heritage is not a collection of documents and laws. Nor is it a community's idealized memories of its founders. Nor is it even the social visions of a community's founders. A heritage is the actual set of priorities that a present generation *considers* it inherited from forebears. These are the inherited priorities that actually govern lawmaking and define what a community considers respectable behavior. It includes the values a community places on schools, laws, govern-ments, the military, and all kinds of welfare and cultural institu-tions. It also includes the personal habits, skills, and obligations that define our priorities, as well as all the connections to family, friends, and larger communities with whom we share those priorities. A heritage is an enormously complex, unclassifiable body of values gained through billions of individual adaptations to concrete circumstances made by forebears to whom we feel affectively bound.

This actual, operating set of priorities may be at variance with what a community's founders thought was their legacy. Sometimes today's priorities are better than the original and sometimes worse. Today's priorities may even be at odds with each other, as people take contrary views on what they consider important in their documents, laws, founders, and leaders. Of course, these internal differences can lead to better or to worse—better when creative members challenge a moribund status quo, and worse when disaffected members sabotage an otherwise noble legacy.

We are born into a heritage, but we learn authenticity only grad-ually. Parents aim to shape their children's growing up by be-queathing their heritage in an affective environment of trust. There is clearly a *mutual* trust going on here. But there eventually emerges an *inner* trust when parents help their children to trust the voices of authenticity within them. And the more clearly children hear the inner voices of authenticity, the more quickly and clearly they learn both the merits and the problems in the heritage that nourishes them.

To recognize the inner voices of authenticity is a lifelong and highly personal task; no one does it perfectly. In the meantime, people make bad decisions, which distort the better parts of their heritage. The very affective support they feel leads many children, students, employees, voters, and religious congregations to simply absorb moral worldviews that have been distorted by the unau-thenticity of their parents, teachers, employers, politicians, and religious leaders. This makes the existential task of recognizing one's inner voices of authenticity all the more difficult.

In a better heritage, the actual priorities by which people act are rooted in authenticity—their obedience to the five transcendental exigences. Most of the customs, the social expectations, the laws and the standards of behavior that people follow are linked back in history to the actions and words of authentic women and men. And even though authenticity does not exclude the possibility of error in the short run, in the long run authenticity is our only resource for discovering and correcting them.

In a worse heritage, the actual, functioning priorities emerged from the unauthentic actions and words of people. Forebears may have similar experiences, but they also may have a shared repression of certain experiences—such as being a victim or a victimizer. They may have understood a great deal about one another's priorities, but not sought to resolve mutual misunderstandings about them. They may have proudly stood up for truth and realism, but without ever challenging their cultural myths about race, sex, money, war, religion or politics. They may have promoted human rights but neglected human duties. Loyal to their own, they may have incited a hatred of others.

In reality, no heritage is simply good or bad. Actual heritages are a jumble of both, rooted as they are in mixtures of authentic and unauthentic initiatives. In the meantime, as children grow up, they may gradually discover the exigence to be authentic persons, including the exigence to authentically scrutinize their heritages. But it is not always clear whether the priorities of youngsters are indeed more rooted in their personal authenticity than in the values of their heritage. If they assume that their heritage is *always* morally wise, they fence in their authenticity with a sign that says, "Question anything except the legitimacy of authorities." But if they assume that they are *always* morally wiser than their heritage, they dismiss the wisdom of past and shoulder the burden of learning everything firsthand.

Certainly, children have little choice but to accept a heritage from their parents. Children who bicker about the rules disagree with how their parents use authority, but not whether parents should set rules. But adults have a choice. An adult authenticity will go beyond loyalty to one's heritage. There are times when one has to play the prophet and challenge the powers that be. If the prophet turns out to be wrong, authenticity requires a humble withdrawal of the challenge. But if the prophet turns out to be right, and if like-minded companions are attracted by the prophet's authenticity, a movement begins. And if these companions hold authenticity in high regard, the movement may blossom. New values arise to enrich the old. Others notice that things are improving, and they sign up to help. Still, the risk continues as the old guard tries to suppress the movement through a campaign of deception and sabotage.

A heritage can feel like solid rock underfoot, compared to our mucky journey toward authenticity. When it comes to beliefs about God, or one's race, or one's family, we want our beliefs to be well founded. But beliefs are not truths housed in some eternal sky. Beliefs are historical realities. The originators of our beliefs are people who felt bothered by their experience: their own beliefs did not help, so they spoke up. The exigence for authenticity prompted their contemporaries to pay attention, to make sense out of the situation, to realize what is really going on, and to join the effort. Newly emerging values are not deductions from abstract principles; they are inductions from concrete experiences of asking and answering moral questions. They are expressed primarily in decisions, commitments, and action. These operative values may also be expressed descriptively in historical narratives and abstractly in ethical principles as part of a community's moral legacy, as well they should be. But revered texts arise from concrete actions. They are the lessons of history learned by our revered predecessors who cared deeply for us, who were yet to be born.

Unfortunately, many people try to bolster their hope by driving all doubt out of their minds. And when doubts are exiled, questions are suppressed and authenticity is compromised. So it is ironic— sad, really—that those who exile doubts so as to defend a cherished belief isolate themselves from the rich sources of authenticity in the very founders whose wisdom they cherish.

This empirical view of a heritage casts a different light on the affective movement in human development, particularly on the moral ideals of loyalty and fidelity. Authenticity alone is the source of anything legitimate in a heritage. And it alone has the power to eliminate anything illegitimate. Affective loyalty to one's heritage, therefore, can best be exercised only through a prior loyalty to being an authentic person. Likewise, fidelity is not essentially to an institution or even to a friend. The primary meaning of fidelity is an obedience to the inner normativity that alone discerns which institutions are worth one's fidelity, how best to be a friend to someone else, and what religious commitments are worth a lifetime of love. This inner loyalty and fidelity are based on an affective commitment to transcending oneself, to deeply love the ever better, not exclusively for oneself, but for everyone concerned.

WE HAVE BLIND SPOTS

A second dynamic that impedes the successful functioning of the normative drives of our nature is the phenomenon of the intellectual blind spot. What a blind spot does is block our learning in certain areas. The field of learning, however, is not just two parcels: What I know and what I do not. Rather it is three: What I know, what can I ask about, and what I lack the knowledge to even ask about. Lonergan names these the Known Known, the Known Unknown, and the Unknown Unknown:[20]

The Known Known	The Known Unknown	The Unknown Unknown
Everything I have learned.	Everything I can try to learn.	Everything I have not learned enough about even to try to learn.

In my first parcel, I know what I have learned: people's names, why the inflation rate is rising, and that racial tolerance is better than racial discrimination. In my second parcel, I *know* what I have *not* learned. I am ignorant about many things, but I know enough to ask questions. Why does my boss come to work so late? Is assisted suicide always wrong? In my third parcel, I *do not know* what I have *not* learned. No question whatsoever occurs to me about certain realities. I am not simply ignorant about them; I am also ignorant about my ignorance. No one in Ancient Greece felt curious about a gross national product.

My world—that world of concerns that goes with me wherever in the world I go—grows as I find answers to my questions, expanding my first parcel by taking over territory from my second. And my second parcel takes over territory in my third as new learning reveals previously unnoticed things, and I ask questions that never occurred to me before. We can characterize each person's learning as moving these two boundaries outward within the total field of learning. Both formal education and personal experience introduce one pupil at a time into these ever expanding fields. As we hit the books and meet people with different perspectives, our answers and questions both grow.

But these are individual worlds. Your world overlaps mine, but not perfectly. Somewhere, between similar data, we often come up with dissimilar and even contradictory knowledge and values. Even people with similar education and experiences can learn different and irreconcilable lessons. There is one embarrassing reason for this, so embarrassing that otherwise intelligent men and women find it preposterous: *We may not really want to learn.*

Besides our wondrous intellectual capacity to reach beyond the stars, we also have the ambiguous moral capacity to push certain issues out of our second parcel, where we ask questions, and into our third, where no questions pester us. And the more successful we are at pushing *questions* out, the less we will wonder what we did to ourselves. We paste a blind spot on our curiosity.[21]

Keep in mind that a blind spot is not an area that appears opaque or dark or confusing. We call it blind because it does not appear at all. Here is an exercise that demonstrates how blind spots escape our notice:

> Close your right eye. And looking straight ahead, notice any gaps in your field of vision. Do you see any areas where nothing at all appears? Probably not.
>
> Now put a ring on the thumb of your right hand. Then stretch your hand out at arm's length, fingers up, palm facing away, with the ring at the same height as your baby fingernail. Again, close your right eye, but now focus in the area of your baby fingernail. What you will notice is that in your peripheral vision, there is an area where you cannot see your ring. You can see it see it if you look a little further to the right of your baby finger, and a little further to the left, but it seems to disappear in an area within 2 inches of your baby finger. The reason this is called a blind spot, is not that we see something blocking our vision, but that we see nothing at all there.

Something similar happens in our intelligence. We may imagine our curiosity as limitless, but when we have areas that we refuse or are unable to question, we will not notice the spots where both knowledge and questions are absent. We might notice second-parcel areas that make no sense, but instead of pursuing questions about them, we bump them directly to the third, where no questions can be asked.

We each have our share of blind spots. However, all is not lost. We can raise questions about blind spots in general. We can ask what kinds there are and what sort of healing is needed for each kind. We can expect that each kind of blind spot will be maintained by an avoidance of certain types of questions. Four main kinds can be distinguished:[22]

- **Neurosis**. A psychological neurosis is maintained by repressing questions into the certain spontaneous fixations or obsessions.
- **Egotism**. Egotism is maintained by suppressing questions about the good of other persons.
- **Loyalism**. Unquestioning loyalty to a group is maintained by suppressing questions about the good of other groups.
- **Commonsensism**. A blanket trust of common sense is maintained by suppressing questions whose answers require in-depth analysis and the study of history.

Each kind of blind spot introduces a bias in our intelligence. Our intelligence favors certain areas over others, so that our questions rush there spontaneously, to the neglect of our blind spots. This distorts where we pay attention and makes us functionally stupid regarding the ignored questions. It appears to be innate to the structure of the mind that these biases are present to some degree in everyone, at least as spontaneous tendencies. To the degree that we fail to take charge of our spontaneous intelligence, certain moral issues recede beyond our curiosity. To understand how each of these blind spots may be healed, we first need to examine more closely how each one works.

Neurosis

Just because we raise no questions about certain events in our psyches does not mean that we have no data on these things. Our third parcel includes many psychological events we experience directly but never wondered about: bad moods, emotional disturbance, and strange imaginations. Indeed, prior to Freud, few people wondered about these inner events in scientific terms.

There are two reasons why we ignore certain inner experiences. An acceptable reason is that these experiences never bothered us. A less acceptable reason is that some experiences do bother us, but we refuse to let this disturbances evolve into explicit questions. I am not speaking about suppression, by which I mean the process by which we *deliberately* drive out certain thoughts or feelings or images. Moral integrity requires that we suppress covetous thoughts, vengeful feelings and bad self-images. Even moral degenerates will suppress inklings to repent, but more about this in a minute. For now, we need to consider suppression's slippery cousin, *repression*, by which I mean the process by which we block certain questions from rising to consciousness *without noticing that we did so.* Where suppression knowingly ignores certain questions in our second parcels, repression moves second-parcel questions into the third, pre-consciously blinding our otherwise open-minded intelligence. Repression is a major dynamic in what we call a neurosis.

As you read this, certain obvious obsessions may come to mind, but later it may occur to you that there are other phobias or cravings that powerfully direct your attention to certain objects and away from the phobia or craving itself. For example, an argumentative man may admit that he can be defensive, but prefer not to ask himself why. He may go to his grave consoled by having always steadfastly held his ground, but ignorant of, say, having always desperately—but unsuccessfully—wanted his father to respect his opinions. Or an anal-retentive mother, always telling everyone what they ought to do, will not wonder why disorder threatens her so. She may chuckle at her obsession for order, but never reflect on why she is so obsessed.

Their habits may just irritate others, but they powerfully inhibit the questions that could liberate the neurotic from this psychic prison. This inhibition happens because, where certain questions are driven out of awareness, obsession tends to move in. Obsessions may be the familiar minor fixations on cleanliness or gossip or making money; they may also be irrational fears or serious addictions to drugs or sex. In any case, obsessions serve as analgesics to dull the pain of unanswered questions about ourselves.

Egotism

Where the bias of neurosis unintentionally avoids learning, through *re*pression, the bias of egotism intentionally avoids learning, through *sup*pression. Egotists earnestly ignore anything that might benefit others at their expense. They are often accused of being driven by their feelings, but, quite the contrary, they domineeringly suppress any feelings of compassion that might divert their attention toward the good of others; more often than not, they manipulate the feelings of others for personal benefit. Nor are they necessarily stupid. Most have the mental capacity to make things better all around, but they dedicate their minds exclusively to getting just whatever they can for themselves. Nor are they necessarily uncooperative. Most are raring to join corporate efforts that benefit themselves, but only as long as they are not required to sacrifice much for the group.

This description of egotists is just a caricature. In reality, we all experience egotistic impulses. We set boundaries to what we think about: "I'm not the sort of person who would ever be concerned about the handicapped." We avoid thinking that our job perks may be excessive. We connive to make comments only when it will boost our reputations, and we spontaneously suppress even thinking about what might boost someone else's.

Still, we feel the tension. Our human nature still urges us to know what is objectively better despite our self-imposed restriction to knowing what benefits ourselves alone. Egotism meets this tension by piling up defenses that grow stronger over time. As we more frequently defend our self-absorption, our egotism becomes a habit. The more we draw on our intelligence to justify our self-absorption, the more we rationalize an "I did it my way" approach to life. And the more successful we are in getting what we want, the more we respect we earn from those who themselves admire egotism. At this point, we hardly have to think at all about suppressing selfless thoughts. We exiled our questions about the well-being of others into our third parcel of learning, completely outside our world.

This view gives us a higher perspective on the popular distinction between self-love and love of neighbor. In the popular sense, self-love means preferring goods for oneself rather than for the neighbor, and love of neighbor means preferring goods for one's neighbor at self-expense. The moral issue comes down to which party benefits: me or my neighbor. But since Aristotle, philosophers note a higher meaning to self-love, namely, a love that seeks what is truly the best for oneself. And what is truly the best includes the virtue of moral objectivity. So a thoroughgoing self-love will break out of exclusive self-regard and pursue an objectivity about the better that sometimes benefits the self at others' expense and sometimes benefits the other at self-expense. Since this moral objectivity is the fruit of authenticity, the moral issue comes down to which voice to obey: authenticity or unauthenticity.

Loyalism

Where the bias of egotism avoids learning what benefits other individuals, the bias of loyalism avoids learning what benefits other groups. So the stronger the loyalism, the weaker the egotism, and vice versa. To their fellows, they are quite selfless. They are praised for their dedication to the community. They may eagerly seek virtue, but only to a point—the point where the dictates of virtue threaten to extend their concerns beyond their group's membership. Their field of moral vision is wider than personal comfort, but it still lives within a fence that divides "us" from "them."

Again, this description of loyalists is a caricature. Everyone experiences a bias against questions about the good of other groups. The "other" groups in question can come in any size: Loyal company employees avoid wondering whether there is anything wrong with "killing the competition." Loyal religious believers spontaneously defend their practices and priorities—often despite concrete evidence that other congregations manifest greater spiritual depth. Loyal patriots measure their pride by how effectively their nation dominates other nations.

Like egotism, loyalism is self-sustaining, but far more powerfully. Where egotism thrives on securing strong personal habits, loyalism thrives on strong social and cultural ties. In an ironic twist of human affectivity, the very camaraderie that can liberate the egotist will only imprison the loyalist. Egotists have only themselves to overcome, and their liberation is usually welcomed by their friends. But loyalists have to overcome the loyalism of their friends, who tend to gang up on dissenters.

Typically, extreme loyalists belong only to a single group, defined by a single cause (The True Believers) or by some countergroup's hatred (The Violated Victims). They view other groups simplistically; their assessments are one-dimensional; dogmatism reigns. Emotionally, camaraderie deepens their commitment to the goals and priorities of the group, and the less they engage with other groups, the less likely they will understand their intentions or notice any readiness to collaborate. But the restrictive effect on moral growth is similar to that of other biases: Minds, by nature expansively curious about everything, are narrowed—for the loyalist, narrowed to what benefits the colony.

Or loyalists may belong to Max Weber's *Iron Cage*—a social order where role assignments are primary. Their loyalty is closer to that of The Violated Victims, but what makes the cage iron is that they do not realize how deeply the social order imprisons them. So The Iron Caged use their minds less to create new ways of doing better and more to carry out directives from the boss. They typically accept their own social structures without question.

So loyalism engenders its own species of blind spot—the cultural myth. We speak of these myths as "what we all know": What White People Do. How Muslims Act. What Homosexuals Are Really After. The simpler the picture, the stronger the myth and the more unrelated to actual lives. For loyalists, plain experience does not undermine the myth because they already rely on the myth to filter out the plain experiences of foreigners and strangers, letting in only the data that prove the myth to be true.

Commonsensism

Common sense is absolutely necessary for day-to-day living. But it is not sufficient. Many of the greatest achievements of humankind were made in theoretical areas: physics and chemistry, historical studies and the arts, philosophy and theology. And while many people of "good common sense" acknowledge and respect these disciplines, not everyone turns to them when life gets complicated. Part of this attitude stems from the nonsense that these disciplines sometimes foist on society. Or it may stem simply from unfamiliarity with what these disciplines aim to accomplish. But whether by design or default, many people of common sense regard their common sense as sufficient for solving most problems. This is a type of blind spot we may call "commonsensism." It is a bias against in-depth investigation of problems.

Commonsensism is familiar: It is chronically vulnerable to the Myth of the Simple—the assumption that progress must be based on simple strategies, simple principles. It assumes that it is always better to take some action than no action at all. It easily spots the quick and dirty solution but is blind to the slower and cleaner solutions revealed to wider perspectives. No doubt, tackling immediate problems is often better than sitting around planning global solutions. But is it better in every case? Do we not make things worse when we tackle immediate problems without some knowledge of the general nature of the problem and its particular history?

A good example is your experience of reading this book. You made it this far, but it has been an uphill climb, and you often had to rest to get your bearings. Are you impatient to get to the end to find out what you should do? (This is a book about morality, after all.) Do you feel skeptical that you will ever get answers to the many questions that occurred to you along the way? If so, then you are now experiencing the bias of common sense against thinking on the levels of systems, theory, and history. It infects everyone. It accounts for all kinds of disagreements about what to do, even among people deeply committed to doing what is really better.

The Effects of Blind Spots

Blind spots are areas of ignorance not only in ethicists, observing situations from the outside. They are also wounds in the mindsets of the people in situations they investigate. When we ask what is going on in our schools, hospitals, or law courts, we can expect to find any or all of these biases. Likewise for what is going on in my spouse, parents, or children. What these situations *mean* is identical to what the people involved mean by them, and what they mean by them is distorted by their psychological fixations, their self-centeredness, their unquestioning loyalties, and their penchant for action and simple answers. In any situation, we will find people more or less intellectually blind. A few may see clearly the areas where their moral vision is blurred by bias, and another few may be totally blind to certain moral issues, but most have somewhat fuzzy notions of their blind spots. So their deliberations drag on, and their resolutions are often based on shallow analyses.

Worse yet, our biases have all the self-propagating features of viruses. Once they settle into a suitable host site, they infect our other intellectual organs. First, we consider them rather trivial, then somewhat benign, then a strength, and eventually a source of pride. Then we spread the virus to others. We brag about being a little compulsive, or "taking care of Number One," or being "loyal to the death," or being someone of "total common sense." Parents teach these biases to their children; teachers press them on their students. The point is simple: The concept of intellectual blind spots helps explain why people with the same inner criteria of authenticity can come to very different conclusions about what is better.

WILLFULNESS

We can uncover our blind spots by analyzing what is going on in our consciousness. We can reach a similar enlightenment through camaraderie with people who succeeded in this effort to some extent. We can, I say. But there is a further question: Will we?

Suppose you are convinced that X is something you ought to do. Suppose, further, that you feel ready, willing and able to do it. Would you ever deliberately *not* do it? I am talking about a situation where you are totally convinced about what you should do, where nothing prevents you from doing it, and where you are willing to go ahead with it. No "extenuating circumstances" force your hand. Is it really possible that you would deliberately and knowingly act against your own better judgment?[23]

In Ovid's *Metamorphosis* (7, 21), Medea complains about an ailment that affects us all. She was heartsick in love with Jason and convinced that she would do wrong to pursue him. But she admits: "I see the good, and I approve it too; condemn the worse—and yet the worse pursue." And St. Paul's *Letter to the Romans* (7:18-19): "Wanting the good is in me, but not the doing. I do not do the good I want, but rather the evil I do not want."

What Ovid conceived as our *fate*, Paul conceived as a *sin* against God. For Ovid, we can be destined to oppose our better selves, even unto death, and the gods seldom lift a finger. For Paul, too, we are opposed to our better selves, although God offers to heal our self-opposition.

The familiar cases of our fate or sin fall under a morality of prohibition: We know what we should *not* do, but we do it anyway. Lying is wrong, but who has never told a lie without any justification? Breaking promises is wrong, but who has never broken a promise, knowing that keeping the promise was the better thing to do? But we find even more examples—an embarrassingly large number—when we think about a morality of doing better: We know what we *should do*, but we do not do it. We realize that we really ought to call a friend who badly needs our help, but we do not call. Or we hear someone spread a lie about someone else, but we do not object. Or we feel impatient with ourselves for not getting the exercise we need, but we do not exercise. This is the easier immorality because we are seldom asked to justify *not* doing something. And although hardly anyone today will call these omissions moral failures, nonetheless they are instances of acting against our better judgment.

The results of this inner disobedience are more far reaching than a right/wrong view of morality. Even when the effects on others are slight, we are loading our consciences with a moral inertia that will make future inner obedience all that more difficult. As the individual conscience evolves, the symbolizing exigence assembles a self-image and a self-affect designed to maintain some order in the ego, so when we knowingly act against our better judgment, our egos will press for consistency. But something has to give. Eventually, through thousands of individual everyday choices, we lean toward one of two opposed meanings of "better":

> The transcending exigence may open us without reservation to what makes sense, to what is real, to what is better, and to the mysterious dimensions of life beyond what we can ever know. Our conscience becomes oriented toward what is "better in itself" and will bother us until we dismantle our self-absorbed habits.

> Or we may narrow our intellectual, moral and affective pursuits to what gives us personal advantages and to hell with everybody else. Our conscience becomes oriented toward what is just "better for me."

So, although most of us fall somewhere between these extremes, moral disagreements can arise from the fact that people can often mean radically opposite things by "better." As our moral habits gel, we become persons for whom better more often means either "better in itself" or just "better for me." When we lean toward "better in itself," we pursue any proposals at all, independent of whether they serve our personal well-being. When we lean toward "better for me," we dismiss ideas about what may be better for others. Even when we move out of "better for me" to a "better for my community," loyalism just replaces egotism, without moving further toward "better in itself."

People living in a mainly authentic heritage feel the cultural supports to pursue what is better in itself, and to pursue it together. As they secure the gains of the past, they also press on to ensure that such improvement continues. So they educate their children about the damage done by any "better for me" ways of living. On the other hand, the cultural dictates felt by those living in a mainly unauthentic heritage encourage them to get what they can for themselves. This typically leads to worsening living standards, and even should a dictator take over, the people will likely believe that subservience will be "better for me" as long as they obey the rules and the roads are well maintained.

WOUNDED NORMATIVE DRIVES

We looked at six distinct factors that can distort the normative functioning of our consciousness—a morally compromised heritage, neurosis, egotism, loyalism, commonsensism, and willfulness. These may be boiled down to two: bias and willfulness. Bias may be any combination of the four types. Willfulness stands on its own. And a compromised heritage is ever the fruit of bias and willfulness. The stronger these factors are, the higher the odds that situations will worsen, along with the declining ability of distorted normative drives themselves to turn things around.

Happily, these incoherent effects of our moral woundedness are not the whole story. There are other dynamics that undo the mischief caused by bias and willfulness. So let us turn our attention now to the ways in which the wounded normativity of our spirits is open to being healed.

6. OUR NORMATIVE DRIVES ARE HEALED

WHERE SHALL WE TURN?

In chapter 4 we described historical improvements as the result of two complementary movements of our spirits—an affective movement by which we live out the authentic traditions of our past in our present and a creative movement that refines our present traditions and explores ways to improve our future.

Then, in chapter 5, we examined how these historical improvements are blocked, delayed, or reversed by bias and willfulness. The affective movement can be distorted by an uncritical acceptance of one's heritage as well as a bias toward loyalism. The creative movement is vulnerable to neurosis and can be biased toward both egotism and commonsensism. And both movements are vulnerable to willfulness.

So we are left with a fundamental question: If both our affectivity and our creativity are so wounded, where do we turn to heal these wounds and ensure any moral progress at all?[24] In the concrete circumstances of our moral fallibility, what liberates us to make moral progress? Most of us assume that there must be an answer, since we recognize that, at least for some periods of history, many communities made genuine moral progress. What is the answer? Practically all moral and religious leaders point to love. Love may well be the power to heal the wounds in our heritages, the distortions of our personal biases, and the willfulness that persistently derail us from doing ever better. Here too, of course, people mean different and even opposite things by love. But now that we identified bias and willfulness as major impediments to moral progress, what comes clear is that the love we hope can liberate us should pass this test: Does it heal bias and willfulness? And if it does, then how? The more insight we gain into how love heals, the more clearly we can distinguish "true love" from its imitators and the more intelligently we can cooperate with that love to improve our lives together.

We will organize our exploration of how love heals in three steps. First we will review the creative movement to understand how our normative drives function to improve living. Then we will review the factors that frustrate or divert the proper functioning of these inner drives. This should then put us in a good position to understand exactly the kind of love, inherent in the affective movement but often ambiguously mixed with non-healing loves, that heals our wounded creativity.[25] Our approach here is like osteopathic medicine. Physicians begin with an understanding of the body's healthy functions, then move to an understanding of diseases that compromise that health, and finally provide an understanding of what further factors in the body can help heal the diseases.

THE CREATIVE HELIX

First, then, how do things improve? Not by fate or magic or superstition or official decrees. Our analysis so far points to authenticity as the key. Things improve where people attentively notice shortcomings, intelligently optimize opportunities, reasonably shun half-baked ideas, and responsibly do what they believe is better. These are the key events in all human creativity.

The creative demand impresses itself on human consciousness all the time. Moreover, it reinforces its continuing functioning. We can understand this self-reinforcing characteristic if we imagine the creative process as winding around and up like a helix:

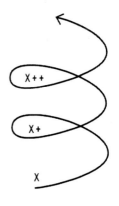

Suppose we have situation X, which includes some things that make sense and other things that could be better. The exigence for authenticity impels us to do better. We notice what does not make sense; we see opportunities for improvement; we validate which opportunities are workable; and we take the appropriate action. Now situation X has risen into the improved situation X+. Then we notice what still does not make sense in situation X+; we see new opportunities, validate new plans, and decide what to do next. Our next action transforms an improved situation X+ into an even better situation X++. And so the cycle spirals upward, as long as we keep following the normative demands of consciousness. This is not a recipe that ensures success in every case. It is simply an explanation of how better situations get that way. It makes it clear that no human situation really improves without human authenticity.

When we say our situations improve because we follow the movements of our inner normative drives, it is not only our external circumstances that improved. As participants, our own ability to make things better improves as well. This is true of any situation. Participants who grow up in environments that have generally been getting better more quickly discover these normative drives in themselves and more willingly yield to their directives. For example:

- The normativity of experience impels children to notice more quickly a difference between what they imagine and what they actually experience.
- The normativity of understanding more effectively impels youngsters to catch on to how getting an insight is quite different from memorizing an answer.
- The normativity of reason strengthens the confidence of teenagers to ask whether the explanations they took for granted—granted mainly by parents—are really valid.
- The normativity of responsibility more forcefully impels adults to recognize that not everything that feels satisfying is really worthwhile.
- Concretely, all this occurs in a context of more or less love, and the more that certain affective environments honor authenticity, the quicker the participants end up improving themselves.

This blossoming of our normative drives does take time. It is no small achievement to catch the exact difference in one's consciousness between the movement of the normative drives and the movement of their opposites. But the more people yield themselves to these normative drives, the quicker they learn to distinguish and trust them and the higher the odds that the creative helix will continue to rise.

THE WOUNDED HELIX

In the business world, promotional speakers praise creativity as an unadulterated good. Religious preachers encourage creativity as sharing in the Creator's own nature. But creativity is vastly over-rated. In chapter 5, we saw that the exigence to do better is hardly infallible. We grow up in the soiled air of a polluting heritage. We have the personal blind spots of psychological fixations, personal egotism, unquestioning adherence to group priorities, and the commonsense preference for the short-term solution. Most baffling of all, even when we have a clear moral vision, we can willfully act otherwise. Bring on more creativity damaged in these ways and nothing really gets better. Praise creativity as an unadulterated good and you inadvertently foster clever ways to make things worse.

So let us take a deeper look at how a damaged creativity rein-forces its own malfunctioning, winding backward and downward:

Suppose, again, we have situation X, which includes some things that make sense and other things that do not. The exigence for authenticity impels us to do better, but now we fail to notice what does not make sense, or fail to under-stand *why* it makes no sense and *how* things might be improved, or fail to validate which initiatives for improving things are workable, or fail to take the appropriate action, even when it stares us in the face. Now, through inaction or

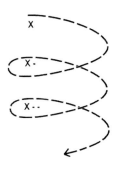

inappropriate action, situation X has fallen into the worse situation X-. At this turn, the additional elements that make no sense now make authenticity additionally difficult. We overlook these additional elements, or skip thinking about new opportunities, or forgo checking our plans for effectiveness, or fail to decide what to do next. Our inaction, or inappropriate action, transforms a bad situation X- into a worse situation X--. And so the helix spirals downward, as long as the normative drives of consciousness continue to be blocked.

Again, we are part of any situation on which we have effect. While we may imagine a declining situation as crumbling houses, disgusting food, unreliable services, unruly children, and the like, we should include our declining ability to turn things around. Our unauthenticity becomes a habit and is easily reinforced by the social norms of a distorted heritage. Each downward turn of the slipping helix only increases the odds against our authenticity successfully halting the slide. So it is that while good situations tend to get better, owing to fewer challenges to authenticity, bad situations tend to get worse as our authenticity itself loses its capacity to face problems that have grown in number and complexity.

While these problems are familiar, we should not forget how baffling they are. For one thing, they occur only in humans. Everything else in nature follows laws and probabilities, and science is dedicated to spelling out these dynamics on every level, from physics on up. But professionals in human studies run into a major obstacle to understanding what governs human nature. While it belongs to our nature to be attentive, intelligent, reasonable, responsible, and in love, we have the frightening liberty to violate our nature.

Declining situations also render otherwise fertile minds increasingly barren. True, not all fertile minds turn fallow. Some historians will still lay out the moral flaws behind the decline of once well-functioning cultures. Some psychologists will continue to expose the fixations that account for their clients' narrowed view of what is really better. Some pastoral counselors will uncover the factors that derail a person's moral development. Some educators will keep on providing students insights into underlying economic and political systems that oppress the masses. But not everyone turns to these professionals for explanations. To say the obvious, an incoherent moral heritage and one's moral blindness cloud the very moral vision that sees the importance of recognizing authenticity in those who possess the wisdom to provide good counsel.

Moreover, willfulness, the malice of deliberately acting against our better judgment, cannot be explained at all. If willfulness had an explanation, we would call it "unintended consequences," and we would not jail anyone. But we call some actions malicious, evil, sinful, or wicked to express our judgment that they are inexcusable. There are no extenuating circumstances that could possibly justify them. This is what human studies find so baffling: How can anyone understand what intrinsically makes no sense? What scientific theory can possibly explain what willfully goes against its own nature? What historian can explain the causes of evil deeds freely chosen?

THE HEALING HELIX

Evidence is everywhere that we humans are, in fact, capable of rising above the forces of a distorted moral heritage, personal bias, and willfulness. Often enough we do transcend our moral short-comings. So let us look at how our wounded creativity is actually healed.

Mutual Love Heals

Consider this: Is it not true, on average, that children from happy families are more likely to grow up as responsible adults than children from unhappy families? Do we not find that kids whose parents tolerate their mistakes express a free-flowing curiosity, while kids who fear correction have a constipated curiosity? Is it not typical that the children whose parents forgive their wrongs and lift them from shame grow up morally mature, while children brought up in a crime-and-punishment home never grow beyond a rule-based morality?

Or consider the times when we are touched by a person's honesty or kindness. Is it ever a person who hates? Is it always someone of a high IQ? Must it always be a person who rigidly adheres to moral standards? Wherever we see people actually doing better, we expect that their hearts are enlivened not by sharp minds or abstract moral standards but by the richness of their interpersonal relationships. More than brilliance or lofty ideals, it is some form of love that liberates people from the fears and spites that block their moral ingenuity.

I will assume this to be true: On average, any liberation we experience from moral shortcomings is directly proportional to the priority of love in our lives. Taking this assumption as true, however, is not the same as understanding *how* love liberates, which is our goal here. The more we understand the inner processes by which love affects morality, the clearer will be our criteria for distinguishing between authentic love and its great pretenders. Understanding how authentic love heals the wounds of our creativity, in turn, will provide any ethics with concrete strategies for improving situations.

So we can now pose our question of how our moral shortcomings are healed in the terms of our evolutionary framework for understanding morality: By what processes does the system of loving relationships overcome the moral deficiencies that seem inherent to human consciousness itself?

Our exercises in noticing the norms in our inner drives give us the structure of an answer. We noticed that there is a helix of creativity, rising from attentiveness to understanding, to reasonable affirmations, to responsible choices. And we saw how this creative helix is damaged; its upward ascent can be frustrated, diverted, even reversed in a vortex of decline. But within this image of a creative-yet-damaged helix, imagine a further, healing helix winding through 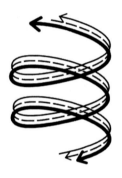 it in the opposite direction. This healing helix represents the affective movement toward doing better. It flows from the mysterious and powerful force of love. That is, when a system of love is at work in a community, the normative drive, "Be in love," works from above downward to heal the damaged normative drives and lift them upward:

> Being in love expands an individual's consciousness to the horizon of a "we" consciousness. One's individual concerns are shared concerns, and the individual imagines his or her activities as contributing to a common good.
>
> "We" consciousness, in turn, liberates the normative demand, Be responsible. It impels one to actively care for others, as well as for oneself.

A liberated responsibility then liberates the normative demand, Be reasonable. It encourages one to be less afraid to face the truth about a situation, however menacing it may appear.

A liberated reason, staring reality in the face, liberates the normative demand, Be intelligent. It strengthens one's curiosity to ask how things got this way and why people put up with with the mess.

A liberated understanding, eager for solid explanations, liberates the normative demand, Be attentive. One scrutinizes all the hard data and takes into account wider ranges of experience, despite the fact that a change one's personal priorities may be in order.

The effects of this inner healing and liberation of consciousness apply to all six of the ways our moral normative demands may be wounded:

In the interplay of authenticity and heritage, a loving environment heightens the odds that youngsters notice, test, and eventually trust the inner demands to be responsible, reasonable, intelligent, and attentive.

A loving environment can relieve neurotics from the fear of what an honest inquiry might reveal about their motives, phobias and addictions. Psychotherapies administered in with an unconditional positive regard have proven effective in helping them lower their defenses and inquire intelligently into their fears and anxieties.

Similarly, the egotists' intellectual myopia regarding the good of others tends to be healed when others befriend them; and while many friendships are based on pleasure or usefulness, any engagement with friends who care for them as persons will often broaden the range of their intelligence to take in the needs of others.

We saw how loyalists tend to be members of single groups, defined by single causes; but when other groups offer them opportunities for better living and invite them to inter-group collaboration, individual members diversify their associations, broaden their perspectives, and widen their concerns as their allegiances branch out.

Love, serious love, is committed to the long haul. And so it dampens the penchant of common sense for fast action. It relies on wisdom born of experience and a sense of history to solve problems at basic levels. Patiently, but tenaciously, authentic love disregards the Myth of the Simple and explores complexities that characterize most moral dilemmas.

Finally, love forgives. When people knowingly choose the worse, worse things happen. Things in the objective situation are exacerbated—first by simple-minded blaming, then by seething resentments, and then often enough by revenge. People in the situation who choose the worse harden their habits of acting against their better judgment, which skews their priorities and narrows their minds and hearts. But forgiveness halts blame and widens attention to solutions. Forgiveness dissolves resentments and refuses to get even. It moves toward reconciliation between offended parties and thereby heightens the odds that better solutions for everyone will emerge.

In all these instances, the healing is far from automatic. But the healing is rendered more likely because people's questions about better and worse have expanded. From our theoretical perspective, the "system" of love among humans is the most comprehensive context of morality.

True Love Defined

So how do we distinguish the kind of love that really heals our wounded creativity and other affective experiences we call "love"? Recall how mutual love is an exigence. As an exigence, love is a dynamic relationship between lower systems and a higher, integrating system that integrates the functioning of lower systems toward higher ends. Specifically, the *exigence* of love is the relationship between the actual lower systems of individuals being attentive, intelligent, reasonable, and responsible, and the more comprehensive system that constitutes the community or the "we" of which these individuals are a part. This theoretical view of love has a surprisingly practical payoff for anyone who has ever wondered, "How do I distinguish true love from mere infatuation?" We can translate our view into this practical definition: *True love is that affective orientation to others that makes one effectively more widely in love, more responsible, more reasonable, more intelligent, and more attentive.*

This definition is simple enough, particularly if you recognized these normative drives in yourself. But the definition also gives us a practical test for distinguishing true love from notions drawn from country-western music or sexual obsession. Put simply, when we feel the attractions that seem like love, we can check to see whether or not they liberate us to follow our inner norms. If our amorous feelings narrow the field of those we would love, if they make us more careless, more unreasonable, more dimwitted, or more oblivious, then we are certainly not feeling authentic, healing love.

Where common sense talks of "falling in love," a metaphor better suited to our theoretical perspective might be "rising to love" and then "staying in love." After all, staying in love requires persistent effort to avoid slipping back "down" into self-absorption or self-identification strictly with one's group. It is no easy thing to distinguish between a love that heals and other affections that corrupt our creativity. We saw how, in the interplay between authenticity and a moral heritage, the emergence of authenticity is a slow and ongoing task. Children who experience only smatterings of healing love in their growing up find it more difficult to know where to look for it and how to recognize it. Wives stick with abusive husbands; teenagers do drugs rather than split from the gang; politicians vote by loyalty to their party rather than let love liberate their sense of responsibility. However, some of those born into affective chaos escape when an affectively healed community invites them out. This happens when a wounded individual marries into a healthier clan. It happens when the addicted find in each other a common hope. It happens when the marginalized feel the outstretched hand of a faith community.

Transcendent Love

Besides the kind of love we bear toward one another, besides the kind our families bear toward other families, besides even the kind we feel for humanity at large, we also love whatever it is that makes anything beautiful, ordered, true, good, and worthy of our love. Earlier we named this love the transcending exigence. But we need to translate this technical term into concrete, recognizable experiences. Grammatically, the beautiful, the ordered, the true, the good, and the lovable are abstract concepts, unsullied features of highly sullied realities. But we do not love abstract concepts. Concretely, we have the "ground" urges toward beauty, order, truth, goodness, and being in love that precede, produce, and stand beyond all our abstracted conceptualizations of them. So we call beauty, order, truth, goodness, and love "transcendentals." We experience them as an inner fire by which we *transcend* the selves we are.

These exigences also *transcend* the specific things we love—be they art, or people, or institutions, or communities. No specific product or person or community exhausts our drives toward these ends. We go beyond specific objects, but without leaving them behind. We still love the specific things by virtue of transcendent features they embody, but these transcendent ends themselves remain fascinating yet mysterious. So when it comes to knowing what these transcendent ends are in themselves, we easily get derailed. Where romantics fixate on inner sensations, and materialists fixate on commodities, neither gives much thought to the unrestrictedness, the ever-beyond, of their craving. Whether we speak of this "beyond" as some ideal, or as love, or as the stars, or as God, at least everyone experiences being drawn toward it. Our abiding questions about our interpersonal relationships—Who is with me? With whom do I share my life?—are no less applicable to the possibility of sharing life with divine company. That is, besides experiencing the exigences to be attentive, intelligent, reasonable, responsible, and in love regarding this world, we also feel an exigence to engage this "beyond" of our transcendental desires in a manner that may be completely personal.

We leave to theologians our questions about the existence and nature of this divine company. Our aim is to understand how the experience of the transcending exigence heals our wounded creativity and liberates our powers to do better. We want an explanation of what happens to our moral horizons when we let transcendent love become an integral part of our lives.

Mutual Love

Most obviously, transcendent love produces mutual love. The pulls we feel toward beauty, order, truth, goodness, and ultimate engagement are the same dynamics that lead us to recognize the same pulls in one another. So we love one another as company in the struggle to live authentically. When our communities break down into mutual animosities, transcendent love can deepen our resolve to forgive and pursue reconciliation. This mutual love heals the fears of the neurotic and invites egotists out of their shells. It is the force behind any liberation of racial, national or religious groups from their own resentments and hatreds of other groups. Mutual love is serious about the long term; it spreads beyond immediate, commonsense practicality to an all-consuming practicality explores the scientific, philosophical, theological, and historical dimensions of situations desperate for improvement.

Transcendent love also beckons us deeper into a mutual love with the divine, although the divine transcendent remains ever dark and mysterious. Many obey the invitation to transcend the selves they are without embracing a religion. Even those who believe that this beyond is an ever-beautiful, all-knowing, absolutely real, thoroughly moral, profoundly interpersonal reality, can only imagine partial aspects of what this divine reality may be. Nonetheless, everyone is familiar with the drive toward it, despite the fact that many have yet to wonder about it.

Moral Vision

Besides moving us into mutual loving, including with the divine, the transcending exigence also gives us moral vision. It leads us to see more clearly what the better really is. In St. Exupery's *The Little Prince*, the omniscient fox tells the prince, "One does not see well except with the heart." And Pascal tells us that the heart has reasons unknown to reason. What they are talking about is not factual knowledge or high IQs. They are talking about moral knowledge—the eye that sees value where logic is myopic and reason is biased. Just as spouses in love are quick to see what is really better for their own families, so men and women who unabashedly love what is beautiful, ordered, true, good, and loveable are quick to see what is better for families anywhere. Here, transcendent love gives us moral vision.

Moral vision may be directly about better and worse decisions in concrete situations. It also may indicate whose word can be trusted and who might benefit from an invitation to see things from a larger perspective. Again, it also may be about what teachings, principles, doctrines, and truths are reliable. In this sense, moral vision enlarges our intellectual vision of all reality by revealing truth where unhealed creativity overlooks it.

Those who engage the divine through religious faith learn a level of moral discernment beyond reasoned principles and even beyond the values that human love reveals. Particularly for Jews, Christians, and Muslims, what is better is whatever the absolutely good and loving God desires. To discern better and worse, they scrutinize their own desires with their eye of love, asking which desires come from God. And to the degree that they are familiar with with the exigence for consistency among the inner norms of their attention, intelligence, reason, responsibility, and love, the more likely they will avoid any Divine Command Ethics that pits faith against reason, or the sacred against the secular.

Hope

Besides a heart of mutual love and an eye with moral vision, the transcending exigence also gives us the guts to hope. Anyone who has struggled against great odds knows that hope can be more painful than resignation. Yet even when we are knocked down, our love of beauty, order, truth and goodness, and engagement can lift us up again.

A major vehicle for this hope is the symbolizing exigence—the exigence that produces affect-laden images by which we represent this mysterious beyond to ourselves. Sometimes we use mimetic images such as the radiant sun or roaring thunderclouds or delicate violets that embody the transcendentals. We may use conjectural images of God or gods, drawn from our experience of wise and noble persons. Or we rely on abstract images of world order or peace or progress or friendship. We experience these symbols as inner linkages of image and affect, and we express them in the outer symbols of music, sculpture, dance, liturgy, ritual, art, incense, metaphor, architecture, and flags. What these external symbols do is firm up our affectivity to keep on hoping, despite awful situations and even awful behavior on our part.

7. THE OPEN ETHICIST

OPENNESS OF SPIRIT

It appears, then, that being open to the transcendent is a basic condition for making life more livable. This is not just an openness to the *idea* of transcendence, but the courageous habit of letting our thoughts and hopes be lifted always beyond present truths and values, beyond present company to accompany anyone in the human struggle. This openness does not lift us out of our humanity; it lifts our humanity from mere exigences to survive to the higher exigences to make sense out of life, to sift truth from error, and to share ourselves in a deeper love for one another. Our openness is infinite. No truth is excluded, no value is excluded, no personal engagement is excluded. It has the power to bring any authentic person to take seriously the religious question what sort of being might be responsible for making us like this and why. And the exigence for openness is ongoing. Should the day ever come when we eliminate slavery across the globe, we will not have eliminated the possibility of slavery because egotism, its main driver, is a permanent alternative to authenticity. The same may be said for wars, driven mainly by loyalism, and for violence, driven mainly by commonsensism, and for every kind of irrational willfulness that religions call sin.

This brings us to the personal question that we ethicists cannot avoid. As wondering persons, we are impelled by normative drives in consciousness to recognize what we ought to do in actual situations. Unfortunately, we are not fully open to doing better. And when we are closed in ways we do not recognize, we will disagree on methods and promote principles and policies at odds with one another.

Openness

What does it mean, then, for us to be fully open to doing better? In the next revolution of ethics, we will have discovered in ourselves an openness surprisingly different than what we may be accustomed to.[26] We usually assume that we are good learners, that we are objective in our evaluations, and that we are open to working with others for the common good. But openness involves something more radical than straightforward expansions of our horizons. It will be an abrupt step upward to investigate the ambiguous workings of anyone's creativity and the healing of its wounds. We will pose new kinds of moral questions—beyond the practical questions about what better or worse initiatives. We will ask what happens in us when we take initiatives in the first place: What happens in us when we learn about situations, and what makes our learning valid? What happens in us when we make choices, and what makes our choices valid? What happens in us when we love, and what additional perspective on ethics does our loving give? In short, the new openness will open onto the realm of method.

Conversion and Horizon

This openness[27] sets us on a long and arduous journey. Long, because issues of method underlie all major moral dilemmas in every imaginable field of human endeavor. Arduous, because coming to grips with what we do when we learn, choose, and love requires conducting inner experiments and exposing our findings to the scrutiny of others. To envision how this radical new open-ness to method might generally occur, it will help to distinguish between an initial breakthrough and the subsequent working out of the basic models of ethics that are implied by the breakthrough. We will call the breakthrough a "conversion" and the resulting developments "expansions."

Conversions are highly personal events. They involve a commit-ment to authenticity in the intellectual, moral, and affective dimensions of our lives. Expansions built on conversions occur first in our personal lives as we change how we learn, choose, and love. But the exigence for authenticity also drives us as ethicists to expand beyond our personal moral decisions into the discipline of ethics that shapes such decisions.

A conversion is not necessarily sudden. The impression of sud-denness may stem from a leap from a partial openness to the full and unconditional openness that colors absolutely everything a person will ever know and value. This is why conversion is often described as a breakthrough. The impression of suddenness may also be reinforced by the vivid reports of some people of their first glimpse into the totality of life and the corresponding inner demands for total openness. But for our purposes, by conversion we will mean a new way of asking questions grounded in a person's actual openness. Our definition specifies nothing about how gradually or suddenly this horizon may open up to a person.

To talk about the new openness of spirit on which an effective ethics can be built, I have been using the term, *horizon*. It suggests a person's *outlook*, *viewpoint*, *perspective*, and *world*. But all these terms can be misleading insofar as they depict a person *looking* at something. But knowing is quite different from looking. Knowing is a matter of asking and answering questions, which has no similarity to opening our eyes and seeing what is out there. So we need to give a technical definition to *horizon* in order to avoid the more common-sense use of horizon to mean "as far as the eye can see." So: *A horizon is the set of answers and questions a person cares about.*

So my horizon covers everything I already know and value. My total mindset includes the set of answers to questions posed by someone, somewhere—answers I take as reliable. My horizon also covers everything I do not yet know, but know enough to ask questions about, and care enough to take the questions seriously. In the terms we used in chapter 5, our horizon covers the "known known" and the "known unknown," but not the "unknown unknown"—things we are completely unaware of.

My horizon may be closed in ways we already discussed—incomplete development, a distorted heritage, bias, and willfulness. When I shove certain questions out of mind, I shut out the realities these questions might reveal; I repress inspirations that might create something better; I chill my heart when love invites. Conversely, my horizon may be open—open to learning about whatever is real, open to creating the better, and open to engaging the mysteries of love, life, death, and ultimate meaning. So when we say that people's outlook, or viewpoint, or perspective, or mindset, is "closed," our evidence is precisely that they impose some restrictions on the questions they will consider. Their world is closed, where "world" means their horizon—the set of questions and answers they care about.

With this definition of horizon in mind, then, we can sketch out the three kinds of conversion that we will discuss in the sections that follow: There is an intellectual conversion by which we learn what we do when we learn, with the result that our horizon is open to learning anything. There is a moral conversion by which we choose a new basis for choosing, with the result that our horizon is open to choosing whatever is really better. There is an affective conversion[28] by which we let love take the lead in our consciousness, with the result that our horizon is effectively open to loving ourselves, one another, and transcendent reality.

These conversions are are not simple additions of further knowledge, better things, and more love. They are radical changes in what a person means by *knowledge, better,* and *love.* Everything he or she knows, values, and loves changes because the originating questions that gave rise to it all become clarified. Just as man cured of lifelong blindness will have a new meaning of "seeing" that changes the meaning of everything "seen," so anyone undergoing these conversions will have a new meaning of "world" because his or her knowing, improving, and loving anything in the world are new. The new horizons do not abandon the old; they incorporate the old within more comprehensive perspectives.

In the next chapter, we will discuss how these conversions open the way to developing the basic ethical categories and procedures that can be validated by anyone. Following upon that chapter, we will discuss how a newly-grounded ethics can establish commonly accepted ways to collaborate with one another in making good moral decisions. But first we need to consider in detail the intellectual, moral, and affective openness, and their originating conversions, that ought to characterize the horizons of ethicists.[29]

LEARNING ABOUT LEARNING

What we call "moral reflection" involves learning about everyday situations. We want to know what is going on before we leap into action. No doubt, different people learn different things about the same situation because they bring different concerns. When your learning nicely dovetails with mine, it is easier to talk about what we should do. But often enough people with the same concerns about the same situation hold opposing views on what that situation really is. In the courtroom, the clear testimony of an eyewitness is viewed one way by the defense and another by the prosecution.

We reconcile some of these differences by learning from each other: someone calls our attention to things we overlooked; or someone raises a question that did not occur to us. But what happens when we do not agree on what "learn" means? This is not a preposterous question. People learning about the same situation can assume very different meanings of "learn." All parties may feel confident that they learned what they wanted to learn and still be baffled about why others do not agree. While they may be dedicated to learning ever more about life, they can overlook learning about learning itself. So their universes of what they might learn are not the same universe.

Most of what we know, of course, comes through believing others. But whom we will believe is a matter of choice, so we will postpone a discussion of belief until our next section on choosing how we choose. For now, we need to explore what happens in first-hand learning, whether our own or in the original learners whose word we believe.

Among the many different assumptions about learning available to the human mind, four in particular stand out. A first assumption holds that learning relies on *sights, sounds,* and *feelings* to reveal what is really out there. A second assumes that learning requires an intellectual commitment to developing *concepts* that correspond to reality. A third regards learning as exploring the *history* of situations. A fourth assumes that learning results from an abiding attentiveness to all these issues, but with an explicit focus on the *different kinds of questions* that lead to learning.

Four Views on Learning

Here, I will describe four psychologists, each one rather overdrawn to represent each of these four assumptions about what learning is. I invite you to consider not only *what* they each learn about their clients, but, more to our point, how their assumptions about learning deeply affect what they are able to learn.

Eve

Eve listens to her clients with a deep and obvious compassion. She helps them express their feelings about the people and the situations that trouble them. She believes that psychic health comes only by looking very hard at real, concrete situations, and letting one's feelings flow freely. But unfortunately for her clients, Eve has no idea of how the mechanisms of repression, transference, and reaction formation can play shell games with the original objects of their feelings. Her clients feel refreshed, having unloaded some emotional baggage for an hour, but the feelings they express will soon enough attach themselves to some other object whose connection to the originating trauma continues to escape notice.

Conrad

Conrad takes seriously every statement his clients make. He expects that all their statements should fit into one of the basic conceptual schemes that he learned in graduate school. Whether or not he admits it to himself, he is committed to the idea that human behavior is always an instance of a concept. "This is a case of obsession." Or, "She has a narcissist personality." He works hard at mastering his craft, but he envisions his mastery as learning all the categories that apply to the psyche. His clients come away with a name for their problem and some understanding of how the dynamics of the named problem works. But they have yet to verify that concepts such as "obsession" or "narcissist" adequately explain how their personal troubles fit into their life histories.

Narella

Narella is quite aware of history. Besides wondering what is going on currently in her clients, she knows that every problem has a history, and it is in the history that she expects to find the pressures, assumptions, expectations, and traditions that shape her clients' mindsets. For analysis, she relies on classical psychoanalysis to uncover formative events in their past, on good fiction and drama to understand how the twists of time affect the heart, and on her knowledge of cultural history to understand their particular ethnic, gender, and religious priorities. For therapy, she leads her clients not only to understand how past traumas led to their present problems, but also to exercise their self-determination by taking a stand on the values they intend to live out in the future. She supports their interpretations of their problems and the values inherent in their choices for change. She avoids injecting her own opinion, even when she thinks their views may be short-sighted. By keeping her criticism of others to herself, she conveys to her clients the idea that the validity of anyone's moral commitments lies in the conviction of the person who holds them; they cannot be fairly criticized by the standards of others.

Abe

Abe seems unengaged at first. This is because he does not take his clients' statements as true. He takes them as just evidence. He plays with mental images of the evidence until he has an insight into plausible connections among the various assertions and behaviors that trouble his clients, and he delicately leads them to the same insight. His explanations usually include the possibility that his clients are faking emotions, shading the truth, or dodging sensitive issues. Should contrary evidence appear, they both reconsider the evidence, looking for a better explanation. Abe brings a host of psychological concepts to bear—suppression, denial, paranoia, and so on—but he relies on these concepts only insofar as they help him understand the behaviors and verbal evidence that his clients present. Dedicated to getting insights, he avoids emotion-laden descriptions of his clients' problems, just as he delays mentioning any technical concepts and summary analyses lest these displace the essential need in his clients to gain their own insights into their behaviors. Like Narella, he also relies on what he has learned about people from reading history and fiction, particularly the many ways that minds can be narrow and hearts can be bitter. But unlike Narella, he does not rest with making judgments of fact that these are the interpretations and priorities of this or that client. He is also morally critical. He flushes out their inconsistent values, aiming to help them discover what parts of their experiences and mindsets are truly better or truly worse.

Differences

Each psychologist has a different view of what it means to learn. None may have spelled it out in a theory of learning, but each stops asking questions at a very different point along the ascent of their learning. Should all four counsel the same client, each may feel confident about what is going on, but each will have learned something very different about this client because each has a different idea of what learning is.

Eve thinks learning is paying close attention to what is out there, or "in here" in the client out there. She takes pride in an objectivity that does not let any word or gesture or tone of voice go unnoticed. She assumes she learns something about her clients when she can vividly picture their situation and deeply empathize with their feelings. For Eve, *learning is assembling emotionally colored mental images.* To her credit, she is faithful to the normativity of experience. While she is counseling, besides listening to every word, she also notices postures, gestures, silences and voice tones. But she has not clearly discovered for herself the further normativities of understanding, reason, and responsibility. She is intelligent; she does understand things. But she has not noticed the difference in herself between experiences of insight and experiences of vivid images and poignant feelings. She is also reasonable; she reflects on what she understands. But she is oblivious of the fact that she is testing her ideas against the evidence of her clients' words and behaviors. She considers herself "in touch" with her feelings, but to her, "in touch" means only that she *notices* her feelings. She does not directly reflect on *why* she experiences them, nor does she scrutinize them for their subtle trickeries. She is also responsible; she is committed to caring for others, but not to the extent of a "tough love" that challenges her clients about wishful thinking or hedonistic values. *What she learns is a cluster of symbols*—a look and feel of a client "out there."

Conrad, unlike Eve, is quite aware of the need to understand. He thinks learning is not only paying attention to behaviors, testimonies and feelings but also understanding how everything fits together. He is dedicated to an objectivity that will not buy any explanation that is not logical, coherent, and comprehensive. He is consciously faithful to the normativity of understanding as well as the normativity of experience. He asks himself *why* his clients behave as they do, and *how* their psyches may be distorted. But he expects that everything is a case of something. He has not discovered for himself that the concepts he is familiar with resulted from insights that occurred to theorists like Freud and Jung. He thinks of his insights, and everyone else's, as revealing which concepts "apply" in this or that situation. In his view, *learning is correlating concepts related to experience.* Like Eve, he too is reasonable; he reflects on his insights to make sure they are sound, but he is ignorant of what makes an insight sound, having detached them from experience and bottled them up in concepts. So he tests his understanding by examining how coherent the resulting concepts are, which leaves little room for revision by someone with more experience and deeper insight into the lives of a wider variety of clients. He too is responsible, which shows in his readiness to deduce what is right and wrong based on criteria of consistency and coherence. But he has no grasp of inductive methods for sorting out the issues of better and worse that fall outside his purview of logic. Also unlike Eve, he monitors and scrutinizes his own feelings for any false signals, but he expects that any false signals will be a case of transference, or screening memories, or projection, and so on. *What he learns is a set of concepts that correlate* with his client's behaviors and testimonies, as well as concepts that explain his own feelings.

Narella, like Conrad, is keenly aware of the need to understand. But for her, understanding is not restricted to logical deductions. She also engages in creative *inductions.* She expects that every person and every situation is unique, and what makes them unique is an interweaving of unique past circumstances and decisions. So she focuses on "context." She asks about concrete events in her clients' pasts to see if she can discern the path leading to their present mindsets. What she expects to learn, and hopes her clients also learn, is a story and, as far as possible, the full story. She goes beyond Conrad's notion of objectivity by encompassing not only what makes logical sense but also what makes historical sense. She expects that people will say one thing and do another, will behave inconsistently, and sometimes will knowingly demean themselves. So she questions how her clients interpret their experiences, seeking to understand their understanding by anticipating also their misunderstandings. She lets their contradictions stand as an unprecedented drama, which, like the great dramas of theater, intertwine insights with oversights. For Narella, *learning is making judgments of fact about what actual people believe and honor.* While she relies on her understanding to entertain various explanations, she is mainly after a reasoned judgment of what her clients' beliefs and values really are. Like Eve, she is quite aware of her own emotions;

and like Conrad, she recognizes certain emotional dysfunctions that affect her own behavior. But unlike both, she is also aware of how her past experiences still "live" in her, and how healing will involve weaving the threads of her own past into a more integrated fabric of life in her future. For herself and her clients, *what she learns is a history.*

Abe knows that learning is not only paying attention to experience, not only understanding experiences, and not only making reasoned judgments of fact about the meanings and values people hold. He also takes a critical stand about which explanations best explain the experiences and which values are actually better than others. He is familiar with the differences between the normativities of experience, of understanding, of reason, and of responsibility. His notion of objectivity combines Eve's concern about experience, and Conrad's concern about understanding concepts, and Narella's concern about understanding how in fact people concretely understand themselves and what their operational priorities really are. But he adds his responsible concern to distinguish between truth and error, and between better and worse. Where Narella makes judgments of fact about people's mindsets and priorities, Abe goes beyond her historicist assumption by making judgments about their adequacy. For him learning is *an answer to the questions, What is intelligible and unintelligible, true and false, better and worse here?* Among the many explanations he considers, he includes the possibility that his client may be lying, or clinging to some myth, or behaving in self-defeating ways. He aims to form an opinion for himself that best explains how his clients act against their better interests, and he watches for the opportunity to challenge his clients' attitudes or behaviors. Abe also wonders about his own feelings, but experience has taught him that his feelings come loaded with his own history and give him only some initial indications of better and worse. He has learned to ask himself, "Which feelings can I trust to indicate what the really better may be?" *What he learns are answers to questions about reality.*

Now all four psychologists are more or less guided interiorly by the normative drives on the levels of their experience, understanding, reason and responsibility. But only Abe *knows* that he is, which is why he more faithfully follows the criteria inherent in these drives. He is more acutely aware of how learning works: *Learning is responsibly asking questions and getting answers about experience.* We grow in learning by conscientiously cycling through questions and answers. Our imagination pictures what we only begin to question; insights give us answers that we express in concepts; and judgments issue in a narrative of a key developments, stubborn myths, and regrettable mistakes. But unless our sense of responsibility aims to undo whatever impedes our full openness to reality, values, and love, our learning will be blind to the issues that we are unwilling to tackle. We might ask the questions, but we will avoid some answers, and any action we take will, by default, be just an exercise of the closed mind and heart.

A Dialectic of Horizons

Now what happens when these worlds meet to discuss the same situation? When egos are at stake, there will be debate, of course. When ethicists are open, there will be a dialog, but dialog still does not mean agreement. Given different views about learning, there will also be a dialectic of these horizons. So, to anticipate the issues about learning that collaborating ethicists everywhere face, let us imagine how these four psychologists might work together to resolve a concrete moral problem.

Suppose that each one has a child in the same grade school. And imagine that Eve, Conrad, Narella, and Abe are sitting side by side at a parent-teacher meeting. The principal explains that an eighth grade boy named Raymond had loaded 38-caliber revolver in his locker, so she wants to discuss what to do. During the dialog, they will each learn something. And insofar as each means something quite unique by "learning," listening to one another creates a live dialectic among their respective intellectual horizons regarding learning itself.

We can expect that Eve will find Conrad rather abstract and unsympathetic to Raymond's feelings, and that Narella overly complicates things by asking about Raymond's past, his social life, and the priorities of his parents. But she may be taken aback by Abe's caution because she does not understand why Abe feels this is necessary, since, to her mind, what is out there is plain to see. She just wants to convince Conrad, Narella and Abe to change *what* they think. Still, she recognizes that the others are not stupid or silly or irresponsible or uncaring; she realizes that she *likes* them. So she feels an abiding inclination to be open to their views.

Conrad would probably try to lead Eve to recognize the moral principles involved and to see some sense in his conclusions about what ought to be done. He may respect Narella for her awareness of the full context of the situation, but be wary of her suggestions for practical action that he cannot justify in principle. He reads Abe's caution as evidence of possibly significant questions that Abe himself cannot clearly formulate. He feels a tension between his respect for Abe's integrity and his own commitment to logical ideals.

For her part, Narella would respect the views of both Eve and Conrad, but she would likely press to get all questions out on the table before jumping to conclusions. She is not out to dispute with anyone but rather to widen their perspectives to include what may appear odd or confusing about the past. She would lay out the many historical factors in Raymond's life and perhaps even wonder aloud about assumptions that lie behind the opinions of the parents and teachers in the room. She listens attentively to Abe because he not only gives her credit for her historical perspective; he also expresses his own opinion not as dogma but as honestly inviting the feedback from the group.

Abe understands the minds of the other three. Like Narella, he is quite aware that minds are like clothes: no one likes to change in public. But where Narella will apparently accept all but the most outrageous views, Abe will not. He will engage the enemy—people's biases, myths, and hardheartedness. But he will do so as strategically as he can, in a sincere effort to enhance their relationship while not compromising his views. So he waits, allowing veiled fears to be revealed, hoping for large gains and settling for the small. His goal is to make a decision based on a collective authenticity that enriches the "we" in the room. Specifically, he deeply desires to expose the myths that may have affected Raymond, his parents, his peers, his teachers, the administration, and, indeed, his three fellow psychologist-parents.

As I say, these four types of learners are caricatures. But because they each align with distinct normative criteria that function in everyone, it should be no surprise that they also align with distinct moral philosophies. Eve's instinct about learning is shared with empiricists, materialists, pragmatists, and positivists. Conrad's is shared with conceptualists, idealists, linguistic analysts, and historicists. Narella's is shared by relativists, postmodernists, and other conventionalists. Abe's is shared by realists, understood as those whose notion of "real" includes the processes of learning which, because they are recognized as normative by nature, but also wounded, give a realism that is also critical.

It is in such live dialectics of horizons that the underlying norms that Abe verified for himself become verified by others as well. As he asks and answers questions, others may notice the priority he places on inner demands over the voices of authority, scripture, abstract universals, and moral sentiments. As their attention shifts from plans to performance, they engage the basic and universal ground for ethics that lie behind all other norms. As long as an atmosphere of mutual respect is maintained, the dialectic of horizons is essentially an invitation.

Of course, we—real people—are more or less aware of the distinct yet interlocking ways these normative demands actually work. Learning about learning takes time and persistence. What we learn is based on the particular mix of awareness of these normative drives that we happen to have. And even when our intellectual horizons may fully open on some issues, on other issues we can easily fall back from Abe's horizon into Narella's or Conrad's or Eve's.

Pining for Certitude

Presumably Eve, Conrad, Narella and Abe want to learn about Raymond and the gun in his locker. As learners, they listen to one another. But they also talk to one another, so they are teachers too. In this fashion, the learning and teaching move along, not aimlessly and forever, but converging toward an agreement about the nature of this situation.

But how do they know when to *stop* learning and teaching? By what criteria will they conclude, "Well, we seem to know what went on here." To see why this is an important question, think of the many discussions where some people rush too quickly to closure and others drag on the discussion endlessly. Both the rushers and the draggers are unsuccessful in learning because they have only a foggy notion of what makes learning "enough."

Why is this? Interestingly, although the impulse to rush a discussion feels quite different from the impulse to drag it out, both impulses grow from a common root. That root is the false assumption that the goal of learning is certitude. Even when certitude does not seem possible and the need for action is pressing, the rushers and draggers regard this as just an unfortunate compromise without giving up the ideal of certitude.

There is a good reason reason for this. In learning about any situation, there are two moments, or phases—learning *what* happened and learning *why* it happened. When we ask, *what* happened, we rely on what someone saw, or heard, or smelled, or tasted, or touched. Except for watching magicians, we trust our five senses. We are certain about what happened because we experience it directly, or we believe someone else who experienced it directly. Here is where we usually find certitude—in the experience of learning *what* happened.

But when we ask *why* something happened, we do not turn to our five senses to gather more data. We turn to our intelligence to play with the data we already have, so that we can consider different ways the data may be interconnected. Eve, Conrad, Narella, and Abe each plays with several different explanations of *why* there was a gun in Raymond's locker. As they listen and talk, each notices data previously overlooked, and each raises questions the others had not considered. If they eventually settle on a single explanation, it is because the explanation answered most of their questions about the data at hand. They think of this explanation as "better than any other," and they leave open the possibility of new data and new questions and, therefore, a better explanation yet.

The ideal here is staying open. Because certitude closes further questions, it is not an appropriate ideal for learning *why* things happen. The problem with the rushers is that they so *enjoy* the feeling of certitude that they ignore new information and new questions. The problem with the draggers is that they so *hope to enjoy* the feeling of certitude that even when they never quite get there, they keep on asking questions that cannot be answered. In both cases, one reason the ideal of certitude resists dethronement is because it promises to relieve the tension of living with unanswered questions. It is the comfort of a mind asleep—embraced by the rushers and longed for by the draggers.

There is a deeper reason why certitude is so alluring, deep enough to evade the notice of many philosophers. The reason is that learning *what* happens seems almost identical to looking. We express our certainty by saying, "I saw it with my own two eyes." Even when we use our imagination to invent something or make a plan, we *picture* this kind of thinking as *picturing.* But this is just an analogy; there is no mental screen and projector in the mind. What we need to do is *understand* this kind of thinking as *understanding.* With learning both *what* happened and *why,* our minds pose questions and test answers. If the principal says she found a loaded 38-caliber revolver in Raymond's locker, one might wonder if it was really Raymond's locker, or if it was loaded with real bullets, or if her account can be trusted. Mental pictures are essential here, but only as the data that our understanding works on. Even learning *what* happened is done by raising relevant questions about data we already pictured, not just by "looking at" the mental pictures.

So the criterion for saying, "Well, we seem to know what went on here," is not some vivid picture, or urgent description by an eyewitness, or a dogmatic pronouncement by some authority. At base, the criterion for this or any other judgment is simply the *absence of relevant questions.*[30] We grasp that the evidence on hand is sufficient to support a certain or a probable judgment. The validation for concluding *what* happened is the absence of residual questions about the data, their source, their reliability, and so on. Similarly, the validation for concluding *why* something happened is a subjective acceptance of a "better than any other" explanation while remaining open to new data and new questions.

Practically speaking, this means that someone like Abe, who has learned about learning, focuses his attention on the questions that bother him. He is familiar with the feeling of intellectual discomfort. The normativity of understanding disturbs him. He asks himself, "What exactly is *the question* that bothers me?" No doubt, Narella, Conrad, and Eve will learn a thing or two, but odds are that Abe's learning will be far more successful because he focuses his mind quite strictly on questions and answers, relying on narratives, concepts and images to help him identify further questions that may prove relevant.

Intellectual Conversion

The point of describing these four types of learners is to clarify how learning about learning involves an intellectual conversion.[31] What is this? *An intellectual conversion is the discovery in oneself and the implementation in one's thinking that learning is responsibly asking and answering questions about experience.*

This discovery about learning is not a discovery of one's psychological peculiarities (the arena of counselors and fiction writers). Nor is this a discovery that most people would call *scientific.* That is, it is not a discovery of some data that others can look at, listen to, smell, taste, or touch, and then verify some hypothesis by pointing to sufficient evidence in the data. Yet the discovery does indeed meet the revered standards of scientific method. It is true that the "sufficient evidence" on what is discovered does not initially belong to the publicly available data of sense but rather to the privately available data of consciousness. Yet it quickly enters the public forum for verification. When we express our inner criteria for saying something is valid, or true, or a best available opinion, our criteria are always open to question. The less people are bothered by questions about our criteria, the more sufficient the evidence for affirming that learning is really like this.

Intellectual Development

This discovery at the heart of an intellectual conversion usually evolves gradually, although the growth does seem to have distinct stages. To children, the real is what they see and hear, or what their parents tell them others saw and heard. The inner needs, fears and hopes that children experience all point to people, events and things they can picture. They are familiar with social institutions, but only as police officers, teachers, lawyers, coins, banks, and city halls—things they can see or imagine. They lay a foundation that some, like Eve, never fully transcend.

With schooling, youngsters learn to form, compare, and combine concepts. People can be categorized by their roles—teachers, parents, grocers, police. Moral concepts of honesty, stealing, lying, fairness, right, and wrong that can apply to any number of concrete, imaginable people, events, and things. This lays a foundation that some, like Conrad, never fully transcend.

Adolescents are taught their history. They learn that present nations are the results of wars and leaders, and that new wars and leaders can always rearrange the global map. They study the ways of different cultures—how they worship, haggle in the marketplace, raise their children, and bury their dead. This opens a new world to them, the world of meanings and values that define all social and cultural institutions. This lays a foundation that some, like Narella, never fully transcend.

Later adolescents come to realize that not all their beliefs are true. In science, they learn that not all hypotheses pan out under testing. Even religious ideas can be tested, as a high school senior once asked a teacher friend of mine, "Sir, is our God the real God?" They learn to form judgments on their own. Having discovered the fault line in human creativity, they test stories for truth. They test explanations to make sure they fit the evidence. They learn that all the beliefs, theories, stories and moral doctrines passed on to them are not unquestionable starting points for their additional learning. Rather they are answers to questions raised by other people in other times. This lays the foundation for a commitment to living in reality and passing judgment on any claim or story. Like Abe, they add to their learning by raising their own critical questions about what they read and hear from others, which often requires some unlearning of what turned out to be erroneous.

Of course, intellectual development does not necessarily stop at adulthood. There is always more to learn, certainly, but there are also entire realms of moral reflection that an adult may or may not understand. In chapter 1, we noted how the mind may or may not differentiate cleanly between common sense and theory. Intellectual development can differentiate in further ways yet. We can open our minds to four other realms of moral reflection—scholarship, aesthetics, religious love, and a philosophic interiority that reflects on realms of reflection as such.[32] Learning the differences among these realms can be a real eye-opener because they each have unique relationships to everyday morality and to ethical theories.

Scholarship.

About scholarship, besides asking about our own everyday priorities, we can also ask about the everyday priorities of peoples in
other times and places. This is neither our own common sense nor
our understanding of theoretical ideas. Rather, it is an effort to
learn about the common sense of other cultures. This is the work of
"scholars," as distinguished from "scientists." Where scientists
learn about general patterns in nature, including human nature,
scholars learn about the ways particular communities live—their
customs, beliefs, commitments, achievements, and tragedies. They
rely on special tools: hermeneutics for interpreting texts and
artifacts, socio-analytical procedures for determining what social
and culture changes occurred, and historical-critical criteria for
assessing whether these changes are for better or worse.

Aesthetics

We can also ask about the aesthetics of our environments—the
realm of art, sculpture, architecture, landscaping, music, drama, and
dance. In all these media, artists draw public attention to values
that have no names—incarnate values. They may be motivated by a
variety of goals, but their success in actually eliciting appreciation
of the beautiful will depend on what they learn about what beauty
does to their viewers and listeners. The goal of this learning is to
elicit specific emotional responses in others, and the means they use
are the palpable media of paint, plastic materials, sound, pathways,
and bodily movements. This aesthetic learning is neither practical,
nor conceptual, nor scientific, nor scholarly, nor religious. Many
artists learn how to evoke affective responses without depending
on any theory, but these make poor teachers. Artists who are more
self-aware ask themselves questions about what beauty does to
someone's mind and heart. They learn that portraying tension and
unresolved patterns can, through disturbing the forms of order, tap
the deep need for resolution in their viewers and hearers. They also
learn how to play with images in their minds until they hit upon
one that best expresses a certain emotional rhythm; any name we
give it detracts from the uniqueness of the experience because it
subordinates it to some general concept. It is this unique, unnama-

ble rhythm in their aesthetic expressions that they hope will stir the exigence for beauty in the hearts of their audiences or viewers.

Religious Love

Further, we can ask about the inner movements that focus our love for the transcendent. These movements are unique to each person. They include worship and prayer, as well as discernment between one's reliable and unreliable inspirations. This is a mysterious realm because experience keeps drawing one forward without ever delivering final clarity or satisfaction. Many begin by feeling moved by symbolic representations of God as creator and savior, and of their created selves as winning or losing that salvation. They advance by purging their lives of egotism and hatred, turning instead to the love of God and neighbor. As they advance, they may learn about God and religion from the theoretical perspectives of theologians, from the scholarly perspectives of historians, and the symbolic representations of artists. But no matter what other realms of meaning they understand, there may come a point of a real assent in which they judge that their abiding dissatisfaction is already both a love *for* the divine and a gift *from* the divine and that the value of divine love surpasses all other value. This real assent brings them to the question of a real *consent*. If their consent is only notional, they allow whatever may be divine to carry on without much interference; they may feel a willingness but not an effective desire. But if there occurs the further, real consent that surrenders to that transcendent love, one decides to subject one's spontaneous desires to an everyday discernment that wants to be moved only by this love. One also learns to rest in that love, through prayerful contemplation and wordless gratitude. Others, however, whose horizons are already open to all knowledge and all value, yet without growing up with religious education, may discover that they have all along been in love with the one whom others call Yahweh or God or Allah. Because their real assent to divine love passed over specific religious traditions, they are usually eager to learn from religions what others learned in their personal surrender to divine love.

Philosophic Interiority

To learn these differences between common sense, theory, scholarship, aesthetics, and religious love is itself an instance of learning. But it occurs in none of these other realms. Rather, it occurs in a sixth realm where we *learn how learning occurs* in any realm. This is the realm of fundamental method, whose data field covers the native methods of mind and heart. We may call this realm "philosophic interiority"—the mode of learning we are pursuing in this book. Our goal has been not to *devise* methods for realms of moral reflection but rather to *discover* and *understand* them. In each of these realms, including philosophic interiority itself, we ask different kinds of questions, and each kind has its unique criteria and goals. Of course, one must know the right questions. So what is absolutely essential for anyone seeking to learn how learning occurs in any realm is some degree of personal commitment to asking the sort of questions that define that realm.

Verification

We considered many interlocking hypotheses about how we learn. I will summarize them here, but it is important to understand these as hypotheses, as more or less plausible explanations of how learning works. They need verification. And the only verification needed, or possible, is your own. If you like what you read here only because of what practical use it may have, you stand with Eve. If you like it only because of its logical coherence, you stand with Conrad. If you like it only because it brings historical scholarship into moral reflection, you stand with Narella. But if you noted what happens when you learn anything, and find that these hypotheses explain what happens in you more thoroughly than any other currently available explanation, then, with Abe, you will have successfully verified what you learned about learning. Moreover, if, like Abe, you appeal to these norms in your discussions with others, and if your appeal to the exigences of consciousness makes sense to them as well, you contribute toward the ongoing, common verification of how anyone learns anything.

By way of a summary, then, here are the main hypotheses about learning that we considered so far:

- What prompts us to learn are distinct normative drives on the levels of experience, of understanding, of reason, and of responsibility
- The fulfillment of each lower drive leads us to the next higher drive.
- These normative drives are the source of everything anyone has ever learned.
- These normative drives do not work perfectly. They are impeded by dysfunctional elements in our heritage, biases in consciousness (personal neuroses, egotism, loyalism, commonsensism), and the willfulness, or sin, by which we act against our better judgment
- Learning about learning does not give a recipe on how to learn. Rather, it gives an explanation about the nature of learning.
- An intellectual conversion is needed to realize for oneself that learning is responsibly asking and answering questions about experience.
- Dialog among people of open minds can function as an invitation to intellectual conversion and as ongoing verification of what the ground of learning is for anybody.
- The range of possible learning includes not only common sense and theory, but also scholarship, aesthetics, religious love, and philosophic interiority.

As ethicists, we can expect that when we share with others not only *what* we learned but also *how* our learning came from struggling with questions, we may well engage them in a sincere examination of the origins of their own opinions. And when new experiences and new questions arise, we can expect that our shared learning will more readily deal with what our current views do not explain well enough. In the next chapter, we will explain how these personal discoveries translate into a set of expectations about what we really can—and cannot—learn about moral situations. But before we do, we need to consider a conversion in how we make our choices.

CHOOSING HOW WE CHOOSE

We make choices every day. We decide to do something, or we decide not to do it, and that seems to be all there is to it. However, from the perspective of evolution, personal choices are elements within the massive and complex moral flux we call history. We make our choices in historical contexts where opportunities rise and fall, owing largely to the results of previous choices. When we decide to direct our resources toward some A, we direct them away from some B, C, and D. And when we decide *not* to do some A, we reserve our resources for some B, C, or D. All decisions are choices among alternatives. For every opportunity we explore, we advance world process in a direction that leaves other opportunities unexplored.

Strategic Choices Shape History

Our choices change history, but not only through the conglomerated effects of innumerable particular choices. We also learned how to *eliminate* huge numbers of particular choices by making one strategic choice—a skill passed down to us from our distant ancestors that we now refer to as a *policy*. We say, "From now on we will ..." or "A better way of handling these issues is to ...." Strategic choices may be collaborative, as when business leaders negotiate contracts and legislators write laws, or they may be individual, as when I commit myself to daily exercise. Strategic choices eliminate the need to refresh our knowledge and consult our feelings at every turn of events. They are the foundation of what we call a *society*, or *the social order*, understood as all the ways people habitually focus their skills on common enterprises.

This social order can break down suddenly, as when disaster strikes and in the absence of police, marauders roam the streets and loot the stores. It breaks down more slowly when big businesses fudge their assets or special interest groups take over the government. The justification is usually, "Everybody's doing it." But nearly everybody forgets that their laws and policies embody strategic choices made by previous generations and refined by their peers. In their place is a hodge-podge of choices made by individuals or subgroups who aim to get what they can for themselves.

The chain of antecedents and consequences of our choices is not limited to the social orders that condition our living. In every choice we also change our selves. We pursue our learning along some paths rather than others. We take on new duties and drop old ones. We strengthen some relationships and let others fade. One day it can suddenly occur to us that the kind of person we are is a result of all the choices we ever made. It dawns on us that we have not realized our full potential. We have become, shall we say, *peculiar*.

So every choice is a change in both external circumstances and in the person choosing. Moreover, depending on how valid people's understanding of a given situation is, and how authentic their priorities are, their choice may be for better or for worse. Then everyone involved in the situation faces a changed situation and shifts his or her priorities to meet it. In this manner, choice by choice, in every waking hour of every human being on our planet, better here and worse there, humans and human situations evolve.

In this mélange, we can distinguish three types of choices that any ethics needs to take into account.[33]

- **Particular choices** include any choice of a particular good thing or event. Our needs and wants drive us to make countless particular choices every day. Some are morally insignificant—whether to order the hamburger or the salad. Others are morally fraught—whether to badmouth a coworker or keep my mouth shut.

- **Strategic choices** are about policies and habits. Leaders choose to set up social institutions by committing groups and individuals to specific routines. These routines churn out a steady flow of particular good things or events. These routines typically outlive their own members, giving the group its "tradition" of how things are done.

- **Fundamental choices** (also called a "fundamental option") include one's choice of the self one is becoming through all one's particular choices and strategic choices. This type of choice is difficult to pin down because it usually sneaks up on us as the cumulative product of millions of choices of the first two types. But moral maturity usually brings one to realize, "What I make of my-

self is up to no one but me." Still, we usually do not attempt such an existential commitment alone. We associate with those with whom we share values; we share
relationships based on what "better" means for us. Such
fundamental choices lie behind every moral standard by
which we critique our social institutions and our particular choices. This commitment to moral standards defines our cultural institutions—such as the judiciary,
humanities education, the arts, and religion.

Not everyone makes all three kinds of choices. Many adults
seldom deliberate before choosing some particular good; they are
content to deal with immediate needs through old habits. Others
accept various policies and habits from parents and authorities
without any scrutiny to ensure that these routines will really
deliver what they promise. Still others let themselves be moved
entirely by impulse or compliance to social pressures without even
a thought about the kind of person they want to be.

In any case, it is all three kinds of choices that change history.
This is what history is—the unfolding of particular, strategic, and
fundamental choices for better or for worse. History's agents are
those who make these choices knowingly, while those who let
others do the choosing just drift with the flow. Collectively,
though, it is the choicemakers—mostly anonymous—who make
things really better or worse. They are the ones who direct the flow
of history while the drifters glide along without argument. In this
perspective, history is identical to the human moral order.

The Elements of Choices

So if we are going to maximize our chances of improving history,
we need to ask ourselves, "What do we do when we choose?" This
is an embarrassing question. We make choices all the time: we
blush to admit we do not know what we are doing.

In any choice, we make two value judgments. In a first, we assess
better and worse about a situation. In a second, we assess our
options for action. These two value judgments are sandwiched by
feelings.[34] Before our first assessment, we have initial feelings about
better and worse in a situation. Likewise before our second
assessment. Following our second assessment, we experience

confirmational feelings about our choice. Then we rely on this newly integrated set of priorities to feel out the next situation. These feeling functions are carried out by the symbolizing exigence in our consciousness. That is, we are aware of an image linked to an affect that moves us toward or away from what the image represents.

Feelings and Value Judgments

The one role feelings do *not* play is to make a judgment about the actual worth of anything. Many people have yet to realize this. Just as to a naïve realist, reality is what we see, so to a naïve moralist, values are what we feel. This typically stems from childhood, where youngsters rely on their feelings as their primary indicators of values. What they like must be good; what they dislike must be bad. In other words, besides our likes and dislikes, besides our feelings for or against a certain initiative, there is the further question of actual value. The meaning of *deliberation* is precisely this: to ask the question of value. And the goal of deliberation is to arrive at a value judgment: This really is (or is not) better.

What is more, once we see the difference between our feelings as indicators and confirmations of *possible* value and our judgments as determinations of *actual* value, we experience the exigence to be responsible for our feelings themselves. We all have trouble with our feelings, and while we appropriately resist those that lead the wrong way, most of us do this haphazardly at first. But as we mature, we notice our personal emotional rhythms; we get to know which feelings to trust and which to suspect. Part of moral maturity is a clear-headed commitment to take charge of our feelings. It means putting a conscientious gap between the emotional pushes we feel and a value judgment about our choices.

Criterion for Value Judgments

What happens when we make a value judgment? When we determine that a certain X is better than many Ys, we transcend the ambivalences of our feelings by affirming that X is objectively better. We open ourselves to undertake actions that change a real situation and ourselves as well. We then experience a change in how we feel, both about the situation and about ourselves. Although this change is prompted by our feelings and is secured by our feelings, it is not caused by our feelings. It is caused by our judgment of value.

The judgment of value, in itself, is simple. We make an affirmation that X is better than Y or that X is plainly good. The fundamental ethical question is not *whether* we make value judgments; it is obvious that we make them all the time. Rather, the question is this: What criteria do we use to make them? When we deliberate about what may be really better, there are many secondary criteria that are often mistaken as primary—the advice of experts, the words of scripture, the commands of authorities, personal habit, and cultural priorities. But as we saw, we also choose—and unchoose—our experts, our scriptures, our authorities, our habits and our inherited priorities. So, prior to these secondary criteria, there must be a more immediate criterion. Let me state it baldly here, and then offer an explanation of how it works:[35] *The immediate criterion for value judgments is the drying up of relevant questions.*

For example, suppose I am offered a job. The exigence to be responsible prompts me toward making a judgment about the value of accepting the offer. The symbolic exigence loads my imagination with feelings about staying in my current job and about moving on. These images and feelings prompt questions about doing better: What would my parents do in this situation? What might be the long-range outcomes of each option? Is it better to be loyal to my current employer or to courageously seize a promising opportunity? What do my friends think is better? What is better for my family? What kind of person might I become in each option?

Of course, I could just go along with old habits or the opinions of others. Or I could just not choose, and stay where I am. But if I make the judgment that one option is probably better than the other, this happens the moment I realize that I have addressed all the important questions. Some questions I may answer easily, others I may remain tentative about, and still others may not turn out as relevant as I first thought. But when no further relevant questions arise, I make a value judgment in the form, "X is probably better than Y."

Moral Conviction

I say that my value judgment affirms that X is "probably" better than Y because in most cases I am conscious of two facts: One is that I may not have answered all the questions that occurred to me. The other is that I realize there may be further questions that never occurred to me. I may lack information about X that would raise new questions. Certainly I lack some of that farsightedness that notices all the opportunities and risks that lie within my range of options. No doubt, I have uncritically absorbed certain values from my culture. The very connotations of my language carry unquestioned priorities about who really counts in life, and how people ought to behave. The ethical principles I rely on may be revised by new ethical theories that would pose unanticipated questions. So I say that X is "probably" better because my value judgment is conditioned by the fact that I simply do not know all the relevant questions. The reason we call some people "wise" is because they know more relevant questions than the rest of us. This permanent possibility of new questions makes it clear that in our choices about particular things, as well in our strategic choices about policies and habits, we can only do our best, and our best can only approach the really better. As we saw earlier, we seldom can expect moral certitude.

Still, we must choose, and very often we choose without hesitation. On what grounds can we justify choosing when we are not certain? Recall from chapter 1 the parallel between the objectivity of our moral judgments and the objectivity of judgments in science. Scientists do not aim for objective truth. They aim for the best available explanation of specific data, knowing that further questions may arise from new data or new scientific models. Their objectivity is an expectation that the exigence to be intelligent and reasonable can increasingly approach full knowledge. They toss out ideas that looked good on paper but did not work out in practice. These exigences are the driving energies in an entire community of scientists, producing ideas that build on each other and are successively validated by experience. So too with our deliberations. We seldom claim moral certitude. Rather, we base our moral judgments on the answers to the questions we happen to have considered, knowing that further questions can arise. Our moral objectivity is an expectation that the exigence to be responsible, working in an entire community of caring people, produces value judgments that ever more closely approach what is really better and that devalue earlier judgments that turned out to be biased or nor longer relevant to the changing times.

So between an unattainable moral certitude and a nihilistic moral relativism, we humans together assume that among all the value judgments ever made there is a massive subset that grasps what is really better and what is really worse. We rely on the ongoing normativity of responsibility, working among many people, to monitor and refine our evaluations of historical trends. We make assertions about what progress or decline has occurred in technology, economics, politics, education, and law. We propose new exemplars, principles, policies, procedures, and standards that show promise of improving life. But we express our commitment to these assertions and proposals by a careful use of language. We claim, not moral "certitude," but moral "conviction"—a state of mind and heart that is fully ready to commit ourselves to a course of action based on best available moral opinions.

Still, this is not to say that all moral judgments are open to revision. There is one judgment that we cannot question. It is the judgment that being responsible is better than being irresponsible. For we cannot responsibly ridicule being responsible. There are also second-order judgments about which we can be certain. These are the judgments on whether or not we actually did *what we were convinced* was better or worse. Initially, to say I did what I thought was better or worse is a judgment of fact, not of value. But a completely certain judgment of value follows immediately. In any situation where we acted against our better judgment, *and are certain that we did so*, the judgment of value regarding this act is certain. Likewise for situations where we are certain that we acted in line with our better judgment. And, finally, there are the innumerable moral judgments that we, as a race, have effectively established beyond question: The Second World War was a horrible tragedy. Rape cannot be justified. The disparity of standards of living across the globe should be redressed. The "beyond question" is the key here. For we are a people who experience normative demands to do better. And this "better" that we actually accomplish builds up a legacy of virtually unquestionable moral judgments for future generations.

Moral Conversion

We saw that the drying up of relevant questions is the immediate criterion for value judgments. And we noted how most everyday value judgments are as open to revisions as any scientific theory because new relevant questions may well be asked. But if the absence of relevant questions is the criterion for making value judgments, we come to a more basic question: How, in everyday decisions, do we recognize whether or not a moral question is relevant? An abstract criterion is easy to state: Moral questions are relevant if they are directed toward the really better. But concretely speaking, people rely on different notions of what "really better" means when they make value judgments. So to examine more closely how we deliberate about better and worse, we need to distinguish between different notions of what "really better" means to actual people.

At the end of chapter 5, we noted a basic difference in what "really better" can mean to a person: A man may equate "really better" with mere preference. He chooses X over Y based on nothing more than his unquestioned predilection for X. In contrast, a woman may equate "really better" with what responsible deliberation reveals. She chooses X over Y because her deliberation aimed at knowing what is better regardless of her spontaneous preference. For those who follow mere preference, it is usually personal interest and personal payoff that makes a question relevant, and nothing else. For those who pursue the notion of "really better," what makes a question relevant is the good that transcends what individuals or groups may spontaneously prefer. The expression, "really better" carries the same objectivity for them as the expression, "really true."

With this distinction in mind, we may now define a moral conversion: *Moral conversion is a choice of the truly better over what is merely preferred as one's criterion for all choices.*[36]

In this definition, moral conversion represents not any particular choice, nor any strategic choice, but rather the third kind of choice: a fundamental choice of a self-transcending criterion for choosing. As a self-transcending choice, it represents an entry into a fully open moral horizon. The person is open to any question about what is really better. It is fundamental because it affects all of one's strategic and particular choices. It is a choice of how we choose.

However, no one's moral horizon is either thoroughly open or thoroughly closed. Children necessarily have a self-absorbed moral horizon. Good parents draw them to consider the "really better" in an objective sense. As children grow into adults, they face a fundamental choice of whether to go beyond their self-absorbed preferences and embrace a self-transcending way of living. They may make this choice inadvertently as a pattern of moral objectivity emerges among their particular and strategic choices. Or they may have discovered one day that putting mere preferences above everything else stings the conscience. The exigence to be responsible may turn them toward an unrestricted openness to what is better in itself, without confining it to what comforts their egos or the sensibilities of their community. Still, they are free. It is up to them to decide whether to carry on in self-absorption or to shift their lives toward self-transcendence.

But wait: Is acting out of mere preference all that bad? Even mere preference now and then does some good. A doctor who advises surgery chiefly for financial reasons will still save lives. What is wrong with that? Nothing—as long as we restrict the meaning of any "that" to outcomes. However, when we incorporate the choosing subject in our meaning of any "that," we see plenty wrong. What counts for really doing better is not only overt outcomes but also covert inputs. The moral quality of any choice includes both chooser and chosen. Because the doctor's choice is not motivated by the exigence to be responsible, we cannot say that better was done. Indeed, the sorry part of the chooser's self-absorbed action that happens to benefit others is that it deepens his or her self-absorption.

Well, then, what about the millions of things we prefer that have no obvious "right" or "wrong" about them? Are not most of our preferences morally neutral? This objection has merit, but only within a legalistic moral worldview where only certain things are prohibited and everything else is allowed. In the fuller scope of the universe doing better, a comprehensive ethics needs to incorporate not only right and wrong but better and worse. Besides an Ethics of Law there is also an Ethics of Better.[37] Besides our history of reflection on what should be regulated by the laws and sanctions of a community, there is also our history of moral inventiveness, daring, and achievement. To resist inspirations to do better where no laws apply is still a moral shortcoming. So in an Ethics of Better there are no morally neutral areas. Everything falls on a continuous scale of better and worse. Any choice based on nothing but preference, ignoring the subjective exigence to intend the really better, will be morally deficient.

Finally, a morality of mere preference has evolutionary consequences: Human preferences are just experiences. They beg understanding, verification, and responsible deployment. Unleashed from these controls of authenticity, mere preferences impede the exigence for authenticity to see what is really better and to do it. A morality of pure preference is an incoherent system, an anomaly in an evolving universe that is ripe for the higher controls of conscience and love. In contrast, a morality of obedience to the normative movements of consciousness is a privileged functioning of the harmony of the universe.

Believing in Each Other

We have been focusing on first-hand learning and choosing. In "Learning about Learning," we looked at what occurs when we understand our personal experience and how knowledge results from judging the validity of our understanding. Here, in "Choosing How We Choose," we focused on how we make value judgments based on our first-hand experience. Now we need to return to our wider context of universal process to see how believing each other is essential to growing in both knowledge and values.

Nearly everything anyone knows and values is inherited. Each person's worldview is a predominantly shaped by believing others. What happens when we are asked to believe anyone? Suppose Lois Lane reports in the *Daily Planet* the fact that there was a bank robbery on Main Street. I believe her if I trust her. It is a factual judgment that the bank was robbed, but prior to accepting that fact, I first make a judgment of value that Lois is worth believing. Likewise for accepting the value judgments of others. If a politician proposes that the city would do better by providing extra security for banks, I consider the values in the proposal, but I also consider whether the politician is trustworthy if I am going to consent to it. The point is this: the mentality of any person at any time is hugely maintained through a network of personal relations based on mutual trust. The facts accepted and the values cherished by most people are rooted more deeply in their *trust* of others than in any supposedly autonomous reason or solitary conscience. To believe each other, we first believe *in* each other.

Belief *in* one another underlies every fact and value we accept on the word of another. What we believe from others blends seamlessly with our first-hand learning. We each have a "mentality," a horizon, made up of settled issues and unsettled questions. Our mentality is a working unity on which we draw to deal with everyday life without fuss about which elements we discovered personally and which we inherited. Our judgments on the trustworthiness of sources are so pervasive in our learning that we seldom notice ourselves making them. Still, when we act on information or priorities received from others and outcomes fall short of our expectations, questions arise about the trustworthiness of our sources. Now the demand for a value judgment falls into our lap. If our sources are questionable, then question we must.

LETTING LOVE LOVE

This brings us to the everyday task of being our own persons while living in the shadow of ancestors and alongside companions on the journey. As sharers of this land we call earth, we are the inheritors of most of our morals, and we make most of our decisions within a web of affective relationships.

The Affective Movement

Of all the many different ways that our affectivity might develop, there are some common elements relevant to ethics. While it is true that autonomy is a key achievement in moral development, we still identify with one another in seeking common goals. More deeply, we recognize "the other" as like ourselves insofar as he or she feels the same exigences to live authentic lives. So, in loving others, we open our selves to mutual engagements that go beyond *doing better* to *being better together*. We experience an inner exigence to let love have its way with us, taking us down that road never travelled as our mutual engagement changes ourselves and our loved ones together. It also lifts us higher as we engage transcendent ultimates. It seems indisputable that the greatest achievement of our autonomy lies in how freely and deliberately we weave our lives in love with others.

Engagement with One Another

I am speaking not only of friendships but also of our love for any humans anywhere. To see how profoundly we identify ourselves with everyone else, suppose astronomers discover an enormous asteroid headed our way, to collide with earth two years from now. They predict its impact will propel such massive amounts of earth and water into our atmosphere that the cloud will block the sun for a hundred years and all but the bugs will die. What will the knowledge of our collective death do to us? Besides the familiar responses of individuals to their own deaths, what might our collective response be? Some will panic, some will preach God's judgment, but a great many will contemplate what it means to face the end of our race. In some ways we will act like the terminally ill, contemplating our past and facing the reality that our life is nearing not just its end but also its final meaning. But unlike the terminally ill, who pass the torch of life to survivors, we will witness together the extinguishing of the torch. Had the asteroid arrived 12 millennia ago, Homer would have spoken about the anger of the gods against us. But today, I venture, we would speak about the impending disaster in scientific terms—perhaps as an "experiment," our planet as the Petri dish in which, all along, we have been conducting tests on ourselves. "Were we a success or a failure? Did we give as much as we took? Did we make a positive difference to the lives we shared with others?" Answers will be mixed, of course, but a cloud of regret will darken the earth. "We should have cooperated more, trusted each other more, and loved each other more." Whatever the answer, the "we" of the question reveals how deeply we identify with one another as a single race, conducting a single experiment, lasting for eons, comprising billions of individual deaths, all driven by the notion of what we should have done together.

Everyone experiences the same movement to open up the selves they are by transcending their mere individuality to become a "we" with others. We disagree with each other, and we act at cross-purposes, but we would feel no stress over our differences were it not for our natural desire to "get together." This exigence to bond with others is part of the "affective movement" we have been speaking about. This movement is a consciously experienced drive to share life. It first shows in the child's drive to be loved. It expands in the adolescent's emerging drive to love others. It matures in the adult's drive to become part of a "we" committed to love *with* others. In its mature state, one's self-love becomes a love of an engaged self. The individual is liberated from the prison of mere self-esteem and healed of the sad wish to be loved as someone useful to the hopes of others.

The affective movement directly expands our moral horizon to include the hopes and fears of others. We saw that we choose practical courses of action after considering the merits of the moral opinions we find in our heritage and fellows. Under the affective movement, we not only *consider* the moral horizons of others; we also *share* them. The horizon of a life shared with others lifts our eyes beyond the moral obligations we personally derive from ethical principles; it rises above the duties we assume by our contracts and promises. Yet, far from abrogating our individual principles and duties, this shared view complements them by always raising the further relevant questions about the life we share: How do our decisions affect others? Who has vested interests in our decision? Whom do we consult about the situation affected by our decision? Who will benefit and who will be shortchanged? What alliances are enhanced and what alliances are threatened?

Surprisingly, this affective movement also expands our intellectual horizon. To a great extent, it works unconsciously at the level of our self-image, driven by the symbolic exigence. Without love, we tend to imagine our knowing selves as being "in here" looking "out there"—an image that colors everything we can know, with all the problems of objectivity that this naïve realism entails. With love, we imagine our knowing selves as sharing questions with others and contributing to a common fund of knowledge. We imagine knowledge less as information to gather into our individual heads and more as contributions to "what *we* know." Together, we are the wondering children of the universe, inheriting traditional knowledge, sifting its errors, revising it to meet present circumstances, and bequeathing an intellectual heritage to future generations.

They say love casts out fear, and presumably this includes fear of the unknown. Earlier, we considered how mutual love has the power to dissolve the fears of learning connected to the biases of neurotic obsession, egotism, loyalism, and commonsensism. We share open-eyed wonder about life, no matter where our curiosity may lead. On the other hand, love does not cast out *all* fear. Mature love is deeply afraid of the magical thinking, mythical ideals, unrealistic hopes, and even the personal disappointments that make staying in love difficult.

Engagement with the Divine

In chapter 2, we identified a "transcending exigence" experienced as desires that are entirely open-ended. In the realm of knowledge, we desire understanding and truth. In morality, we desire to make life better all around and to live as better persons. In personal engagements, we desire friendship; we desire to care for our communities; and we desire to be engaged with whatever may be the deepest source and ultimate beyond of all our desires. When we consider the evolution of humanity—not descriptively as the emergence of species over time but theoretically as the present reality of stacked systems in every human—we cannot avoid wondering about what sort of completeness integrates the upward dynamic of our intellectual, moral, and affective systems.

Although we often speak of this desired beyond as God, from the perspective of ethics it is particularly important to notice the inner movement toward engaging it. Only by making this inner movement a key theme in ethics can we set the table for genuine dialog among people of any religious perspective. Some believe there is no God. Others believe *in* God, but hold different truths *about* God. But prior to this believing, there is the inner movement of desires—for beauty, order, truth, goodness, and interpersonal engagement. They arise without our devising, and they are never fully satisfied. They are a form of love that springs from mysterious sources and moves toward a mysterious beyond. And so it seems natural to raise questions[38] about these desires: Whence and whither my love? Whence these inspirations and desires to open yet more? Whither lies this further beauty, order, truth, value, and personal engagement? Why are we drawn so?

These questions affect everything learned by anyone, provided only that we let the questions bother us. When they do, we may well regard all moral situations as engagements of people who experience the pull of transcendent love and the many counterpulls of a distorted heritage, biases, and willfulness. Ethicists who dismiss the question cut themselves off from understanding people for whom God is not only a value but a supreme value from which the value of everything created flows. They also cut themselves off from understanding people who take seriously their experience of transcendent love without reliance on religion. Indeed, they cut themselves off from fully engaging their own desires. Those who dismiss the question include not only atheists who consider it meaningless but also dogmatic faithful who think they already have all the answers.

Those of religious faith who let the question bother them know very well that it cannot be fully answered in this life. Yet because their world includes a supernatural order that is real and that really engages their natural lives, they cannot dismiss questions like these: Are we each alone, seeking to find God, or is each of us already a part of a loving "we" with God? Are our inner thoughts and feelings really hidden from God, or might they all be completely known to God? Might some of our loves be also a generous share in God's own inner self that loves?

To live a life fully open to the affective movement is a high achievement, but it does seem quite common. Everyone has some experience of love's invitation. Those who completely reject it fall back into a dim isolation, while those who accept it enter the realm where things and people and destinies come together. They welcome mutual concern as more than an idea, more than an intellectual view of reality, more than an obligation. They welcome other persons and the new selves-in-relation they have become as holding the richest possibilities of becoming the selves they feel called to be. They recognize in one another the transcendent exigence that loves beauty, order, truth, goodness, and engagement without restriction. Some commit themselves wholeheartedly to philanthropy and some wholeheartedly to religion. Yet even though everyone experiences the affective movement, and many praise it, it is quite another matter to understand *how* this movement affects

morality and what implications this understanding has for ethics. It
requires plowing through reflections such as these.

Affective Conversion

It seems plausible to say that as people deepen their friendships and
expand the field of those for whom they care, they learn to trust
love itself. They would trust the inner affective movement that they
neither caused themselves nor received from their friends. Yet it is
doubtful that they open themselves to love because they first decide
to trust love. It seems more in line with ordinary experience to say
they first feel drawn into relationships and, once engaged, discover
a richer, more joyful self. Looking back, they would identify the
experience of being drawn as already love. Similarly, a commitment
to religious love cannot be justified beforehand by any appeal to
personal experience of being a richer, more joyful self. Like human
love, religious engagement too is experimental; believers discover
the taste of a uniquely rich joy only after yielding to the movements
of love for a personal, divine, beyond. Any such yielding to love is a
surrender to an unknown. It is not by reading books like this that
one knows the worth of love and of committing oneself to love.
Without waiting for a look, you leap.

I appeal to your experience of love to recognize that a conversion
is necessary. A conversion is a total opening in one's horizon
through some form of commitment. Recall that I use *horizon* to refer
to everything a person cares about. A fully open intellectual horizon
requires an *intellectual discovery* of the unrestricted range of our
questioning. A fully open moral horizon requires a *moral choice* of the
unrestricted range of what may be truly better. Similarly, a fully
open affective horizon requires an *affective commitment.* What, then, is
an affective conversion? *An affective conversion is a wholehearted
commitment to the unrestricted range of love.*

Like other definitions in the realm of method, this one invites you
to verify the terms. A "wholehearted commitment" is a personal
choice to direct your affections where love points. The "unrestricted range" of love goes beyond arbitrary limits of love—limited,
say, to possessions, to health, to success, to friends, to a group, or to
the created world. Such a conversion obeys the impulses of the
affective movement to share life without restrictions. It is letting
the love in us love all the way. It cherishes the "we" that one

becomes with others. While intellectually prudent about dangerous liaisons, it puts no apriori exclusions on who might belong to one's potential fellows. It brings one to the brink of welcoming the "we" that one may always have been with the divine. By itself, an affective conversion opens one at least to the question of God, while those who engage God enter a horizon by a conversion more properly called religious.

Expanding Horizons of Love

Consider this: When we trust love, our horizon expands from mutual love to transcendent love, but saying our love expands does not necessarily mean that we notice the expansion. Still less does it mean we use religious terms for it. Love can—and often does—expand at the lower registers of consciousness. The heart feels this affective development, but the mind does not notice, at least not to the point of asking questions about what is happening within.

This obliviousness about inner experience is evident in the typical philosophical discussions about whether God exists—usually concerned strictly with a question of fact: Is there a God or not? But the question whether God exists is asked by people who, presumably, are also concerned that their own lives are rising to the level to which they *should* rise. To admit that one's existence falls short is to admit an openness to a self-transcendence that is not yet fulfilled. Moreover, this openness may have no intrinsic limits. In practical terms, when anyone raises the question of whether God exists, an appropriate response might be, "Do you put any limits on your openness to what is beautiful, meaningful, true, good, and shared in love?" This is not a trap of logic. It is planting a moral question that likely resonates with a person's deepest desire. It remains an existential question: Shall I let love carry me beyond the person I happen to be?

Obliviousness also shows among people who, while living in a faithful obedience to the promptings of love, focus more on the outer objects of their love than on the inner experience of being in love. While they certainly experience poignant feelings of attraction and devotion, their attention is fixed on the persons to whom they are attracted and devoted. But the day may come when they consider what is happening to their hearts. As they wonder about this love that seems to have no limits, their intellectual horizon opens onto the intricate world of inner experience—a world familiar to mystics, psychologists, and even some philosophers.

One way of tracking how transcendent love expands is to tease out three distinct, but overlapping horizons of people in love. A *basic* horizon opens up when, existentially, they notice what love is doing to their hearts. A *notionally transcendent* horizon opens up when they understand their being in love in the language and concepts drawn from their respective cultures. An *actually transcendent* horizon opens up when they deliberately and conscientiously count on this love to shape their everyday decisions. I want to detail these three expansions further because it will help anticipate what sort of affective horizons ethicists might bring to a dialog and how, in particular, religious commitments affect formulations of ethical principles.

Basic Expansion

When an Eloise says to an Abelard, "You are so good," she is not talking about some property of his person. She is not classifying him among people called "good." Rather, she recognizes in him an active and continual striving for the better. If, as Aristotle proposed, the best friendships are based on a mutual fostering of character, what makes Abelard loveable to Eloise is his obedience to the normative drives to learning, to doing better, and to being in love. And Abelard is drawn to the same in Eloise. The transcending exigence in both draws them closer to each other as they converge on the beautiful, the intelligible, the true, the better, and to sharing life in the mystery of love.

This *experience* of mutual love is familiar. I doubt that any person or group whose authenticity is deepening lacks it. Still, to deliberately wonder "What is happening to me?" is a distinct achievement. And only some of those who pose the question will consider that they are being drawn by a force not in their possession toward a place not of their choosing. Eloise reaches a basic clarification about love when she recognizes this force as an objective event— not in the sense of "outside of me" but in the sense of "actual, real." She recognizes love itself as a transcending force. Then she meditates as much on the inner movements of love in her heart as on the attunement of her five senses to the sights and sounds, the memories and images, of her beloved Abelard. Then a revelation breaks through: "The desire I feel within is not just *for* Abelard, and *with* Abelard, but also *beyond* Abelard and me together." She recognizes that love is by nature a reality that invites a person not only to share life with another but also completely opens the field into which loving persons are drawn.

Notionally Transcendent Expansion

Another expansion of transcendent love comes through the clarification provided by the inherited concepts and language for the inner experiences and the outer goals of that love. A girl growing up *within* a religious tradition may be taught terms such as God, Allah, or Yahweh; Heaven or Nirvana; jihad or Holy War; Brahman or Tao, sin and repentance; grace and wisdom; covenant, redemption, sacrament, pilgrimage, blessing, salvation, faith, charity, and so on. The meaning of these terms will deepen as she reads her scriptures and listens to her catechists. Her conscience will be shaped by the inherited values of her religious tradition. She will be encouraged to love the divine with all her heart. For a boy growing up *outside* of a religious tradition, the expansion of this clarifying process may occur through literature. It may begin when he feels touched by Shakespeare's *King Lear* or Cervantes' *Don Quixote*. Or he may find existential expressions of the same transcendent love he feels in Tolstoy's *Confessions*. He feels not only a deep spiritual kinship with other searchers but relies on their language to express his own transcendent love. A married couple with little interest in religion or literature may have discovered in Plato or Kierkegaard the words and technical structures that help them talk about the many transcendent dimensions of the love they each feel.

Actually Transcendent Expansion

An actually transcendent expansion occurs when one moves beyond understanding the meaning of terms to a personal, deliberate, and loving engagement with the movement of love. Commonly this expansion is fully actualized when one welcomes the love as from a transcendent lover and in the terms provided by a religion. Still, it is not joining a religion that fully expands one's horizon but the commitment to letting the movement of love fully expand. Their being *in* love is being *in* something more than themselves—something like being *in* a marriage, but in something that possesses them, engages them, brings them to a mysterious destiny, one infinitely beyond what they can ask or imagine. They discount the intensity of loving affection in favor of a real assent to the reality of love, and of a real consent to being totally engaged by it. Being in love gives them a new eye for transcendent values that the affectively converted have always seen—now in the wisdom of sages, now in the word of prophets, now in the message of scriptures, now in the deeds, the words, and the life of historical persons. Their love is marked more by gratitude than by striving. They aim to speak *from* and *with* love even when not speaking *about* love.

The founders of great religions made this real consent, and they invited their disciples to do the same. From then on, both the fertilizing and the pruning of the blossoming movement were left to those who, it was hoped, would recapitulate in themselves this engendering consent to such a union with God. Religious rituals were designed to reenact the original journeys, meals, exercises, and sacrifices of the founders, so that later generations might more readily actualize their transcendent love through these symbols.

People's horizons become actually transcendent outside of religion when anyone lets love take over completely. Some may never have heard an authentic word of religion; others may have heard nothing but unauthentic words from religion. But being in this love gives them a hope in ultimate meanings and in a certain immortality of anything good they will ever do and of anything good that they are. It gives them a love of neighbor that is nonexclusive and an eye for transcendent values in everyday life that are beyond reason.

Overlapping Affective Horizons

These three expansions are not distinct "steps" as one's affective horizon opens. Commonly, these expansions occur the way musical themes develop. Sometimes the brass leads, sometimes the winds, and sometimes the strings, but an advance in one slows until the others catch up to fill out the movement. In any case, to deal with ethical questions, it is essential to recognize that a person may have made this commitment to being in love without necessarily putting it into words, religious or otherwise. When it comes to discussing moral issues, the question is not how far ethicists should allow religious doctrines and language to shape their moral principles. The question is how fully they allow their transcendent love raise relevant questions and how clearly they express their thoughts and desires as motivated by this love.

Healing the Ethicist

It should be apparent by now that the implications of an affective conversion for ethics are first the implications for ethicists themselves. As we saw in chapter 6, an open affectivity heals a creativity wounded by biases in our intelligence. Where this healing occurs in ethicists, it not only widens the scope of their personal concerns; it also expands the range of questions they can ask about the public moral issues they are committed to resolving.

For neurosis, we may imagine that the ethicists' experience of love dissolving their obsessions gives them a first-hand familiarity with the tricks of repression. It would alert them to the possibility that people's public condemnations of certain behaviors are fueled by repressed fears about quite private matters. So they tread delicately, probing for that narrow gate where one can disagree with people's moral opinions without enflaming their fears. Indeed, sometimes ethicists need to probe their own over-the-top emotional responses to publicly debated issues.

For egotism, an affective commitment to the full range of love certainly opens their horizons beyond self-absorbed concerns. But it also would give them a higher viewpoint on that most revered principle in ethics—the autonomy of the individual. True, the appeal to the autonomous individual conscience is necessary to drive a stake in the ground against outside pressures to conform without argument. Still, it can hardly stand alone against all moral problems. Even ethicists who, like Luther, say, "Here I stand; I can do no other," will likely add, "...but I do not stand alone." Their values are hugely inherited from ancestors and widely shared with companions.

Probably the most stubborn obstacle to an expanding affective horizon is loyalism, mainly because loyalism thrives on affective bonding. Where egotists look for personal payoffs in the future, loyalists look to shared stories of the past—particularly stories of group accomplishment. It is said that Margaret Mitchell, author of *Gone with the Wind* and the compelling stories of Confederate gumption in the Civil War she heard from her uncles, was in her teens before she learned that the Confederacy lost. Among ethicists, this kind of group pride may show in a group fixation about a single moral issue or in a hero-worship of ethical theorists such as Kant or Rawls. Ethicists whose affectivity is not hemmed in by group pride hear the same deep concern in foreigners. They probe for common ground in the shared moral question rather than in the comforts of belonging to the club.

An open affective horizon also has an indirect but important effect on commonsensism. Ethicists may rely on the social sciences and historical studies to understand moral problems, but those who are affectively closed pit answers against answers, doctrine against doctrine, philosophy against philosophy, authority against authority, while those who are affectively open speak heart to heart, listening for the underlying question behind the sometimes dogmatic opinion. They avoid debates between the bullheaded; they prefer the dialog with the open-minded. They include their own horizons as possibly part of the "moral problem" they discuss, asking themselves questions like: "What's going on among us from a social and political perspective? What moral anthropology have I assumed without question? What economic interests are driving my decisions? What historical events have shaped our present moral questions?"

Finally, the affective movement has the power to heal one's personal habits of acting against one's better judgment—willfulness and sin. This healing may be characterized by a single word: forgiveness. Certainly an ethicist can regret personal willful decisions privately, but when someone else forgives him or her, the "we" of whom the ethicist is a part is made stronger, and any future individual willfulness becomes also a sin against an "us."

Unfortunately today, ethicists of all stripes—philosophical and theological, professional and lay—exclude questions that ordinarily are prompted by their experience of the affective movement. Why so many ignore questions about love is difficult to say. In some cases, it is because they have not heard anyone seriously ask how far love can go. In other cases, they heard the question quite clearly, but their egos, frightened at the prospect of losing autonomy, suppress it. In either case, they have grown accustomed to being drawn by a blinkered horse.

8. METHOD

THE ETHICIST

We launched our exploration by observing that ethics needs a method that is commonly accepted and whose effectiveness can be verified. Then we proposed that we can discover this method if we clarify what actually happens in people who actually improve situations. After identifying norms inherent to consciousness itself, we identified three conversions that define an individual's fully open horizons on learning, choosing, and loving. Our next question is how the inner norms and openness of the ethicist might clarify how ethicists can work together effectively. As we will see, the essential requirement is that they engage one another on the level of these conversions. Specifically, their collaboration will rely on a "mutual sharing of horizons."

In this chapter, then, we will first describe the changes in ethicists that the next revolution in ethics would bring about. Then we will detail how a mutual exposure of horizons prompts these changes in them. Finally, we will identify the specific tasks of ethics that flow from this mutual exposure of horizons.

Merging Horizons

What effects will the next revolution in ethics produce in ethicists themselves?[39] Recall from chapter 1 that this *revolution* is the appearance in humans of certain general dynamics of *evolution* by which higher systems emerge and integrate lower systems. This appears in the ethicist as the emergence of higher functions of mind and heart, which, far from abolishing any currently successful functions in ethics, order them within a higher system of questions and answers. In the ethicist, then, the emerging functions may be conceived as a stacked set of systems:

The highest system is affectivity. We experience the affective exigence as an abiding movement toward complete openness to sharing life. There are the familiar dimensions of collaboration, friendship and loyalty as well as its more mysterious dimensions of engaging the divine. An *affective conversion* is the opening of affective consciousness to an unlimited field of love.

An open affective horizon reveals values to our moral horizon—our second-highest system, as it were. Our value judgments may be guided by personal inspirations, by deductions from moral principles, by the dictates of authorities, and by social conventions. Where moral horizons are narrowed by bias, affectively converted ethicists aim to widen them to encompass what is objectively better, without regard for personal satisfactions. Moreover, people with affectively open horizons see value in welcoming the stranger, forgiving a wrong, enduring hardship, living in faith, and overcoming in themselves any tendency to act against their better judgment. We named opening of consciousness to the unlimited field of "better" as a *moral conversion.*

An open moral horizon in turn, reveals the value of learning, including the ongoing effort to spot the narrow-mindedness of psychological obsession, egotism, loyalism, and commonsensism. It promotes an *intellectual conversion* that opens consciousness to whatever may be true, including the truth about how we learn anything. It sees the value of in-depth analyses of complex moral situations and of understanding the historical developments that led to them. Expecting to find willfulness or sinfulness everywhere, it looks to therapies of forgiveness rather than the futile attempts to analyze what is essentially irrational.

So while our discussion so far moved upward—first on learning, then choosing, then loving—our *experience* of expanding horizons moves downward as expanding affective horizons expand moral horizons, and as expanding moral horizons expand intellectual horizons.

Knowledge of Morality

Ethicists whose horizons have expanded through these conversions come to know certain key features about morality. We discussed many of them, but here are the main points:

- Ethics may be profitably conceived as the theoretical reflection on morality, and morality as the field of everyday decisions.
- The ultimate base of all moral judgments lies in normative drives in consciousness. There, our fundamental

"shoulds" are the experienced impulses to be attentive, intelligent, reasonable, responsible, and in love.

- The ultimate scope of ethics is as wide as the scope of all moral judgments—ranging from a negative ethics of avoiding evil to the immensely larger field of a positive ethics of doing better. We formulated the difference as an "Ethics of Better" that incorporates an "Ethics of Law."

- Morality is an ongoing, historical process—the actual unfolding of improved situations driven by women and men who choose the truly better. The moral stands we take are not ahistorical absolutes but rather contributions toward improving the specific historical situation in which we happen to find ourselves.

- Moral judgments are conditioned *cognitively* because our understanding of moral situations is usually provisional.

- Moral judgments are conditioned *morally* because of several factors. (1) Moral ideals are mostly inheritances from the morally imperfect culture we happen to be born into. (2) Our conscience matures through several stages. (3) Our moral orientation toward the truly better as opposed to the merely satisfying may be minimal, partial, or full. (4) We listen to the wisdom of others, but often without considering who is really wise.

- All moral judgments are subject to critique. General moral judgments may be expressed in moral standards and policies as well as through narratives of noble behaviors. But all such general judgments have birthdays, parented by people vulnerable to bias and capable of irrational choices.

- Despite these impediments to making truly objective moral judgments, we can make objective judgments about what is truly better. The judgment that X is truly better is more appropriately called a conviction than a certitude. Our convictions deepen regarding the value of certain persons, proposals or actions insofar as we reach answers to the relevant questions.

- Some moral judgments are objectively unrevisable: The moral judgment that being attentive, intelligent, reasonable, responsible and loving is better than their opposites is absolutely unrevisable. General moral judgments about the value of human life are unrevisable. Specific formulations of moral standards about birth, friendship, war, freedom, death, etc. are increasingly unrevisable as historical experience provides increasingly comprehensive answers to relevant questions.
- Being in love liberates our morality. It occurs palpably in friendship and loyalty; it includes all efforts to improve the lives of others; and it occurs in a less palpable but unlimited manner in welcoming love itself as the highest human value.
- The question of God cannot be excluded from ethics. The transcending exigence, which presses us to seek beauty, order, truth, goodness, and interpersonal engagement, is entirely unrestricted. The transcending exigence is a form of love, which prompts the question, "Whither and whence and why this love?" Answers will vary but the question is the same.

Symbols of the Moral Universe

These achievements in knowledge about moral process do not occur merely by reading. Most occur in people who take seriously their everyday experience of the movement toward total openness. This is because, prior to their learning about morality, they experience this openness as *being moved*. Recalling our definition of a symbol as an image linked to feelings, we may say that this movement of openness is carried by symbols that represent not only the objects we seek to learn about or improve or love; it also represents our own selves in the often painful movements of learning, improving, and loving.

Across cultures, symbols of the moral universe vary widely. But while different cultures have different images of the moral cosmos, the affective component is transcultural. This component is a movement, an emotion, an inclination, a drive toward a transcendent beyond. Everyone is familiar with the *experience* of this movement toward the transcendent. Still, there are plenty of people, ethicists included, who dismiss the possibility that a transcendent reality may be doing the moving. This includes atheists, of course, but it also includes many people who are committed to religion. They may be totally dedicated to doing better and searching for a hidden God, but might also imagine the transcendent movement strictly as their personal search for God, and not also as God's gift of their searching heart. Their symbolization of "everything" excludes the experience of the search, despite the obvious fact that searching is not an exploration they chose but rather a gravitational pull on their desires. Typically, they expect that God must enter human life in no other way than to provide answers to their autonomously-generated questions about life's meaning, and to issue orders on how they ought to behave. This one-way symbol of transcendence is what shapes the Pelagian exclusion of God's initiative. It also shapes the dogmatist insistence on religious truths to the exclusion of the historical memory of the search from which these truths first emerged.

The problem with these one-way symbols of transcendence is that they focus on *images* of the divine without noticing the associated *affects* that make up these symbols. All our images of the divine are ambiguous, of course. They generate different concepts and names for transcendent reality, and these variations are often the source of disagreements and antagonisms among believers. But the persistent experience of always wanting the better is not the result of a deliberate choice. To ignore its givenness is to arbitrarily exclude key inner data and smother the natural question about their burning desire, "Who lit this fire and why?" So the more attention we pay to the experience of the search, the more likely we will understand the moral standards of others. To put it succinctly, while differences among *images* of transcendent reality typically start the arguments, our common *affects* have the power to settle them.

THE FUNDAMENTAL METHOD

We assumed that the fundamental "method" of ethics is whatever may be the methods of our minds and hearts by which we actually do better. It includes what ethicists know and the symbols that simultaneously carry their moral imagination and move them affectively. The strategic component of this "method" will be a mutual exposure of these intellectual and symbolic horizons[40] that brings to light the sources of authenticity and unauthenticity that lie at the root of all progress and decline.

What Method Is

This "method" of a mutual exposure of horizons is hardly automatic. Its effectiveness depends totally on the normative drives of consciousness urging each person to pay attention, to understand, to make reasonable judgments, to make responsible commitments, and to live in love without arbitrary restrictions. When we carry out these inner demands, we obey the exigences that define our nature. We discover that the authentic self we hope to become is an open self, a self-transcending self. Moreover, the affective exigence to share life with others naturally triggers the realization that everyone else seeks this satisfaction of spirit that comes with being self-transcendent. This is why a more open horizon in one person will likely be attractive to the person with a less open horizon. When engaging those whose horizon is open, the resentful feel invited to an affective conversion, the self-absorbed feel invited to a moral conversion, and the confused feel invited to an intellectual conversion.

Obviously, this is a special sense of "method."[41] Its ordinary meaning is a procedure devised to produce specific kinds of improvement. In some cases, like baking, we clearly know the outcome: if we follow the recipe, we get the cake. In other cases, we do not know the outcome, but the method includes course correction procedures like "problem solving" and "conflict resolution" and "brainstorming." Most procedures taught in ethics courses are instances of this second kind of method. We start from certain general moral principles, but as we apply them to specific cases, we adjust our sights according to principles like "proportionality" or "double effect."

While these procedural methods have proven their value, it is important to understand that they are *devised* procedures. That is, we used our wits to formulate the principles and the rules for proceeding and adjudicating. But the fundamental meaning of "method" is the method of our wits themselves—the ways we learn, make choices, and share life in love. We do not *devise* these methods;

we *discover* them. What ultimately counts, of course, is to verify in ourselves what is likely going on in anyone with whom we seek to do better. What we learn about our own inner norms of consciousness not only helps us speak our mind more convincingly; it also helps us understand the opinions of others more thoroughly, and probe for clarifications more effectively. Most importantly, as we probe together for clarifications and agreements, we verify for ourselves that the same norms lie behind the views of everyone else. As we engage in frank exchanges on *why* we say X is better than Y, we either revise our views on what occurs in everyone or we verify that the same inner norms underlie their views, just like our own.

Method on the Move

In one sense, this mutual exposure of horizons is nothing new. Ever since the question of "should" appeared on our planet, there have been fruitful discussions of moral options. If our exercises to notice the norms of authenticity are on target, then it was authenticity that made these discussions fruitful. They were dialogs among people whose horizons were basically open and openly shared. Yet the mutual understandings that occurred were usually expressed in *descriptive* terms: "I see where you're coming from" or "I completely resonate with your struggle." What is needed to ensure the effectiveness of ethics as a theoretical discipline are accounts of these horizons in *explanatory* terms—the categories and models that express the basic events in learning, choosing, and sharing life.

Only recently have philosophers proposed to *explain* what inhibits—and what promotes—the fruitfulness of a moral discussion. Earlier we noted how Kant, Darwin, Engles, Nietzsche and Freud undermined the Enlightenment's glowing optimism by *explanations* of the dark ways of our supposedly enlightened minds. On the positive side, there are developments in scholarship and anthropology that recognize how documents from a culture are to be taken *not* as true, but only as evidence. To transform a document into knowledge, it takes a mind curious about what historical developments really occurred—developments usually proposed in terms that are qualified and open to revision. In psychology, Victor Frankl, Abraham Maslow, Irvin Yalom, and others have widened psychology's horizon beyond mental illness to deal with existential pursuits of meaning in life. In philosophy, Robert Doran, Frederick

Lawrence, Bernard Lonergan, Eric Voegelin, and others, by illumi-
nating how the human spirit raises questions and seeks ever better
answers, provided models for assessing the horizons of practitioners of the human studies—historians, exegetes, philosophers, theologians, psychologists, sociologists, economists, cultural anthropologists, and political scientists. In none of these developments have
theorists *devised* a new method for studying humans. Rather, by way
of a Second Enlightenment,[42] they proposed systematic explanations of the innate methods we humans use to understand the past,
our inner selves, our social interactions, and our destinies.

Unfortunately, at least in these early years of the 21st century,
philosophical explorations of the fundamental methods of mind and
heart have made little headway in human studies. One reason is
that experts typically resist new paradigms which Thomas Kuhn, in
his *Structure of Scientific Revolutions* (1962) explained as based more on
social taboos against breaking ranks than on professional critical
investigations. Another reason for this lag is the lack of awareness
among these professionals of the current shift in philosophy from
concepts and language to method. And even those who are aware of
methodological issues probably look long before leaping. After all,
fundamental method pivots on conversion, and under conversion,
everything changes. One's personal memories and hopes, one's
relationships to friends and coworkers, one's notions about
morality and ethics, and even one's God are revealed in a new light
that can be simultaneously stunning and frightening.

Most ethicists today work out of methodological models based
loosely on the views of influential moral philosophers. Their models
may be internally consistent but inconsistent with each others'. A
duty-based ethics will say X is better while a virtue-based ethics
will say Y is better, and a utilitarian ethics will say Z is better. To
the degree that any model relies on loose descriptions and analo-
gies, it lacks the explanatory terms and relations rooted in the
personal discovery and articulation of what happens when anyone
learns, does better, and loves. While many people easily recognize
when things go well or badly, few possess clear diagnostic criteria
for explaining *why*. So they promote policies that may indeed be for
the better, but they cannot give convincing explanations to anyone

else. Nor can they propose any intelligible therapy that can heal moral problems at their real roots in people's horizons.

A mutual exposure of horizons requires a new standard of method. It asks all ethicists to deal explicitly with the ultimate sources of their own moral views. It asks them to lay their ethical models on the table for the scrutiny of others. The payoff is triple. It refines ethical theories, purging them of the ambiguities of mere descriptive associations. It expands the scope of ethical theories by the requirement that they provide a comprehensive explanation of all the factors that *constitute* better living, all that *impede* better living, and all that *heal* the impediments. And it functions as an ongoing test to validate just what these three kinds of factors really are.

If a mutual exposure of horizons is essential, we must not forget how discussions on this level are no picnic. Sharing of horizons includes the familiar discussions of moral actions and ethical concepts, but it also includes taking the time to get to know one another. It means listening to one another's personal stories and the stories that embody the ideals and memories of their communities. After all, this is the major way we learn about anyone's affective horizon. It also means exploring the reasons behind the moral views of others, not so much to immediately challenge these views as to first sound the depths of what meaning of "better" others have chosen—along a hierarchy ranging from the merely self-absorbed, to the objectively worthwhile. And it means the deeply engaging work of helping one another clearly connect any unique philosophical category or ethical model to the common movements of self-transcending consciousness. Such discussions will occur not only in an evening's roundtable conversation but also in semester-long symposia and along the multi-year sequence of books and articles that build upon or criticize earlier views.

THE TASKS OF ETHICISTS

It is time to get specific. How do we get from mutual exposure of horizons to actually doing better? Here is a sketch of the links:

- A mutual exposure of horizons among ethicists brings to light their respective degrees of intellectual, moral and affective openness.
- The exigences of authenticity prompt ethicists to recognize in one another where a fuller openness is desirable.
- An analysis of the normative demands of authenticity and of the several ways our moral creativity is wounded reveals specific questions, in explanatory terms, that may be asked about any moral situation.
- These questions form an ordered set, or "model," of moral process that can be verified or improved by anyone.
- Doing better is the cumulative result of pursuing answers to these questions.

In other words, those scientists, scholars, philosophers, theologians and practitioners who make up the community of ethicists face a challenge to ground their methods in personal analyses of the norms of consciousness. In this challenge, an essential task is to develop commonly-accepted *models* for formulating moral guidelines.

Three Kinds of Models

Now there are many kinds of models. Those that mainly rely on descriptions (and there are many) do not help much for asking questions that seek explanations, so we will pass them by. Among the models that rely on explanatory terms, three in particular seem essential:

1. *The Historicity of Morality*

The first model is about the historical nature of morality itself. The evidence is everywhere that the human exigence to do better is always active. Where classical moral philosophers discussed the "good," they aimed to establish eternal, fixed principles and firm assertions about "right" and "wrong." Similarly, moral theologians rooted their moral views in revered scriptures; they proposed ideals in the form of canonical narratives and saintly exemplars. But since the emergence of empirical science and, in particular, the theoretical framework of evolution, no one can ignore the fact that the good is reached concretely by ever aiming to do better. To put it concisely, the good is a concrete history.[43] What a model of morality's historicity would provide is an account of how moral standards and behaviors emerge and change over time, how different cultures end up embracing different values, and how objective history is rooted in normative, subjective events.

2. The Foundational Elements of Morality

A second model lays out the foundational categories and structures of morality. Such a model would function like Mendeleev's periodic table in chemistry. It should aim to be comprehensive, with all elements related to all others, and with no additional elements appearing at the same level of explanation. Suppose, for example, that "authenticity" is identified as a basic element in the model. Then ethicists could no more formulate theories of ethics without reference to authenticity than a chemist could formulate a new theory without reference to atomic weights. By explicitly connecting all any structural elements of morality to the norms of consciousness, such a model provides an integrated set of questions about ethics and morality—an "integral heuristic structure."[44] Since these norms are presumably experienced by all, such a model can help ethicists to uncover latent contradictions among principles before they are put into practice and the damage is done.

3. A Framework for Collaboration

A third type of model governs collaboration. Certainly a model for collaboration should cover all the traditional functions that fall under "ethics": gathering and interpreting data, tracking history, formulating moral principles, implementing plans for action, and gathering feedback on outcomes. What is new in the next revolution is to incorporate these tasks under an umbrella that includes the collaboration involved in a mutual exposure of horizons about learning, choosing, and loving, and a commitment to the foundational elements of morality.

Validity and Effectiveness of the Models

We will expand on each of these three models in the next chapter. As you read, keep in mind that their validity is open to question, depending on how well they align with what we discover about the actual normative functions of consciousness. Like scientific theories, the needed models will last only as long as they provide us the best available explanation of moral experience. To the degree that we become more familiar with these models, we can expect our language to change. Key terms would be more clearly defined as part of a comprehensive model of self-transcending persons and communities. The change in language, of course, must express verifiable insights into what occurs when anyone learns, chooses, and loves.

The mutual disclosure of horizons leads to doing better by increasing the likelihood that women and men in human studies will converge on an ethics approaching the same degree of agreement among themselves that we find among practitioners in the natural sciences. They will agree on the fundamental normative drives because these are verifiable. They will further agree on the fundamental dialectical process whereby moral issues can be assessed, not exclusively by their outcomes but also by the horizons, worldviews, and priorities of those who make the choices that change their situations. Where the validity of categories in the natural sciences stands on independent but public experiments, the validity of these categories stands on public dialogs where the mutual exposure of horizons occurs. While this process does not guarantee agreement on what the better may be in specific situations, it does provide the explicit criteria and a commonly-accepted process for distinguishing better and worse. In this process, we would have our commonly recognized and effective method in ethics.

9. MODELS

THE HISTORICITY OF MORALITY

We have been speaking of "good" not as some static feature of things but rather as a moving enterprise of people doing better. An ethics that provides guidance to this enterprise will employ a model of morality that reveals its deeply historical features.[45]

Ongoing

One obvious feature is that morality is an ongoing process of assessing the past and planning the future. At any moment in time, everything we consider good or bad has historical antecedents and future possibilities. And when we consider whether anything is good or bad, our interest goes beyond forming an opinion; eventually we want to make a choice. Sometimes we choose to change situations, and sometimes we choose to keep them as they are. But both are choices that change our moral reality. Our concerns about *good* and *bad* are always expressions of larger concerns about *better* and *worse*.

Constituted by Nature and History

A less obvious, but more important feature is that moral situations are defined partly by nature and partly by history. For among the "things" whose value we assess, there is a fundamental difference between the material products of nature and the immaterial products of history. Material products include wood, oil, food, and clothes. These things are constituted by atoms, molecules and cells. The related moral issues are chiefly about the appropriateness of a choice by the chooser.

In contrast, products of history include economies, laws, and agreements. These things are constituted by acts of meaning—the ideas and commitments of the people involved. When these people gain insight or change their priorities, the significance of economies, laws, and agreements changes as well. This is why the related moral issues include not only the appropriateness of a choice by the chooser, but also the appropriateness of thing chosen. For example, economies are implementations of people's ideas, and where these ideas are biased to favor the wealthy, these economies are inappropriate objects of choice. Similarly, laws are expressions of ideas, and where these ideas are biased to benefit politicians, these laws are inappropriate objects of choice. Again, agreements depend on ideas about what the parties give and receive, but where the parties silently withhold full commitment, the agreements are less comprehensive than they appear. So a historical dimension of any moral situation is that these objects of human choice are themselves constituted by ideas and commitments, which may be more or less biased.

Since actual situations are a mix of both nature and history, they have two interlocking dimensions—actions and meanings. In technology, for example, what high-tech devices *do* is save labor, speed up travel, give wider access to information, enable new forms of recreation, and provide greater material security. But the *meaning* of technology depends on the historical motives of the people who use it. Likewise for sex: Some norms may follow from a nature-based analysis of its general reproductive function and other norms from a psychological analysis of its specific affective function. What sex *does* can be seen by analyzing its physical nature, while what sex *means* depends on the affective histories of the partners. What "good sex" means depends on what they mean by good. Likewise for death: What happens to the dying person depends on his or her physical make-up; but what it means—tragedy, or rest, or triumph—depends on the life history of the dying person. So moral standards regarding any human reality must take into account both what its nature is for every person and what its historical meaning is for specific persons.

Concrete

A historical-minded model of morality will also be based on the insight that the "good" is not a property. Properties are abstractions by which we classify objects, actions, and events: My car is blue; her hike was slow; his wedding was noisy. These statements are answers to questions about what *sort of* thing this is. But when we say: My car is great; her hike was healthful; his wedding was a mistake, we are not speaking about abstract features. We are speaking of the concrete worth to particular persons of this particular car or hike or wedding. These statements are answers to questions we raise not to know what *sorts* of things they are but rather to know their specific *value* to persons in light of any action they might take. The "good," in other words, is not an abstract feature or quality revealed by our exigence to understand. Rather, it is the concrete value that engages our exigence to be responsible in light of the direction of our lives.

Provisional

Another feature of this historical-minded model is to expect that practically all our moral judgments will be provisional. With most moral issues, as we saw, we cannot expect the kind of certitude that comes with asking simple factual questions. If we ask *whether* it is raining, we can walk outside and remove all uncertainty. But if we ask *why* it is raining, we must deal with explanations about atmospheric pressure, wind speed, humidity, and the like. Because explanations can differ, we settle for the best available.

Similarly, if we are certain that it is raining, we may ask whether we *should* we cancel a picnic. We would take into account the preferences and priorities of all the people involved and then settle on what seems better. Yet even then, we often change our minds about what is better because the situation changes. These changes may be external, as when the forecast changes or we learn more about people's preferences and the availability of shelters in picnic areas. Or the changes may be internal, as when the same people, with no change in their resources, shift their priorities and raise new concerns. In other words, changes in the moral horizons of participants can change situations, and often in fundamental ways.

Principled

Again, recall that some moral judgments cannot be revised, particularly the judgment that being authentic is better than being inauthentic. And between those moral judgments that are highly provisional and those that are completely unrevisable, there are judgments that become unrevisable in practice. These are the familiar moral "principles" that have proven their worth in the crucible of history. They may be general: Thou shalt not steal. Treat others as you would like to be treated. Tell the truth. Pay utmost respect to persons. Or they may be discipline-specific: Obtain informed consent (medicine). Solve problems at lowest feasible level of authority (subsidiarity in social systems). Advertise truthfully (business). Deliver on your promises (politics).

These principles are not absolute in the sense of being the absolutely primary starting point of any ethics; this honor belongs to us as persons suffering the exigences of authenticity. Rather, in the manner that case law complements civil statutes, the meaning of any such moral principle becomes more secure over time as it successfully meets newly emerging moral questions.

To grasp the actual meaning of such principles, it is not enough to connect them to certain duties or rights based on an analysis of human nature, enlightening though these connections may be. We also need to seek enlightenment about the historical circumstances and moral questions from which the formulations of these principles arose. At the same time, as new forms of war, science, medicine, economics, politics, communications, and business appear on the human scene, the meaning of these principles *widens* to the degree that they provide answers to newly emerging questions. Their meaning will also *deepen* as their prescriptions become unquestioned assumptions about the good life: Don't lie, cheat or steal. Be kind and compassionate. Understand problems before proposing solutions. Protect life. Precepts like these become practically synonymous with the transcendental and unrevisable precept to be responsible. Or their meaning will become *historically fixed* to a place and time in the past when they no longer provide guidance to newly emerging changes in science, technology, economics, marketing, law, political orders, the arts, and education.

Correlative to Cultures

Yet because some moral principles take on deeper meanings in specific cultures, both their formulations and their historical manifestations can vary significantly, culture to culture. So there is a tension between universal, core norms of consciousness and actual standards of moral behaviors lived out in local cultures. Across the globe, we see great differences in political economies; in the degrees of respect different cultures pay to elders, police, and teachers; in the levels of honesty expected regarding library books and taxes; in what being a good neighbor means; and in attitudes toward capital punishment and amnesty for illegal immigrants.

These practices all have histories. Any claim that one is better than another must take these histories into account.

Correlative to Horizons

Besides being ongoing, constituted by nature and history, concrete, provisional, principled, and correlative to cultures, whatever may be "good" or "better" is also apprehended within a person's mentality. That is, objective moral worth is always a correlative of someone's subjective range of relevant questions, including the worldviews and priorities which he or she inherits as historical sediment. Any justifications of a moral position, whether based on philosophical reflection or religious commitment, occur in people whose horizons may be more or less open. So a historical-minded model of morality will keep in a single view both the value of the objects chosen and the horizons of the people doing the choosing.

FOUNDATIONAL ELEMENTS OF MORALITY

Besides needing a model of the historicity of morality, we also need a model of the "elements" of morality—its foundational categories and structures. These elements, in turn, must be related to the normative criteria in consciousness, so that the model forms an intellectual bridge between our inner, experienced normative drives and our outer, formulated standards, principles, and policies.

The payoff is essentially strategic. A model of foundational elements would give us a set of questions to pose about any moral situation. Some ask about the connections between individual needs, the social order, and cultural norms of the times. Others ask how morality develops—and fails to develop— both in the individual and in cultures. Still others ask about one's own intellectual, moral, and affective horizons, as well as those of fellow ethicists. Taken together, this model aims to be comprehensive. Keep in mind that a model is neither "true" nor a pre-packaged explanation of everything. This model is question-generating: it orders the questions while keeping the door open to further questions that arise from new developments. To promote agreement among ethicists, it links these questions to verifiable events in consciousness. Still, by way of warning about the terrain ahead, to understand the model requires some effort, but by way of encouragement about panorama to be reached, it will be worth the climb.

Moral Situation

We already identified many of these foundational elements, so now we need to show how they relate to one another. First, then, consider the deceptively simple notion of a "moral situation." Here is a definition that can help us link together key moral elements in a single view: *A moral situation is any cluster of events about which a question about better and worse occurs.*

Note that this definition applies not only where the participants ask about better and worse choices but also where reporters and historians ask whether situations are improving or worsening. It covers not only actions we call "immoral" but any action intended to doing better. It also covers interlocking events as they occur in our institutions of science, technology, economy, politics, law, education, religion, and the arts. By defining moral situations by moral questions, our aim is to retain the perspective that morality is a matter of humans asking, "What is concretely better here?"

A Hierarchy of Values

In chapter 7, we noted how the fundamental issue of a person's moral horizon is whether "better" means "merely preferred" or "better in itself." Here, we need to notice that the changes in a person's moral horizon from "merely preferred" to "better in itself" involves scaling an objective hierarchy of values. From philosophy's earliest days, we have wondered whether some values rank higher than others.[46] In *The Republic*, Plato presses Glaucon to rank these four values: agreeable pleasure, knowledge, medical care, and justice. Thomas Hobbes provided an initial answer to Plato's question by proposing that the fundamental human value is the preservation of life and the promotion of happiness, adding that a social contract would make happiness more attainable if people are willing to yield some of their individual rights to gain the benefits of collaboration. John Locke went further than Hobbes by adding our natural duties to society and to one another through mutual care. So we can see in Locke's work the following hierarchy of values:

- The *vital values* of self-preservation and health are fundamental.
- The *social values* of cooperation are higher ends.
- The *cultural values* of carrying out one's duties to the community and to mutual care are still higher than social and vital values.

Implicit in this hierarchy, although in need of development, are two values that our exercises on the norms of consciousness reveal as ranking higher yet:

- There is the concrete *value of the person*. It is actual persons who reason and reflect—philosophers like Locke who would rank the vital, social, and cultural values in that order.
- At the top of this hierarchy are *transcendent* values. There are the transcendent values of beauty, order, truth, goodness and love that are found in real places, events, things, and persons. Also, there are the correlatives in a person's unrestricted openness to all beauty, order, truth, goodness, and love, particularly as actualized through one's unrelenting creative endeavors and their unrestricted affective commitments to family, to nation, to the divine.

The objectivity of this hierarchy depends on how well it meets our relevant questions. So, to rouse as many questions as we can, it will help to put some flesh on these bones. Imagine, then, a "pure" progress from a moral horizon based on spontaneous preferences through a hierarchical series of ever more self-transcending preferences.

We spontaneously prefer the *vital* values of comfort over discomfort, health over sickness, strength over weakness, protection against weather and intruder over exposure and risk. We develop habits of eating, dressing, and housekeeping.

Somewhat less spontaneously, we prefer the collaboration that eases the tasks of harvesting food, sewing clothes, constructing homes, and blazing trails. We recognize the value of an integrated *social order*. Some philosophers treat this matter under the heading of the *social contract*. This value is made real by the achievement of a society where everything works.

At a third level, we prefer common moral standards. We see the value of promoting a living *culture* based on what is objectively worthwhile rather than merely preferred. The association we naturally make between culture and the arts finds its justification here insofar as the arts educate the feelings of a community to prefer harmony and higher aspirations over their opposites. Many philosophers treat this matter under the heading of a *common good* (although not all distinguish between the social value of mere agreement—which is hard to distinguish from moral conventionalism—and the cultural value of a common recognition of what is objectively better).

At a fourth level, we accept the value of our own *persons as originators and embodiments of values*. As originators of value, we commit ourselves to live out these values in our lives, with full knowledge that our engagement with others will test, modify, and refine these values in each other. Here we experience a normative demand for consistency[47] among the drives we experience to be authentic, self-transcending persons. It results in the personal integration of what contemporary philosophers call *moral autonomy*, in the sense of accepting oneself as a genuine source of true values. At the same time, as embodiments of value, we demand the highest level of respect simply for our being.

At a fifth, topmost level, we recognize that an openness to whatever is truly valuable means taking seriously the question of *transcendent value*. Having recognized ourselves as responsible and loving sources of value, we experience a "pull" to open ourselves both to the ultimate source of the values we happen to be as persons and to the ultimate fulfillment of all things we call "good." Whether expressed in humanitarian or religious terms, when we experience how love in us reveals and promotes values beyond what logic can dictate, we suffer the persistent question of the mystifying source and ultimate purpose of this love. It results in

a personal commitment—open-minded and full-hearted—
to participation in the mystery of the open-endedness of
our living. Without the experience of a normative drive
toward transcendent values, no philosopher would be in-
clined to crawl out of the cave of mere sensation. No one
would want to dignify and enhance life wholeheartedly
and without reservation. Nor would anyone feel the pull to
worship a divine source of one's love and engage the divine
giver in a union that fears not death. This is the area explored under the headings of *transcendental ethics* and of *theological ethics.*

In the life of any individual or group, the ascent to higher notions
of value is not quite so "pure." Nor is the ascent driven by logic.
Indeed, some people use logic to justify staying right where they
are. Rather it is driven by the two interplaying drivers of history:
the cognitive, creative movement in which we ascend the hierarchy
of values through personal experience, insight, verification, and
decisions; and the affective, healing movement where our being in
love reveals values that elude cognition alone. By itself, a cognitive
grasp of the hierarchy of values lacks the power to make us change.
Where the cognitive factor maps the way, the affective factor pours
in the fuel for the driving. Most of us inherit our values from our
parents. They stress the vital values of safety and health, the social
values of cooperation and planning, the cultural values of truth-
telling, fairness, promise-keeping, and duties. They gradually
launch us to discover for our autonomous selves the full range and
real limits of our abilities. On our own, if we know we are loved, we
may discover the meaning of a self-transcendence that is fully open
to learning, to doing better, and to love.

This affective movement is richly colored by feelings, but, to milk
the metaphor, the hues change as we mature. To embrace these
successively more comprehensive notions of value requires successive adaptations of our feelings. As we saw in chapter 7, we
maintain whatever moral perspective we happen to have through
symbols, and symbols are images linked to feelings. So as we
embrace more comprehensive notions of value, we imagine life and
feel about life in new ways. We become new sorts of persons. Our
habitual priorities are reoriented—from exclusive concern for our

personal comfort and safety, to social harmony, to the common and objective good, to personal, autonomous authenticity, and ultimately and without restrictions to all things that embody true values.

Typically, members of small groups of high moral vision identify affectively with noble leaders. They live together; they eat together. The leader's desires are their desires; the leader's vision is their vision. It is the affective movement that draws them forward together. Before any laws are written, members discover within themselves the same sources of life that inspires their leader. Eventually the leader dies and the followers take on the task opening the minds and hearts of new members to the same total openness experienced by their founder. Of course, the openness of any founder cannot be passed on to the next generations by rules alone. As Socrates explained to Meno, virtue cannot be taught. Religions elicit this openness to a divine order by rituals of re-enactment such as the Passover, the Way of the Cross, and the Hajj. Nations, in stark contrast, tend to re-enact military victories that celebrate only the ambiguous freedom that revels in crushing other nations. Or they may celebrate achievements of new political orders founded on the high standards of liberty and equality, but again, unless moral development expands from the third level of high cultural standards to the fourth level where the hearts of individuals are converted to a fully open moral horizon, lofty social visions tend to settle down to mere conventions—agreements on standards of efficiency and effectiveness without personal commitments to the truly better.

The Structure of Morality

In chapter 7, we outlined three types of choices—particular, strategic, and fundamental. To expand these into a model of the structure of morality, we now need to align these types of choices with how they affect—and are affected by—the lives we share with others. So, in the following chart, the third column depicts the communal aspects of these three types of choices. At the same time, we can align these types of choices with three distinct and analogous meanings of "good".[48]

Individual Exigences	Type of Choice	Communal Aspect	Analogs of "Good"
Spontaneous Needs. Wants.	Particular	Cooperation. Spontaneous intersubjec- tivity.	Particular Goods
Intelligent inquiry. Insights. Development of habits and skills.	Strategic	Institution, setup, process. Roles and tasks.	Good of Order
Responsible assessment. Judgments of value. Conversions.	Funda- mental	Personal relations.	Terminal value

The first two columns are clear enough: Impelled by three levels of exigences, individuals make three types of choices—particular, strategic, and fundamental. The third column lays out how their choices affect, and are affected by, their communities. The fourth column highlights the fact that the "good" we seek is not a univocal notion but rather has three distinct but related meanings. If you will bear with some repetition in content, to understand them as elements of a more comprehensive question-generating structure, it will be helpful to describe the communal aspects of each type of choice, row by row.

As individuals with spontaneous wants and needs, we instinc-tively seek all kinds of particular goods—whether some material commodity or a particular service. At the same time, we are spontaneously intersubjective. We spontaneously seek the compa-ny of others and often ask for help in getting the particular goods we seek. Here, "good" means little more than "desired." Together, our spontaneous needs and wants combine with our spontaneous intersubjectivity to form the *primitive base of a community.*

We are more than mere spontaneity. As intelligent, practical thinkers, we also get insights into ways to get our particular goods regularly. When a single instance of cooperation for obtaining a particular good becomes routine, the "setup" emerges for churning out this particular good continuously. Setups include our economy, our technology, our health care system, our political apparatus, our military, our transportation system, our sciences, our legislatures, our training schools, ... any imaginable institution. Our social routines can also be less formalized, as we see in friendships and holiday celebrations. But these too are governed by shared insights into how to work together more effectively to get what we want. It is our intelligent and reasonable subjectivities that put the "order" into our social order. The social order becomes objectively intelligible, and threats are recognized by the degree to which this "order" shows gaps of disorder. By the same token, the objective social order changes our subjectivities because our participation in social processes requires that we develop certain skills and habits and assume certain roles and commitments which powerfully shape the direction of our personal development. Here, "good" means effective and efficient regularity. It is the events of insights, validated by judgments, which create the good of an orderly delivery of particular goods. These events provide the base for a *social order*, understood as the intelligent ordering of peoples' skills and habits for collaborative ends.

We are also more than mere intelligence and reason. Being responsible, we assess both the worth of our particular goods and the setups that deliver them. Further, as affective evaluators, we cherish one another as companions in life, caring for each other without any further justifications based on duty or role or payoff. Besides *recognizing* the values that currently inform our living, we also *impart* values. We bring forth children whose value is inestimable. As parents and teachers we impart our values to the young. As companions in life's struggle we enrich the quality of the community we form with others. We also impart values by selecting those particular goods and social structures that promise to make life better. So we develop religions, humanities education, the arts, a judiciary—the public institutions aimed mainly at fostering values that give moral direction to the social order. Finally, as sources of new values, and promoters of existing values, we are the "originating values" who impart the "terminal values" embodied in particular goods, social orders, and new, living persons. Here, "good" means "objectively better." It is by the exigences of responsible choice and mutual love that we discern true values in the particular things we seek, in the social institutions that deliver them, and in the persons with whom we care for our world. The presence of responsibility and love provides the base for a *culture*, understood as the responsible and loving ordering of a people's moral orientation toward improving life.

The Significance of the Structure

This model of a moral situation does not represent an ideal moral order. It proposes no moral principles from which we can deduce the value of any specific option. Because it identifies relevant questions without assuming answers it is entirely empirical. But this does not mean that it ignores moral norms. On the contrary, by including the third row about originating and terminal values, it points directly to the empirical evidence of our directly felt normative demands to be authentic, to orient our moral consciousness according to an objective hierarchy of values. It also interrelates the relevant questions one can raise about moral situations. In this fashion, the model clarifies that our inner normative drives are the foundation of all objective values and gives an ordered set of questions we might raise in any situation.

Note too, that the different meanings of "good" in the first and second rows require distinct kinds of moral imperatives. Usually, choices of particular goods may be immediately assessed as better or worse. But choices of any setup, arrangement, routine, or institution can be extremely complicated. In the world of finance, the fine print in insurance policies, mortgages, business contracts, and global banking masks dangerous risks. In the world of employment, the kindhearted family breadwinner can unwittingly contribute to an economy that oppresses the poor. In most cases of a Sophie's Choice—a choice between two evils—she is caught in a rotten setup. Who chooses the setup itself depends on the form of government—a collectivity of voters in a democracy and one person in a dictatorship. Here, moral imperatives include educating the public on debt, the economy, global well-being, and the importance of participation in choosing setups. They require that complex institutions make their operations and constituencies transparent.

This model may well appear coherent, even plausible. But a mere conceptual grasp of these relationships is not enough. What we need is a corresponding working knowledge of ourselves as affective, moral, reasonable, intelligent and attentive human beings. The more we verify in our own lives that moral situations really are laced with all these normative elements, the more habitually we will ask the relevant moral questions. A fully open ethicist does not stand back and judge the rightness or wrongness of situations. He or she plunges in with an abiding concern, a second nature as it were, that thinks in structured questions like these.

Moral Progress

When we talk about a moral situation, we point to how "good" things are at present—the good people, the good ideas, the good products and services. But we also talk about how things are "going," hoping they are changing for the better. To keep this sense of moral progress front and center in ethical reflection, we proposed a historical-minded model of morality. So the above tri-level meaning of "good" which applies to a moral situation at a single place and time, needs to be incorporated into a more comprehensive model that clarifies the kinds of questions we can ask about its *movement*—whether worsening or improving. We may envision this historical movement as a sequence of moral situations—a succession of the tri-level charts, if you will, each one representing snapshots of the individual and communal aspects of particular goods, the good of order, and operative values at a point in time.

In chapter 6, we proposed that things improve to the extent that our creativity is unhampered by bias and willfulness. This is a pure case, of course, since human consciousness is morally wounded by bias and willfulness. But to understand the process of moral progress itself, we need to bracket, for the time being, those factors that impede progress. We may call this account of moral progress "genetic," because it is analogous to the genetics of cellular growth, botanical growth, fetus growth, and so on, which outline the factors of growth when growth occurs, and leaves to a further, closer analysis the factors that impede growth.

Diversity in Cultural Progress

To a great extent, the moral progress of a culture depends on how well its members integrate the several realms of moral reflection. Everyone is familiar with thinking in symbolic forms and elemental logic. Many are also familiar with analytic thinking—the realm traditionally associated with "ethics" and rules about right and wrong. Some are also familiar with historical thinking—the realm we associate with an ethics based on narratives about a culture's wondrous accomplishments and tragic mistakes. A few are also familiar with the realm we associate with method.

These differences in realms of moral reflection mean that a society's reception of new ways and new moral principles will be similarly stratified. In cultures where moral philosophers and historians have no voice, symbols alone shape the priorities of the masses. We see this not only in totalitarian regimes like the former Soviet Union, but also in Western democratic societies where humanities education has been replaced by job training. In cultures where philosophers and historians do have a voice, symbols are combined with reasoned analyses and historical exemplars to convince the educated. But even here, it is only the educated that are directly affected. In cultures where the method-minded also have a voice (currently small and rare), it takes symbols, reasoned analysis, historical consciousness, and open dialog about horizons and foundational commitments to actually do better.

Because our human condition is a growth process, communities everywhere and always face these issues of developmentally stratified moral development. No doubt, moral education needs to be tailored to make sense within the hearers' horizons, but it should also draw members out from an unquestioning acceptance of their culture's priorities into an understanding that can lead them to question those priorities. Moral education should extend back in time to reveal the origins of all moral standards as historical results of social and cultural experiments. It should also widen to understand contemporary differences in moral standards across cultures. With that step—the realization that a moral heritage is a legacy of people like ourselves trying to improve their lives—the exigence for method in ethics comes clear.

Diversity in Individual Progress

Woven through the moral progress of a culture, there is the moral progress of the individual. What sort of model might represent *normal* moral growth? Theorists like Lawrence Kohlberg and Carol Gilligan offer stage-based models. Kohlberg bases his on Piaget's study of the cognitive developments in children. Gilligan criticizes Kohlberg's model as based only on evidence from men, proposing instead a model based Freud's theories of ego development, along with her studies of relationship-building in women. Subsequent studies reveal overlaps in both theories: Women show strong characteristics of an Ethics of Justice that Kohlberg finds in men, while men show strong characteristics of an Ethics of Care that Gilligan finds in women.

The more fundamental issue here is method. The models that Kohlberg and Gilligan present are based on standard ethical concepts verified through empirical evidence of observable behaviors and forced-choice surveys. (Kohlberg's classifications are based on the *concepts* of punishment/reward, approval/disapproval, duty/guilt, and personal rights/standards, while Gilligan's are based on the *concepts* of survival, selfishness/other-centeredness, goodness as self-sacrifice, truth as self-worth, personhood as relational, and nonviolence.) But, if I may hammer this point home again, a generalized empirical method will account also for the data of consciousness and, as a result, reveal universal normative demands. This should allow us to complement those empirical studies that identify developments that *actually occur* by normative studies that identify developments that *ought to* occur. That is, we may understand *normal* growth not simply as clustered around statistical norms but also as aligned with moral norms. Moreover, because the method will define moral *concepts* by appeal to the data of consciousness, we can anticipate that empirical studies will converge toward common concepts that investigators can verify for themselves and use as common parameters in their empirical studies of different populations.

A Hypothetical Model

This model of moral progress in cultures and individuals is based on the evidence of distinct realms of moral reflection and distinct stages of personal moral development. Further empirical research is needed to identify more precisely the concerns and resolutions that define each realm and stage of progress. In any case, actual people develop at different rates, with some surprisingly open at a young age while others remain closed long into their dotage. Actual societies develop at different rates too. Small societies springing from charismatic leaders make rapid advances. But as they attract followers, their social institutions become more complex, and their culture demands a system of education, adjudication, religion and the arts to prevent the moral achievement from being diluted by mistaken ideas and diverted toward ambiguous enterprises. The challenge is to structure the expanding culture and still let it breathe its nascent moral air.

The Historical Task

This model also supports a historical-minded approach to ethics by providing an ordered set of questions about the drivers of moral progress in any social group. So ethicists act as historians as they analyze actual chains of situations that characterize an improving moral tradition. Conversely, historians act as ethicists when they name which developments made things better and which made them worse. For example, a historical investigation of any thriving group, association, village, city, nation, corporation, or religion may investigate the below-upward (creative) vector of moral development by asking questions such as these:

> What symbols of "trouble" captured the attention of participants? What ethical concepts, principles, and theories were used to justify changes? What really were the driving concerns and the resolutions? What effect did these concerns have on the community's ways of collaborating, on how it circulates money, and on what habits and skills were instilled in its members? What symbols of "happy life" or "community cohesion" secured the allegiance of the group's members?

At the same time, historical investigations may pose further critical questions about the above-downward (healing, affective) vector of moral development:

What personal relationships carved the channels that spread better ideas so effectively and so quickly? What religious or humanitarian commitments opened members to a fully open moral horizon? What underlying intellectual, moral, and affective openness characterized the leaders of the community? What are the symbols of hope and challenge that captured everyone's imagination?

In our eagerness to attack moral problems, we can often overlook these personal, institutional, and symbolic dimensions. So it is particularly important in any ethical reflection on concrete situations to identify what above-downward elements contribute to doing better. Questions like the above identify what actually has helped improve a situation (or at least slowed its decline); they lead to further questions about what specific resources are needed to accelerate moral development.

Moral Dialectics

The above genetic model depicts some general features of how the moral character of any community or person develops. If the realms and stages of development are defined in normative terms that can be verified in consciousness, then moral education will aim to facilitate discoveries of these normative patterns of development. Indeed, such an education seems essential to the moral progress of both cultures and individuals.

Still, there are other, more intractable differences that arise from the historicity of morality itself. This is evident from differences across cultures. Each culture is defined by the meanings and the values it built up over time—not by education, not by philosophy, but by the dialectics of historical process. Globally, we may have a thousand distinguishable cultures, each with a unique good of order, each enriched by the contributions of matchless, self-transcending members. Yet a thousand distinct instances of a good of order can lack a common good of order. Appeal may be made to a classical ethics of virtue and moral standards, but these are permanently vulnerable to being measured by loyalist notions of a common good—just the good of our community. Only the few for whom the virtue of justice lifts their eyes to other communities feel any guilt about avoiding responsible concern about their troubles.

Understanding Historical Differences

Clearly, as individuals and communities, we differ from one another far more than the beasts and their herds differ within their species. From the point of view of evolution, subhuman species lack our variety because the changes they undergo are driven by fixed principles of their respective natures. In particular, they lack our primal ability to freely form images, and consequently cannot entertain alternative reactions to threats and opportunities. This freedom that distinguishes us from other animal species is made possible by a triple differentiation in consciousness. By imagining whatever we please, we enjoy the ability to inquire intelligently about our spontaneous priorities and to assess them responsibly. That is, we have three distinct drivers of the decisions we make:

- Our spontaneous priorities—a nature we share with animals.
- Our intelligent inquiry—our nature as intelligent.
- Our responsible assessments—our nature as moral.

Earlier we named these the *structural elements* of any moral situation. But from the point of view of developments over time, these may now be regarded as the ongoing *drivers* of moral change. These drivers are not only distinct; they also head in somewhat opposed directions, and because they do, the resultant moral progress is significantly more complex than mastering further realms of reflection or undergoing stage-like growth. This is because, besides being distinct and opposed, all three drivers govern the changes we undergo in the remarkable manner of being changed themselves. Every person and every community is peculiar is because the dominance of each driver rises or falls at every choice of every individual.

So we may imagine a Community A dominated by its *spontaneous priorities* and intersubjective bonding. A dominance of raw, passionate demands narrows the range of its members' intellects by mocking intelligent inquiry into any situation. Urgent demands for intersubjective bonding regard urgent feelings as more important than responsible commitments. Community B may honor *intelligent inquiry* so highly that it ignores some of the spontaneous but vital needs for the health and safety of its members. At the same time, it may turn a deaf ear to the cultural voices of a humanities education, the arts, a judiciary, and a religion that would challenge proposals that look good on paper but would make life worse in practice. As long as intelligent inquiry fails to give spontaneous priorities and responsible assessments their due, the community's intellectual potential becomes stratified—an elite obsessed with its grand plans and a proletariat obsessed with food, shelter, and mutual comfort. Its culture, which normally would test whether the grand plans will really improve life together, becomes co-opted by the demands of entrepreneurs for business efficiency and of politicians for a compliant citizenry. Community C may cling so strongly to *responsible assessments* that it belittles the spontaneous priorities of men and women whose spontaneity may actually be governed by the voice of authenticity. At the same time, it may downplay the power of intelligent inquiry to reveal the complexity of moral issues. A typical outcome of such an unintegrated moral vision is moral dogmatism. It would impose codes of ethical behavior without appeal to people's understanding. It justifies its pronouncements by claiming noble motives and issuing dire warnings of anarchy.

It is not my intention here to draw three boxes for classifying specific communities. The distinctions are not conceptual labels but heuristic structures. They represent three basic types of dynamics that historians and sociologists might bear in mind when investigating specific communities. They clarify the relevant questions that may trigger insight into what is going forward in any community.

Lonergan names this process of an ongoing mutual conditioning of opposed but linked drivers a "dialectic."[49] It moves beyond a first-order analysis of realms and stages of healthy growth to a second-order analysis of the historical interplay of the drivers that underlie the actual moral growth of any person or community. So a dialectical model of moral development will anticipate that any community will be a moving, concrete resultant of the mutual conditioning of these three drivers. In any community, the perceptions of its members, their patterns of behavior, their ways of collaborating and disputing, and all their shared purposes are the concrete result of how their spontaneous priorities, intelligent inquiries, and responsible assessments conditioned one another up to the present day.

Again, the interplay between these three linked but opposed drivers spawns the various kinds of "wounds" to our natural creativity, particularly our biases and willfulness. But by way of a third-order analysis, Lonergan also points out that these kinds of dysfunction occur in people who also experience the healing power of love. The love of friendship, family, country and religious commitments are powerful antidotes for both neurotic obsession and egotism. The global love that seeks the common and genuine good of all humans can dismantle the loyalism to which friendships, families, countries and religions are prone. A global love is ready for whatever work may be necessary to rise above a commonsense naiveté about life—ready, that is, to take on the analyses of science, the lessons of history, and the wisdom of philosophy and theology. Finally, there is the unrestricted and universal love of a totally open affectivity. Whether it is expressed through formal religion or through a secular, personal commitment to self-transcendence, this total openness welcomes the power to love and works with that love. This totally open affectivity empowers people to act with the charity that transcendent values often require. It gives a moral vision, an eye of faith that sees transcendent values in ordinary life. It gives the existential persistence to overcome obstacles, in the confident hope that all shall be well, despite all current evidence to the contrary. As I say, everyone experiences the healing power of love, but it is one thing to experience it and quite another to recognize the movements of love in one's experience and to discern between those inclinations that close one's horizon and those that open it.

The Dialectical Task

There are all sorts of dialectical relationships possible between these drivers of our choices, and this makes it extremely difficult to unravel the historical origins of priorities held by any person or community.[50] The choices of individuals flow together into the river of a community's history. We cannot see very far upstream, where the ongoing mutual conditioning of spontaneous priorities, intelligent inquiry, and responsible assessments shape those uncountable choices. Any past sources of unauthenticity and authenticity blend in smoothly with the present habits of individuals and the policies of communities.

This is why, besides the general, scientific, and normative categories of realms of meaning and stages of moral growth, we also need historical accounts to bring out the unique twists and turns of moral living in specific communities. We need a mutual disclosure of horizons to bring out basic differences in what these twists and turns do to ethicists themselves. The mutual exposure will reveal some differences as perspectival, as people of different cultures share their histories of moral progress and as various experts share their unique perspectives. Mutual exposure will reveal other differences as developmental, as youngsters develop into mature adults, or as less developed nations learn from more developed nations how to make life genuinely better. But there will remain the dialectical differences between radically opposed horizons. In chapter 7, we contrasted opposing views on learning, on choosing, and on loving. We underscored their radical opposition by noting that personal conversions are necessary to fully open ourselves to the unrestricted range of our learning, choosing, and loving.

At base, then, the dialectical nature of morality is between authenticity and unauthenticity. Authenticity is an abiding obedience to the normative drives of experience, understanding, reason, responsibility, and love. It is naturally open to learning what learning is, choosing how one chooses, and letting love take the lead in one's heart. Unauthenticity is some form and degree of disobedience within. It generates any number of conflicting views on learning, choosing, and loving. The unauthentic person is alienated from his or her true self, just as an unauthentic community is alienated from the exigences for authenticity that its members will feel anyway. Typically, these persons and communities will then justify their mindsets and morals by some form of ideology.[51]

So a major methodological task of ethicists is to reach agreement on a dialectical view of moral problems. We sketched out such a view here, inviting you to verify that it corresponds to your experience. Where it does not correspond, the invitation stands, awaiting improvements. But at least this much seems evident: A dialectical view will acknowledge that moral situations are complex, and that this complexity is constituted in large part by the mindsets and priorities of the people involved. It will understand that people's mindsets and priorities will always be shaped by some unique combination of their spontaneous needs, intelligent inquiry, and responsible and loving care. And it will anticipate that the resulting tensions will be ultimately between being authentic and being unauthentic.

Should ethicists agree on this dialectical nature of morality, they may consider a two-pronged tactic for engaging moral issues.[52]

First, they employ a hermeneutic of suspicion. As they take on the task of tracing the history that led up to present situations, they ascertain, as best they can, what were the main lines of progress. Then they identify the factors that contributed to deterioration, keeping in mind the myriad possible combinations of sullied heritages, bias and willfulness—in leaders, in their followers, and in the social institutions that embody these dysfunctions.

Second, they employ a hermeneutic of recovery. As they assess moral situations, they also identify the many possible combinations of mutual love, moral vision, and existential persistence—again, in leaders, in their followers, and in the institutions that embody these virtues. They look to love as the most powerful source of forgiveness we know of. They look to faith, conceived as the eye for value illuminated by transcendent love. They look to hope, conceived as the desires made confident and persistent by transcendent love.

Finally, if you can bear another distinction, this two-pronged engagement occurs twice.[53] This is because morality is always historical and "history" has two different but related meanings. There is the *living history* that historians study: the interplay of choices and behaviors of actual people. And there are the *historiographies*—the books that historians write. The goal of a dialectical engagement is to assess the *living history*, but to do so, ethicists first need to assess the *historiographies* on which they depend and the horizons of the historians who write them. Biased historians will present views of developments that are not only inaccurate but also slanted in favor of certain group priorities. Once ethicists separate the wheat from the chaff in the *reports* of situations, they take on an assessment of actual historical developments.

Comparisons

To understand more fully the significance of this dialectical model of moral development, it will help to compare it to other typical models. Today, many textbooks distinguish ethical models based on the dominant principles employed—such as duty, or utility, or happiness, or virtue, or natural law. But if, as we propose, ethical principles are always products of the methods of mind and heart, then we can detect the underlying reasons for differences if we classify models by the dominant method they each employ.

As far as I can tell, most proponents of models that fall short are not opposed to a model based on dialectics of authenticity and unauthenticity for the simple reason that they are not aware of it. So in a perspective of a friendly dialectical engagement, we should aim to recognize certain merits in each model and, after identifying shortcomings, suggest ways they may relate to the more comprehensive perspective of dialectical method.

Ethical Positivism. I use the term "positivism" in the sense proposed by Auguste Comte (d. 1857), namely, that human knowledge is limited to what is supported by the data of sense experience. Generally speaking, "ethical positivism" applies to systems based on positive laws, since these impose sanctions based strictly on observable behaviors, without any consideration given to supposed virtues or motives. So theories of Ethical Positivism will also encompass the various theories referred to as "Legal Positivism"—such as those proposed by John Austin (*Lectures on Jurisprudence and the Philosophy of Positive Law*, 1997), H.L.A. Hart (*The Concept of Law*, 1994), and Ronald Dworkin (*Law's Empire*, 1986). Besides the legal arena, ethical positivism is also evident in the policies of corporations that appoint an Ethics Officer (usually an attorney) or establish a Code of Ethics to scrutinize employee behaviors for violations of rules.

Of course, laws are vital to better living. Any ethics worth its salt will disallow imputation of motives and accusations of bad will as grounds for sanctions. What counts is observable behavior—claims and promises that can be supported by evidence. A robust ethics will also retain the pedagogical effects of laws in the moral growth of youngsters who, according to most studies, necessarily move through a stage of an "Ethics of Law," even though, within an

"Ethics of Better," laws serve mainly to draw certain outer boundaries of human behavior to protect people's freedom to pursue and accomplish what is better.

Ethical Positivism also applies to any ethical models based on the natural sciences. We see this in ethicists who assume that human morality is rooted in laws of nature in the same fashion that material reality follows the laws of physics and chemistry. They overlook the radical difference between nature and history, and the corresponding difference between the natural sciences and human studies. When anomalies in material reality show up, investigators in the natural sciences propose theories that better explain the phenomena. But when anomalies in human morality show up (when will they not?), ethical positivists face a dilemma. Some assume that there must be an explanation for immoral behavior, since there are explanations for everything in the field of the natural sciences. They have no method for dealing with the freedom of imagination and freedom of choice which only humans manifest. They lack procedures for tracking how meanings and values originate, expand, and collapse. They assume that we simply cannot act against what our judgment says is better. So they seek explanations by pointing to causes: dysfunctional families, genetic predisposition to violence, or addiction. The reality of willfulness is beyond their ken. A group of sociologists studying race relations may lay out respectable explanations of why racial suspicions run so deep; they may identify certain causes of hatred; they may propose solutions. But unless they allow that there are people who freely embrace hatred with no justification, their solutions will not go to the irrational roots of hatred because they are fixated on what "causes" it.

Others recognize very well that our lives are defined by meanings and values. But because they assume that scientific data must be restricted to the data of sense, they look to the tried-and-true scientific method of *correlation* to explain moral behavior. They gather quantifiable data on outcomes, on prevailing attitudes, and on typical behaviors of representative sample groups. Why do people steal? Research indicates that the mere opportunity to steal is a far stronger predictor of stealing than factors like religious observance and family stability. This finding certainly supports the principle that even good people should be monitored and account-able, but it does not explain *why* people steal. By focusing on the data of sense, ethical positivists cut themselves off from the wealth of data in consciousness that can provide an explanation of the inner motives, inner symbols, inner biases, or inner, unexplainable acts of willfulness that lie behind all irresponsible acts.

Ethical Naïveté. A second model is the opposite of anything institutional or scientific. It is an expression of the bias we called "commonsensism," namely, the belief that common sense is sufficient for quality living. It assumes that moral guides must be available, simple, and unchanging. The reasoning can be compel-ling: Moral guides should be available to the ordinary person; otherwise, only the educated could be moral, and average people would have no grounds for criticizing the behaviors of others. Moral guides should also be simple to understand; otherwise moral deliberation would drag out, leaving urgent moral issues unat-tended. And moral guides should not change with the changing times. Morality is more than mere preference; it has absolutes. And absolutes are exactly what changing times need to ensure harmony and continuity.

There is also a compelling religious reason. Granted that being good is not easy, a good God would not make it difficult to under-stand *how* to be good. A popular, but fuzzy term for this view is "fundamentalism," the belief that the fundamentals of life must be obvious. Whether it appears in the context of religion or of ethics, it has a severely limited intellectual horizon. Sometimes it shows in an unquestioning adherence to the moral commandments in religious scriptures, as if they were dictated verbatim by God or angels to scribes who never experienced a question. It typically produces eloquent preachers who would scold the world into goodness. Sometimes it shows in an unquestioning obedience to moral leaders, as if all their pronouncements were mystically protected against any sort of unauthenticity. But in reality, the "fundamentals" of moral living are indeed complicated, which becomes evident to anyone who looks deeply into the face of evil. So, perhaps a kinder name for this model is "Ethical Naïveté." It would regard "fundamentalists" not as dialectically opposed to learning but rather as living at an earlier stage of intellectual development.

Ethical Optimism. Then there is the model that stands on some single, basic moral principle as the basis for all moral growth, despite the fact that ethical optimists do not agree on what this principle might be. One takes a stand on good will, another on enlightenment, a third on altruism, a fourth on virtue, a fifth on duty, a sixth on consequences, and so on.

Essentially, such single-principle versions of ethical models align well with the "genetic" model we discussed above. The analog is botany: the seed is there; all we need is the fertilizer of a good moral education. On the positive side, this approach does develop creative programs for improving our lives together. After all, who doubts that better ideas and better education will produce better living? Who doubts that good will, enlightenment, altruism, virtue and duty are vital to moral progress? This notion has enjoyed a terrific appeal over the centuries. Hegelian, Marxist, and Darwinian views of history are largely genetic, insofar as they support the liberal thesis that, in the long run, life automatically improves, and that wars, disease, and economic crashes are inevitable adjustments in the forward march of history.

But earlier we saw that a genetic model gives us only a first approximation to actual historical reality. If we go on to a second approximation, we uncover how bias blinds the mind to certain otherwise excellent questions and how even the people who ask the questions will not necessarily act on the answers. By failing to recognize the roles that bias and willfulness play in history, the genetic approach simply cannot develop effective strategies for healing people's moral dysfunctions and restoring crumbling situations. So we might categorize these genetic models as "Ethical Optimism." At its root, ethical optimists fail to see the dialectical character of consciousness and how the inner dialectics of authenticity and unauthenticity in persons always drives the choices that make outer history.

Ethical Relativism. A fourth model is based on the assumption that moral norms are relative to the people who hold them. Proponents of this view recognize that all societies have moral norms, but they propose that these norms arise solely out of an agreement among their members about priorities. They reject the position that universal norms may be identified by reflection on human nature or on what we do when we make choices—norms that can oppose what is merely conventional in any society. Also, they are prone to disregard the lessons of history, particularly when the history is not their own. Committed to moral self-determination of the community, they are slow to study what other communities already learned about living better.

This position has recently been elaborated as a "postmodern" ethics. Generally speaking, postmodernism is a cultural movement that celebrates diversity and promotes local self-expression with an intentional disregard for universal standards. In this gross respect, it shares the approach of "situation ethics" as proposed by Joseph Fletcher (d. 1991). There are a number of philosophers that allow the name "postmodern" to signify their views despite significant differences in their theories. Deeply concerned for the well-being of ordinary people, postmodernists view the modern world as rife with individualism and in tatters under the breakdowns of local communities that used to share in the risks and benefits of life together. They are driven by the perception that certain long-standing ideals have failed us—the Enlightenment hope for better living through science and universal standards of reason, the Classicist assumption that philosophy can provide a total view of the universe, the Romanticist celebration of the individual, and religious views that God's providence governs all things. Relativist ethicists are encouraged by the skepticism of Hume and Nietzsche, as well as by the success of disciplines that suspect human nature—specifically, the suspicions of nineteenth century historians about traditional historiography, Freud's suspicion of the unconscious, and Marx's suspicion of the mental comfort that an economy and a religion engender in the proletariat.

The dialectical model supports these suspicions but opposes the view that morality is nothing more than agreements. It takes a stand against any agreement that violates the normative drives of consciousness. Moreover, taking its stand on authenticity, it goes beyond a hermeneutic of suspicion to a hermeneutic of recovery. It outlines ways to recover what is authentic in the writing of history, in the psyche, and in the economic mindset. Indeed, the dialectical model pinpoints a key factor missing in most relativist models, namely, an inquiry into the data of consciousness. There, relativist ethicists might discover the normative drives common to all humans—drives that provide the basis for moral standards that cannot be reduced to strictly situational assessments. They would still object to the totalizing metanarratives that oppress ordinary people, but they would possess the critical tools for identifying what such metanarratives lack. They would celebrate diversity of perspectives rooted in unique experiences, but oppose the diversity rooted in bias and willfulness. They would still honor the ironies of human life, but find hope in the discovery that certain meanings, truths and values can be objectively established as authentic elements in any community's heritage.

The dialectical model also brings into the light the one great danger of any relativist model, namely, its susceptibility to loyalism. Because relativists abandon the pursuit of objective ethical norms, they lack any positive program for resolving differences in what two different communities take as conventional. Nor do they possess a therapeutic program that can dissolve the group hatreds that have led to practically every civil and international war in history. At the same time, because many relativist ethicists also promote the mutual care that enriches local communities, they uncritically nourish a loyalism that will not only neglect the good of other communities but also, in many cases, pour fuel on hatreds already on fire.

Ethical Categories

The foregoing structures of the moral situation, moral progress, and moral dialectics give an ordered set of foundational ethical categories.[54] To *express* our moral opinions, all we need is a command of our commonsense language. But to *justify* our opinions in ways that are intelligible to others, the next revolution in ethics will require a language that is technically defined and commonly accepted. A technical language for ethics is crucial for the mutual exposure of horizons because it supports the clarity, the coherence, and the consistency needed for effective communication. Ethicists already use scores of familiar categories: justice, rights, subsidiarity, autonomy, beneficence, virtue, duty, authority, and so on. Still, the familiar disagreements about what these mean makes moral discourse difficult. The aim of the generalized empirical method is to identify the *experienced normative drives* common to the consciousness of anyone as a foundation for working out moral standards, policies, plans and communications. Then, to discuss how outer moral directives are rooted in common inner normative drives, the categories we use should also mean the same thing to all involved. In the next chapter, we will review how these categories would be generated.

A FRAMEWORK FOR COLLABORATION

Besides a model of the historicity of morality, and besides a model of the foundational elements of morality, we also need a model for collaboration. We can assume that every ethicist relies on some collaborative model more or less explicitly, and with more or less success, depending on the adequacy of the model. Its adequacy, in turn, depends on how well it aligns with the questions that collaborators can actually raise. The range of those questions, finally, is a function of how open their horizons are to learning, choosing, and loving. This is why an adequate model of collaboration must integrate the actual, functioning horizons of ethicists with the ethical tasks they take on. Specifically, the model must integrate both a mutual exposure of horizons and a foundation in personal conversions with the more familiar tasks of understanding moral situations and deciding how to improve them.

Functional Specialization

In theological studies, Bernard Lonergan proposed that theologians conceive their tasks as ordered into eight specialties with clear functional relationships to one another.[55] These specialties themselves align with the questions that collaborators actually raise. The model we will consider here is based on this same classification of questions into eight distinct tasks. But rather than present a compete conceptual explanation of the model right away, it seems better to begin with the simpler, though less adequate, models we are already familiar with and appeal to your experience of further relevant questions in ethics to assemble a comprehensive model.

Recall, then, the four levels of moral reflection that we discussed in chapter 1: action, concepts, history, and method. While these levels represent ideal types never found in pure form, they have the merit of bringing the distinct functions of consciousness into strong relief.

First, are reflections of people like Eve: people of action. In their horizon of naïve realism, moral reflection means sizing up a situation and then taking action:

Size up the situation ...   ... and then make the adaptations needed for effective action.

Second are people who, like Conrad, rely also on ethical concepts. In their conceptualist/idealist horizon, situations cannot be sized up without some analysis of the situation. Nor can action be taken without understanding how the relevant moral guidelines relate to each other and what planning is needed to coordinate efforts toward effective action.

... by analyzing its moral   ... then creating ordered
elements, ...   guidelines and planning
                                                       coordination, ...

Size up the situation ...   ... and then make the
                                          adaptations needed for
                                          effective action.

Third are people who, like Narella, rely also on historical narrative. Besides analyzing the general features of a current situation, they seek to understand the specific tradition of meanings and values that participants bring to it. This includes not only conceptualized principles but also the moral standards expressed in vision statements, historical narratives, exemplars, and the emblematic stories of a community's origins. From there, the meanings and values most relevant to a situation are clearly expressed as moral standards. It is by drawing on these standards, in turn, that ordered sets of guidelines are proposed and plans for appropriate moral action are coordinated.

... by retrieving the meanings and values in the tradition of partici-pants,...	➜	... then expressing the proven priorities of the tradition as moral standards,...
... by analyzing its moral elements,...		... then creating ordered guidelines and planning coordination,...
⬆		⬇
Size up the situation ...		... and then make the adaptations needed for effective action.

Fourth are people who, like Abe, not only acknowledge the value of experience, of concepts, and of historical awareness, but also scrutinize the tradition for errors, myths, and bias. As they conduct this scrutiny openly, the criteria they rely on for assessing others are exposed as grounded in partial or full conversion. In this manner, the mutual exposure of horizons may reveal radical oppositions. Those who have opened their horizons fully to what might be learned, what might be better, and with whom one might share life, have undergone the basic expansions of intellectual, moral, and affective conversions. They express their commitments in a foundational model that shows the historical character and the structural elements of morality, as we did in the first two parts of this chapter. Upon the foundation of conversions, they select the moral views of a tradition that can be rooted in conversion, express these proven views as moral standards, coordinate them with one another in collaboration with others, and make the adaptations needed for effective action.

... by scrutinizing both the reports and the values of the past, engaging in a mutual exposure of horizons,... ➜	... then grounding one's commitments in conversion, expressing a foundational model of the moral subject in community and history,...
... by retrieving the meanings and values in the tradition of partici- pants,..	... then expressing the proven priorities in the tradition as moral standards,...
... by analyzing its moral elements,...	... then creating ordered guidelines and planning coordination,...
Size up the situation ...	... and then make the adaptations needed for effective action.

It is the top level of this horseshoe that is the breakthrough to the next revolution in ethics. It alone specializes in exposing the normative sources that are actually operative in any tradition and that are potentially fruitful for a community's well-being. By bringing any underlying conflicts of affective, moral and intellectual commitments into the open, it counts on authenticity actually operative in ethicists to recognize where conversion and its expansions are needed. It alone lays out the foundations of morality in terms that are verifiable in the consciousness of persons who are affectively, morally, and intellectually open. It proposes a model of the moral subject in community and history. Without this level, the normative drives of consciousness are still operative, but covertly, and without the discrimination that explicit attention to horizons can give.

We may now simplify this model of collaboration:

From Past ...		...To Future
Dialectic	➜	Foundations
↑		↓
History		Standards
↑		↓
Interpretation		Coordination
↑		↓
Research		Communications

The first four functions retrieve the past, and the second four move to the future. Each of these eight functions has its unique goal and methods. At the same time, each function has a dynamic relationship with the other functions.

Research is important for ensuring that all the relevant data on a moral situation are captured. One does not "size up" a situation by looking at it. One first begins with the data of people's experience. The task here is to identify which data are relevant. An experienced detective arrives at a crime scene with questions born of experience that a rookie lacks. Still, data alone remain ambiguous without the next specialty, *interpretation*.

Interpretation is important for understanding exactly how people *understood* their experience. This usually entails understanding what the authors of relevant documents meant. (What did the framers of the U.S. Constitution intend? What did Mohammed mean by a *jihad*? What do Kierkegaard's journals reveal about his philosophy?) Interpretation is also important for understanding what individuals mean by their rituals and aesthetic expressions. This sort of *interpretation* stands in need of the next specialty to situate it in the flow of history.

History is important for identifying what is going forward in the moral life of a community. People often accept legends about their heritage and about one another's lives without question. The aim of the specialty *history* is to move beyond legends by laying out the more complex changes involved in moral living. It also traces the emergence, modifications and applications of ethical theories. For example, an ethicist may ask, "To what prior issues was Kant responding with his deontological moral principles? And how did his followers in future generations apply or alter his views?" Still, knowing the history is one thing; but assessing better and worse in what is going forward falls to the next specialty, which exposes basic horizons.

Dialectic exposes the horizons operative both in the persons involved in a moral situation/tradition and in the authors who report on them. The goal is to bring those mindsets and priorities under the spotlight where a discernment of values can take place. Historians carry out this discernment when they pronounce a certain cultural or theoretical movement as enriching or decadent. Psychologists carry it out when they challenge the moral legitimacy of their clients' behaviors and commitments. Philosophers carry it out when they name certain ethical theories as adequate or inadequate. At this point, the retrieval of the past is relatively complete; but because this retrieval contains opposing views, it awaits the first, foundational step in moving toward actually selecting the better and rejecting the worse.

Foundations expresses the fundamental models of morality as rooted in intellectual, moral and affective conversion. The goal is to provide a verifiable model of humans being authentic in community and history. That model is expressed in categories that represent the converted horizons within which moral guidelines can be expressed. As we can expect, it requires an intellectual conversion that has learned about learning, and a moral conversion that has chosen the truly better as the criterion of any choice. What may not be expected is that an affective conversion is needed as well. A converted affectivity is what impels ethicists not only to take the world's needs to heart but also to develop friendships with other ethicists and nourish the affective components of their professions through presentations, committee work, writing, training, and participation in conventions. The achievement of these conversions becomes the foundation for establishing moral standards.

Standards refers to any type of general moral guidelines issuing from converted horizons. These are the traditions and initiatives whose roots are brought to light by *dialectic*, whose validity is tested by ethicists from a horizon of the three-fold conversion, and whose expressions are formulated in the categories provided by *foundations*.

The content of these moral standards may be about the attitudes, virtues, and habits that are basic for authentic living. They may recount the histories of communities whose efforts reveal what authentic living looks like in practice. They may set forth general moral ideals such as world peace, universal education, and protection of the unborn, as well as visions of "best outcomes" in specific situations. They may promote the policies of institutions that have proven effective in improving life. Because moral standards are necessarily general and expressed in mixed forms, they anticipate the next tasks of coordinating moral standards within a comprehensive system and coordinating the plans that guide their implementation.

Coordination organizes into a coherent whole the variety of moral guidelines emerging from *standards*. Because the values represented in narratives, biographies, myths, visions, principles and policies can conflict, *coordination* aims to resolve these conflicts. It aims particularly to clarify ambiguities inherent in the symbolic/practical expressions of standards that appear as vision statements, narratives, exemplars, or myths. *Coordination* also lays out concrete plans for coordinating specific moral initiatives with other disciplines such as psychology, social work, financial planning, and, of course, with other ethicists who may not be operating within fully converted horizons. It coordinates moral policies with institutional policies of schools, governments, corporations, and religious groups. Now the stage is set to make changes.

Communications makes the changes that bring moral initiatives to bear on real life. It tailors the message to specific audiences, depending mainly on their present levels of intellectual, moral and affective development. It adapts the presentations to the requirements of various media. It aims to persuade or lead others to take specific actions or implement specific policies.

The point of distinguishing these functions and calling them "specialties" is that each has its proper goal and criteria. Yet because these goals are related in a movement from past to future, from *research* all the way to *communications,* it is important that ethicists understand the entire movement. This keeps them from inadvertently overstepping the bounds of their particular specialties. Surely it would be a mistake to point out shortcomings in a situation before its history has been completely vetted, or to propose moral policy straight from a historical study, or to jump to implementing ideas when the coordination of planning is not completed. Even though individual ethicists may indeed specialize in several of these eight specialties, it remains a collaboration. The ideal is that every ethicist has a "line of sight" from concrete moral situations, through all eight functions that must occur and through the personal conversions of collaborators to the actions proposed to make situations better.

This model of collaboration is supported by the fact that each of the four levels corresponds to a distinct normative drive in consciousness. So, *research* and *communications* are guided by the normativity of experience, both by attending to the data on a situation and by attending to a concrete, noticeable change for the better. *Interpretation* and *coordination* are guided by the normativity of understanding. *History* and *standards* are guided by the normativity of reason. And *dialectic* and *foundations* are guided by the normativity of responsibility. Conversion, the personal commitment to intellectual, moral and affective horizons that are fully open, is guided by the normativity of love, particularly as its realization in affective conversion prompts one to be fully open morally and intellectually. But because this commitment arising from conversions is personal, it stands outside the collaborative dimensions of the model. Still, as we will see in the next chapter, it reigns as the foundational reality on which all the collaborative specialties depend.

Impacts of the Model

Does anyone actually follow such a model? Explicitly, not many. The model as formulated here has yet to be recognized by that critical mass of experts that any discipline needs for a paradigm shift. Implicitly, however, the model reveals the group of functions that in reality, but not always knowingly, enters into any moral reflection that results in people doing better. It takes its stand on how people actually conduct moral reflection, and, through *dialectic*, it sifts the valid from the invalid kinds of reflection. It clarifies the functions of the more familiar specialties of research, analysis, historical accounts, moral principles, coordinated planning, and implementation. But it also introduces *dialectic* and *foundations* as specialties that keep methodological issues on center stage.

To the degree that the model hits off the key elements and their interrelationships, it should make explicit what actually goes on when situations improve. As a *discovered* method, the model is open to revision, depending on future discoveries. Yet in another sense the model is not open to revision. Because it is based on what occurs when we notice, understand, verify, and evaluate situations, any revision will result from our having noticed some shortcoming, understood what is needed, verified that our understanding is supported by the evidence, and evaluated a proposed revision, all motivated by some form of love. In other words, anything we do to revise the model—a praiseworthy goal—is evidence of an unrevisability at the base of the model.

10. PRACTICAL ETHICS

THE PROCESS OF ETHICS

S ome ethicists think of their work as "applying ethics" to various situations. The expression unfortunately suggests that ethics is essentially a stable set of ideal values to be applied in this or that case. As I hope is clear by now, ethics is not an application from on high. It is an ongoing, collaborative process of clarifying whether or not value statements and the resulting choices are expressions of our common normative drives within.

We described this collaboration as a horseshoe of functions. Now, to understand how this collaboration is ultimately practical, we need to set this model into a fully concrete context. So we will add two links that bend the horseshoe into a circle, namely, the concrete situation upon which ethicists reflect and the concrete conversion in the reflecting ethicist:

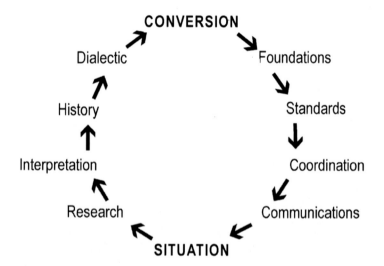

At the bottom of the circle is the concrete situation—the goings on that provide material for *research, interpretation, history,* and *dialectic.* As the source of materials, it lies outside collaborative reflection on it. At the top is the conversion of the ethicist. As an entirely personal event, it too lies outside the collaboration needed for moral progress. It is prepared for by *dialectic,* and is expressed in *foundations.* It grounds the moral *standards,* guides *coordination* among the standards, and shapes the *communications* that result in an improved situation. As new situations are improved, still further new opportunities and challenges arise and the cycle continues.

Such is the collaborative model. It may be complex but it is still intelligible. Ethicists who understand how these several functions of ethics are interrelated will more intelligently conduct their investigations and more clearly express how their views are based in norms inherent to their authenticity. It is a result of their authentic openness that the likelihood of genuine moral progress is heightened. We are now in a good position to put flesh on the bones of these specializations. In the remainder of this chapter we will explain how their specific functions interconnect to form the rising circle of moral progress.

OPENING HORIZONS

At the top of the circle is the conversion of the ethicist. On its left, *dialectic* prepares the ethicist for conversion by clarifying the differences in basic horizons that underlie opposing moral and ethical views. At center, conversion itself is a personal commitment to fully open horizons. On its right, *foundations* expresses the basic horizons of the converted ethicist. Taken together, *dialectic,* conversion and *foundations* make up the elements of ethics where actual methods are revealed through the opening of horizons.

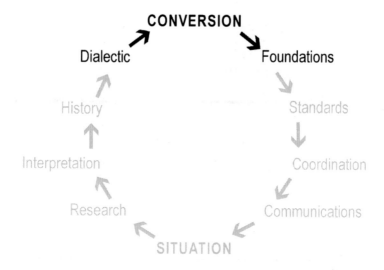

The specialty *dialectic* engages ethicists with one another as whole persons. The more effectively this mutual engagement reveals basic differences, the more clearly ethicists will personally notice the inner exigences to learn about learning, to choose how they choose, and to let love open their hearts. Where mutual horizons are more fully revealed, one feels a stronger interpersonal attraction to those women and men whose horizons are more fully open than to those whose horizons are less open. One more readily embraces the questions about what learning really is, about what the fundamental criteria for choices really are, and about the frightening extent to which an unrestricted love may take one.

Yet just feeling the attraction and embracing the questions are not yet conversion. A conversion is a personal discovery of, and commitment to, a full openness of mind, heart, and self. To the extent that ethicists live in a converted horizon, they recognize the importance of the specialty, *foundations*. Here is where they express their personal commitments to be fully open. Intellectually, they refer to the elements of consciousness in a way that clarifies how our inner normative drives shape their views on what can be real, worthwhile, and affectively engaging. Morally, they talk openly

about their commitments to choose true values over mere satisfactions. Affectively, they engage like-minded ethicists in an animated
spirit of moral inquiry and a common care for all people.

What is involved in opening horizons? Since *dialectic*, conversion,
and *foundations* each involves distinct functions and purposes, let us
lay them out to see how they interconnect.

Dialectic

The need for *dialectic* emerges from the realization of three fundamental facts:

- All moral norms originate in the normative movements of
  consciousness.
- These normative movements are subject to development,
  are easily distorted by bias, and are often resisted by
  willfulness.
- The effects of distorted development, bias, and willfulness on moral views are not readily noticed.

The goal of *dialectic*, then, is to bring these differences to light.
Everyone is familiar with differences in opinion about what should
or should not be done, but ethicists look also to differences among
views on the various factors that raise moral questions in the first
place. For example, these differences may be about any of the
following:

1. What situations need attention
2. What the people involved in a situation meant by their
   words and deeds
3. What was going forward in a community's history
4. What is better and worse in these situations and these
   historical developments
5. What commitments are fundamental to human authenticity and what ethical categories best express these
   commitments
6. What ethical principles and moral narratives should be
   our moral guidelines
7. What ethical system best organizes these guidelines and
   coordinates social policies
8. How best to communicate what should or should not be
   done

These, of course, correspond roughly to the eight functional specialties. However, in *dialectic*, while the first four aim to encounter the past in a variety of manners, the second four move to the future on the basis of foundations in conversion. But the eight specialties are not eight desks along an assembly line. They are groups of operations. Ethicists simply need to know which group they are focused on, no matter in what order. In this respect, as soon as assertions emerge from the second four types of concern appear, they belong to the past, however recent that past may be, and thereby are subject to the scrutiny of *dialectic* to uncover the roots of differences. As ethicists who are grounded in this generalized empirical method collaborate with those who are not, differences can appear in any of the specializations. These differences are essentially exigences to engage in the mutual exposure of horizons in the style of *dialectic*.

Again, within *dialectic* itself, there are assessments of assessments. This occurs because *dialectic* deals with the concerns raised by the normative drive of responsibility, and being responsible involves not only assessing the results of *research*, *interpretation* and *history* but also an assessment of one another's assessments.

Strategy: Reveal Horizons

How does *dialectic* work out in practice? All ethical reflection aims ultimately to resolve differences in moral views and converge upon agreements about what is truly better. The specialty *dialectic* contributes to this end, not by attempting to resolve things right off the bat but by clarifying the roots of differences. This is no easy task. One persistently difficult part of *dialectic* is overcoming our fear of understanding the perspectives of others, particularly the foreigner and the marginalized. Perspectival differences like these will always be with us, but it is one thing to acknowledge another's perspective but quite another to blend the two in a more comprehensive perspective.

There are also differences in the know-how that comes with study in a particular field: those who know more, studied more; and study is difficult and often unrewarding. But besides such deepening, there are also the widenings that vastly open our horizons beyond common sense—particularly into the realms of theory, of scholarship, of the arts, of religious transcendence, and, most importantly for *dialectic*, of a generalized empirical method in the realm of philosophic interiority. Like perspectival differences, such developmental differences will be always with us.

But despite these difficulties, welcoming the stranger usually leads to a mutual enrichment of horizons; and a willingness to learn, when met with the skill to teach, usually converges on similar moral views. What remains are the radical differences that still diverge and eventually oppose one another. These too we will always have with us. The strategy here is to encounter one another's full intellectual, moral and affective concerns, confirm and enrich those views that are rooted in full openness, and alter or reverse those rooted in partial openness. This strategy is ultimately supported by the fact that all people experience the exigence to be authentic, so that when they encounter people of more open horizons, they might more readily recognize any ingrained habits that keep their horizons closed and more eagerly desire to expand their horizons.

It bears repeating that what ethicists mean by "true" or "good" or "love" will mean one thing to the unconverted and another to the converted. It affects the concrete range of questions that ethicists are capable of raising about the moral problems of their day. Consider the issue of capital punishment: Absent conversion about learning, ethicists may assume they can safely ignore scientific data on the costs and efficacy of executing criminals, the historical origins of the practice, and any philosophical and theological reflections on the value of human life. Absent conversion about choosing, their assessment of capital punishment may be based solely on the emotional contentment they feel when they pronounce it good or bad. Absent conversion about loving, they may assess capital punishment only by its effectiveness in maintaining a social order. In all three cases, the unconverted may or may not support capital punishment. But because they have radically different views on what *learning* requires, what *better* means, or what priority *love* ought to have among humans, their opinions on external moral issues cannot be convincingly linked to the inner normative drives they in fact experience. The converted, too, may or may not support capital punishment. But because their fundamental concerns about learning, choosing, and loving are essentially the same, they will more easily convince one another to support or oppose specific policies on the issue. In either case, it is the mutual exposure of horizons that counts. It taps the inner demands for authenticity in all parties; it invites the unconverted to widen their horizons while it prompts the converted to converge on a comprehensive position.

In practice, we can expect some surprises. Those who think they are fully open may discover that they are in fact closed to discussing certain moral issues with which others feel quite at home. And those who regard themselves as novices in ethics may discover they already possess the unrestricted openness that can ground their further explorations in ethics. To lift the curtain on those horizons, it does little good for us to profess what we think our fundamental horizons are. After all, our horizons include a million questions that cannot be systematically summarized. Moreover, because of biases, our horizons often exclude relevant questions. It will be far more effective to discuss specific moral questions or ethical theories and let the range of our openness be evident to others by the specific moral concerns we express.

Tactics: Amplify & Assess

Within the field of what is uncovered by *research, interpretation, history* and *dialectic,* the strategy of a mutual exposure of horizons can be carried out through two tactics. A first tactic *amplifies* current findings and assessments by filling in gaps of data and making connections that corroborate what is already known. Amplifying brings to light any differences that were overlooked, so that hidden assumptions about learning, choosing, and loving are brought into the light. In the last quarter of the 20th century, we saw this played out in the change in attitudes toward withdrawing life support from the dying. Ethicists struggled to work out appropriate criteria for "allowing" and even "hastening" death. Both those who opposed the practice and those who supported it "amplified" the issue by pointing out the current practices of other countries and some potential long-term consequences. What surfaced was a variety of deeper views on the sanctity of life, on the meaning of "suicide," and on the principle of patient autonomy. It became evident that the intellectual horizon of some ethicists excluded the historical contexts of classical and religious prohibitions of suicide; instead, they regarded the prohibition as a moral principle from which concrete decisions can be logically deduced in any situation. Other ethicists were strictly focused on the wishes of the dying individual; they seemed unaware of any difference between decisions based on mere wishes and decisions based on being responsible for what is truly better all around. Another revelation was the blanket refusal by some ethicists to consider that a "beyond" to this life may even be a relevant question.

A second tactic *assesses* what may be better or worse in specific situations and trends. As amplifying adds to our knowledge of moral situations and trends, assessing goes on to evaluate them. It is when we move toward evaluations about what has been going forward that we encounter the past most concretely, as we come to know the persons, their motives, their hopes and fears. We also have reasonable views on the historical currents in which their lives flowed and of which they were largely ignorant. But most deeply, we come to know their agonies from within, as it were. We know the truth of the past, not as mere facts, but as the truth of a people like ourselves on a search for ever deeper meaning, ever better living, and an ever wider allowance for love.

Again, making these assessments requires the preliminary assessments of how reliable are the interpreters and historians who inform us about them, which brings us to a familiar problem: Ethicists reporting on situations or trends may express their assessments in nearly opposite manners. Some may invite their counterparts to wider perspectives, only to discover, upon amplifying the ramifications of these presumably wider perspectives, that they are not wide enough. Others may aim to embarrass their opponents for shortcomings and shut them out of the conversation. So a further dialectical assessment is needed—the task of assessing the assessors. Common sense says this is nothing new; we scrutinize one another all the time. But within a collaborative model of ethics, the dialectical task includes the work of baring one another's intellectual, moral and affective horizons.

Spirit of Engagement

Manners matter. This is particularly true when mutual exposure brings to light one's own shortcomings. Offensive remarks usually generate defensive responses, but in the specialty *dialectic* these defenses shield the very oversights that need correction as well as those partial insights that need amplification. On the affective level, for example, an atheist may reveal deep respect for the abiding question of an unrestricted love, while a devout Muslim may have never personally noticed such a love. On the moral level, contradictions may appear in ethicists whose words promote self-sacrifice but whose actions reveal self-absorption. On the intellectual level, oversights may come to light in positivist, consequentialist, deontological, or critical-realist theories. On the practical level of careers, ethicists whose jobs depend on maintaining certain standards in business or finance or education will cling to positions that they may not genuinely embrace from the heart.

The most effective way to reveal one another's basic horizon is to engage one another as whole persons. Engagement is more than understanding, more than knowledge, more than appreciating values. Engagement aims toward an affective commitment. This may be to one's contemporaries, and even to the giants of the past, in a sort of cosmic friendship based on an inherited vision. In any case, despite differences in understanding, knowledge, and values, engagement trusts that the normativity of love can move us to transcend these differences and heal the deeper wounds of spirit that we share.

For my part as an ethicist, I must be humble enough to acknowledge my sources and how fully I have understood them. I must first make this acknowledgment to myself. This means being unafraid to admit my ignorance, despite my fear of appearing stupid. It means I should discover in myself those beliefs I hold so dear that I spontaneously protect them from criticism—and then courageously open them to criticism. It means leaving my allegiance-based commitments at the door—as Republican, or Jew, or union worker, or attorney, or artist, or CEO, or principal—while bringing the wisdom born of my allegiances to the table.

Equally difficult is moving behind the protective screens held up by others. The more experienced I become in uprooting bias and shortfalls in conversion in myself, the better prepared I will be to address them in others. As good collaborators know, it takes great sensitivity and respect for another's allegiances. It means learning to *invite* the other person—and be invited—to honestly explore alternatives. It means unlearning the combative techniques of debate, dodging rhetorical techniques when others use them, and learning a way of dialog between hearts as well as minds.

Still, there will always be impasses where even hearts cannot meet. A typical cause is egotism. Some leaders seek money, others seek fame, and still others seek power. These kinds of egotism apply across the board, from political leaders to leaders in academics, science, marketing, law, the arts and so on. Another typical cause is loyalism, where minds are closed to the benefits of other groups and dedicated to finding reasons to justify blocking their advance. Here, the spirit of engagement should aim for the sort of "respectful combat" that can disagree on content while maintaining mutual respect and being open to friendship. It comes down to a form of lobbying that rises above the familiar trade-offs between groups and reaches a level of persuasion and accommodation about what is really better. In many cases, it will be particularly helpful if both parties can rise above the bias of commonsensism and examine the issue from the long view of history and the deep view of scientific analyses.

Is Dialectic a Method?

Taken together, amplifying and assessing the results of researchers, interpreters, historians, and other dialecticians, and doing so in a spirit of affective engagement, amounts to improving those results that are compatible with the three-fold conversions, and to reversing those results that are not compatible.[56] This is indeed a method in essentially the same sense that the natural sciences have a method: it produces results that are progressive and cumulative. Certainly there are blind alleys and oversights, but it falls within the field of *dialectic* to name which alleys are blind and replace oversights with insights.

Why should we count on this method of *dialectic* to improve the human condition? The more fundamental question is, Do we have any alternative? Other than the normative drives of our authenticity, there are no other, more fundamental, criteria by which we can do any better. We also have history on our side. Within any valid improvements in our life together we can discern a dialectical sifting of better from worse through open dialog among participants. By making this sifting a specialty in ethics, we raise to the level of formal process what has happened informally ever since we first appeared on the planet.

Conversion

It is ultimately personal development that makes the difference between doing better and doing worse. In *dialectic*, ethicists collaborate on revealing this personal development to one another in the hope of inviting or advancing conversion. In *foundations* they collaborate on a model of morality designed to raise and formulate the right questions. But the personal conversion of the ethicist lies outside this collaboration. *Dialectic* reveals the fundamental issues about learning, choosing and loving, but it is up to the ethicist to embrace the fully open horizons of the three conversions. Once embraced, the ethicist works out the *foundations* that express the terms and relations of those horizons that he or she will use to express moral standards, to coordinate principles and policies, and to communicate moral views.

Earlier we noted how these conversions are not sudden transformations. In each, there is an initial breakthrough to the new, unrestricted horizon, followed by a gradual expansion. As participants in an ongoing collaboration, ethicists cannot claim they have completed the expansion. But as they engage in the specialties of *foundations, standards, coordination,* and *communications*, dialectical engagement can be counted on to continue broadening their horizons and purging any views that are not consistent with the three conversions.

Foundations

In chapter 9, we described how *foundations* in ethics develops a model of the moral subject in community and history. The goal is to provide assertions and categories that represent the converted horizons within which subsequent moral standards, coordinating systems, and concrete communications may be expressed. As grounded in the normative exigences of anyone's consciousness, these assertions and categories will be verifiable. These conversions will show not only in the intellectual views and moral standards of ethicists but also in an affective engagement with one another and in an affective engagement with at least the *question* whether a supreme being lovingly invites a total affective engagement as well.

From the beginning of this work, we have relied on such a foundational model of the moral subject in community and history. Here are some of the main assertions we have presented so far:

- Moral norms originate in human consciousness, which contains the fundamental normative drives on which all externalized moral norms depend.
- These fundamental normative drives are found in the experienced exigences to be self-transcending, or authentic.
- Authenticity is a compound exigence to be attentive, intelligent, reasonable, responsible, and in love.
- Our consciousness may explore distinct realms of moral reflection, each with its specialized criteria: common sense, theory (empirical sciences and systems-based theories in philosophy and theology), historical scholarship, aesthetics, religious transcendence, and philosophies that follow a generalized empirical method.
- Inner symbols (the inner links between images and affects) can both maintain and upset our priorities. But it is by value judgments that we choose our priorities.
- Beauty—whether natural or artistic—symbolizes the transcending exigence. This is the experience of always seeking more truth, more values, and more profound interpersonal engagement in the pursuit of being our best.
- Morality regards historical realities, not abstract qualities.
- The history of ethics reveals three revolutionary transformations: (1) From symbolic/practical to universal moral standards; (2) then to historical-critical reflection; (3) then to method in ethics.
- Most of what we know and value are not first-hand achievements but an inheritance. As inherited, they are

subject to judgments of value on the reliability of their sources and applicability to new situations.

- The normative drives of consciousness are prone to distortion by bias (neurosis, egotism, loyalism, common-sensism) and willfulness (acting against one's better judgment; sin), which compromise a moral heritage.
- A creative movement in history brings moral progress. But creativity is wounded by bias and willfulness. An affective movement in history heals a wounded creativity by reversing the inner inclinations of bias and willfulness and repairing their effects in concrete situations.
- Differences among ethicists may be *perspectival* (the perspectives gained from their life experiences), *developmental* (the greater and lesser knowledge, skills and abilities as one matures), or *radical* (radically opposed views on learning, choosing, and loving).
- Radically deficient stands on learning, choosing and loving are remedied by intellectual, moral, and affective conversions, respectively.
- A collaborative model of ethical reflection identifies eight distinct but related tasks in ethics. It justifies this view by an appeal to a personal verification of what occurs when we learn, choose, and love.
- The *data* for ethical reflection are drawn from concrete situations as well as from inner events of mind and heart. The *criteria* are drawn from the concretely functioning normative drives of consciousness.

As a structured set of categories that represent verifiable elements in moral process, these assertions help us pose questions in ways that can produce answers compatible with each other within the full foundational model. In other words, these statements comprise the *heuristics* of ethics—the features of answers to moral questions that help us pose those questions. Just as algebra does not give any answers but rather specifies the conditions that an x must meet, so *foundations* does not pass moral judgments on situations, but rather the conditions for validity that such moral judgments must meet.

Questions formulated in technically-defined assertions and categories like these result from reflection on what occurs when we make choices. The intellectual task of ethicists specializing in *foundations* is to refine these questions. They do this by keeping up to date on studies of how people maintain world views, develop their symbols, engage one another in shared living, establish social and cultural institutions, and deal with such transcendent mysteries as death, love, fidelity, hope, and inspiration. They refine their heuristics also by monitoring the progress of ethics itself in the specialty *dialectic* as new meanings and trends come to light. Besides these structured questions, there are many other familiar ethical categories whose meaning can be rooted in an analysis of self-transcendence. I have prepared short articles that define, in terms of self-transcending operations, the following 31 familiar ethical categories:

Authority and Power	Principles and People
Autonomy and Self-Transcendence	Rights and Duties
Consequences, Ideals, and Obligations	Right and Wrong
Macroeconomics and Global Progress	Stories and Moral Imagination
Metaphysics and Self-Appropriation	Transcendent Value and Religion
Natural Right and Human Rights	Value and Consciousness
Objectivity and Subjectivity	Virtues and Values
Praxis and Practicality	

I thought it better to leave these articles to the appendix, since they each go into a depth that might distract from the present focus on functional specialties in ethics.

THE FUNCTIONING GROUP OF SPECIALIZATIONS

The foregoing section on "Opening Horizons" present the elements of *dialectic*, conversion, and *foundations* that make all eight specialties a well-functioning group. As a group they represent the new dimension in the next revolution in ethics.

Engaging the Past

In the four specialties on the left side of the circle of ethical reflection, ethicists engage the past in the richest possible manner. The range of this engagement stretches from the dawn of history to the present day. So they may assess evidence of Neanderthal respect for the dead as well as this morning's business meeting about terminating employees.

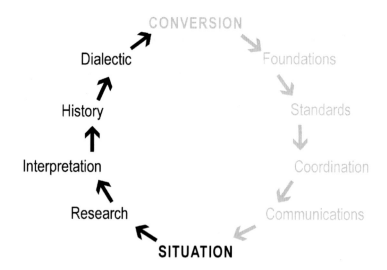

This engagement involves gathering facts, discerning people's assumptions and intentions, and seeing the larger historical contexts of the lives of individuals and groups. But because engagement is a two-way street, ethicists go beyond information-gathering on the past to allow the past to challenge their present horizons.

Research

How does this two-way engagement occur in *research*? Here, ethicists gather data for correlations and functional analyses. The surface qualitative evidence—some revealing values explicitly (such as personal letters and autobiographies) and others revealing values implicitly (symbolically in poetry, art and architecture, and quantitatively in data on how people spend their money). Of course, researchers in all human studies may do the same. But in the specialty *research*, ethicists should be on the lookout for clues about the priorities that shape people's decisions and about the authenticity of their heritage.

As they consider what data are relevant to moral issues, ethicists may grow more aware of certain limitations in their own moral horizons. For example, which of these pieces of evidence would best reveal the moral priorities of bank CEOs: their credit card statements, their attendance at religious services, or their length of vacations? The simple effort to answer for yourself could well lead to a discovery about your own moral priorities.

Interpretation

There is a similar two-way engagement in *interpretation*. Here, ethicists analyze the data from *research* to propose what people meant by their statements on moral issues, by their actual behaviors, and by their literary and aesthetic products. Again, analysts and exegetes in the human studies do the same. But as ethicists pay particular attention to what people meant and preferred, they aim is to support assessments of the moral worth of these particular meanings and preferences. Here are some typical areas:

- Among official statements (such as constitutional documents and policy statements of governments, religious bodies, businesses, and schools), ethicists aim to understand the intent behind them and any conflicts between the formal policies of an enterprise and its real policies as evidenced by which rules are actually enforced.
- Among sources of information, they seek to understand which sources people trust. This involves understanding the policies and constituents of various media.

- In financial records, they identify the actual priorities of a group or an individual by tracking where the money flows.
- In psychotherapy, they aim to understand how individuals understand their own lives, with particular attention to what they mean by "better."
- In social systems, they reveal a community's priorities by analyzing the behaviors, choices, and trade-offs of its members, with particular attention to disparities between the haves and have-nots.
- In macroeconomics, they aim to identify where the pure profits of supplier companies are directed so that, in *dialectic*, an assessment may be made whether the current economic climate would benefit more by reinvestments or by raising the wages of their workers.
- Among cultural symbols, they analyze the persons, institutions, and human accomplishments that a community regards as noble or degrading.
- And among the writings of philosophers, they seek to understand their underlying intellectual, moral, and affective commitments.

Here too, as ethicists dig into the meanings and priorities of real people, they may unearth limitations in their own moral horizons. A woman majoring in political science may pick up *Markings*—reflections by Dag Hammarskjöld, former secretary of the United Nations. She will not find much on political science there, but she will find nugget after nugget of political wisdom born of his heartfelt concern for people all over the globe. A book like this can open her affective horizon.

History

This mutual engagement also occurs at the level of history. According to Lonergan's model, the specialty "history" aims to elucidate what is going forward over time unbeknownst to those who contribute to and yet are affected by this movement. It leaves to *dialectic* any moral assessment of these movements. Today, for example, there appears to be a "secularization" of all sorts of institutions and attitudes formerly wed to religious belief. What will historians say about these our times in decades to come? Historical insight here will be welcome, especially by those who feel baffled by the loss of religious sensibilities, despite their strenuous efforts to stem the tide. What they seek is understanding, not lament; insight, not condemnations.

To focus only on what was going forward at any time without passing moral judgments is a skill in its own right. It means tabling questions about better and worse. It is difficult enough to tease out of hundreds of documents a previously unnoticed pattern of events without tackling the quite different task of passing moral judgment on them. Ranke's *History of the Popes, their Church and State* (1834-1836) traced the intricate involvement of the Roman Catholic Church with politics without passing any moral judgment. He set the standard of fairness for historians ever since, even though at the time his fellow Protestants criticized the work precisely for being "neutral."

Historians' most obvious contribution people's moral horizons is to destroy cultural myths about wars, geographic rights, commerce, economics, social justice, and the like, since many a high-minded moral opinion floats too far above the intricate tangles of reality. Their less obvious but certainly more constructive contribution is to force their readers to really engage the past, and to understand the struggles of people who, like themselves, must always deal with ambiguity and risk. That very effort leads ethicists to wonder about their own assumptions about national destiny or cultural achievements. As they consider the currents of individualism, or of materialism, or of fatalism, they cannot help but wonder about their own views on life.

Dialectic

In *dialectic*, as we saw, ethicists amplify and assess the findings of *research*, *interpretation* and *history* with a view to engaging the past as fully as possible. They point to areas of research that will better validate current opinions about the nature of moral problems. They promote the meanings of some documents as worthy of attention, and they demote others that omit or misinterpret authentic values. To the histories that focus on what actually happened, they add evaluations both of actual events and of the mindsets of the historians who wrote about them. They not only learn about the past; they not only distinguish between the better and the worse of the past; by a full engagement they also allow the past to speak to them as thy muse about what currents in history may be carrying them along right now.

At the same time, the more they expose to one another their own social, cultural, philosophical and religious commitments, the better are the odds of engaging fellow ethicists at all these levels. In this forum of a mutual exposure of horizons, it becomes more likely that views consistent with conversion are strengthened and views inconsistent with conversion are left aside. The strategy, again, is not to debate but to lift the curtain on basic differences. It is not to bargain by trade-offs but to deliberate together on what is actually better or worse. It counts on the natural exigences to be fully authentic persons both to impel the unconverted to open their horizons and to remind the converted that their openness is an ongoing demand.

Engaging the Future

Ethicists also engage the future in the richest possible manner by means of the four specialties on the right side of the circle of ethical reflection. The range of this engagement stretches from the present day to any foreseeable future. So it may cover decisions about removing a patient's life support this afternoon as well as global standards for use of fossil fuels.

Engaging the future differentiates into four specialties. In *foundations*, ethicists express the fundamental intellectual, moral, and affective commitments that arise from their conversions. In *standards*, they canonize narratives of the past and lay out a vision of a better future; they establish moral principles and set institutional policies. In *coordination*, they organize the *standards* into a coherent philosophical system and collaborate with other disciplines in human studies—historians, exegetes, philosophers, theologians psychologists, sociologists, anthropologists, and economists—to develop policies that dovetail with one another. In *communications*, they adapt the moral message to a variety of audiences and to differences in media.

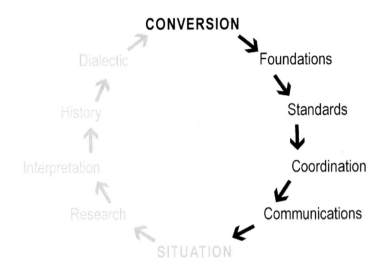

But full engagement is even more. Ethicists not only have a moral message for the future; they not only work with others in making life better. By a full engagement they also share with others affectively. Their message is not just information; not just advice; it is a personal witness. It carries the weight of the prophet who experiences the tribulations of life and who speaks for those who are heavily burdened. This should not be surprising, given that the model is based on an affective conversion in the ethicist. This full affective engagement appears in each of the four specialties that engage the future.

Foundations

Foundations, as we saw, specializes in expressing the intellectual, moral, and affective horizons of converted ethicists. Each of these expressions has its own character. The intellectual horizon is expressed in the special categories for stating moral standards, explaining moral systems and processes, and directing moral action. These categories are interconnected so that they form a comprehen-sive "model of the human"—a network of terms for asking ques-tions about individual persons living in a community with an ongoing history. The moral horizon is expressed in criteria for better and worse that they incorporate in their "models of the human," particularly the normative demands inherent to human consciousness and the exigence to align feelings with the assent from vital, to social, to cultural, to personal, and finally to transcendent values. The affective horizon is expressed in references to the full, unrestricted range of self-transcendence dominated by love. That is, within their formulations of a "model of the human," there is a straightforward acknowledgement that the pull to self-transcendence has no a priori limitations and that the question of God cannot be excluded from ethics.

Standards

Standards expresses fundamental moral guidelines rooted in conversion. These guidelines may appear in strongly incarnational form: Vision statements about best outcomes describe long-term objectives, set measurable intermediate goals, and recommend specific procedures. Based on conversion, best outcomes are not only the material conditions of life; they also include a deepening of authenticity in participants. Then there are the edifying narratives of the origins of one's company, church, clan, or nation, such as the history of Poland's Solidarity movement. We have the emblematic myths about human nature, such as Homer's *Odyssey*. We have personal moral exemplars, such as Gandhi and Mother Teresa. And we see expressions of moral qualities in a variety of aesthetic forms, such as drama in Shakespeare's *King Lear*, poetry in Hopkins's *Wreck of the Deutschland*, and sculpture in Michelangelo's *David*.

Guidelines may also appear in conceptual terms. There are the familiar prohibitions like "False advertising is wrong" and admonitions like "Treat others as you would like to be treated." There institutional and professional policies that appear in descriptions of "how we proceed around here" and in the more juridical manner of a code of ethics.

Now any hedonist can teach moral doctrine. While the above examples show the *forms* of doctrinal expression, the *content* determines whether or not they fall within the specialty *standards*. That content has been sifted by the specialty *dialectic*, so that elements incompatible with conversion are removed and elements compatible with conversion

are amplified. The language for expressing moral policies and principles are drawn directly from the categories worked out in the
specialty *foundations*. Similarly, narratives, visions, myths, exemplars
and aesthetic expressions need to maintain their own powerful
language of hope, but since that language by itself is typically diffuse
and ambiguous, it anticipates commentary in the specialty *coordination*,
which we will look at shortly.

If the specialty *standards* is rooted in intellectual, moral, and affective
conversion, then expressions of moral standards engage those who
welcome the moral guidance in all three dimensions of conversion.
Intellectually, moral standards carry agenda; they express values meant
as guides for action. Unfortunately, people tend to call upon moral
standards more to prevent actions deemed "wrong" than to promote
actions deemed "better." But positive moral standards are important
for the young as they learn how best to get involved in politics,
participate in workplace negotiations, raise a family, and so on.
Positive standards are also important for adults as new technologies
and new financial instruments raise new moral questions, which we
currently see in discussions on genetics research and on regulatory
standards for banks and global corporations. In *standards*, ethicists may
legitimately condemn what should *not* be done, but their main concern
regards what should be done, which demands no small measure of
intellectual creativity.

Morally, standards are promoted by the personal endorsement of
the ethicist. Rooted in their conversions, they do not just "teach"
moral standards; they also bear witness to them. Their aim is to
evoke a real assent to the values they express. This is quite different
from the notional assent to values that function mainly to identify
ourselves as members of "constituencies." A real assent to values is
reflected in taking personal responsibility in actual situations. It is
one thing, say, for a woman to teach the ethics of nuclear warfare
and quite another to get arrested for protesting on the Capitol
steps.

Affectively, the ethicists who promote moral standards share the
joys and sorrows of those who seek moral guidance. They do not
dictate these standards to others; as morally converted, they first
share the life experiences that raise the moral questions, and as affectively converted, they then *share a welcome* of the moral standards

that point toward what is better. Here is where the edifying narratives, emblematic myths, and moral exemplars also come into play. As symbols of the community's values, they provide the emotional energy and the fellow feeling that help each person pursue those values in the face of opposition. One identifies with the finest hours of one's history.

In these respects, ethicists specializing in *standards* strengthen a community. They express common judgments about incarnate values in the community's heritage. They promote a shared commitment to achieving common purposes, and they encourage the mutual commitments to pursue those purposes together. This is a far cry from any moral authoritarianism that in fact inhibits genuine moral growth.

Here, in proposing standards, is where ethicists make statements about right and wrong. They may express them as moral principles or as the policies of a social body. In the perspective of a generalized empirical method, right and wrong are not reified ideas in the heavens. They are history lessons. Ethicists discern the meaning of statements about right and wrong in *dialectic* by evaluating historical movements. Converted ethicists select the lessons best suited for improving life in the future, and they formulate the lessons succinctly as principles or policies, using terms drawn from the models of the human developed in *foundations*—terms such as authenticity, openness, bias, conversion, hierarchy of values, and being in love. Knowing that standards arise from history and speak to people in history, and they fill out their meaning by referring to that history. Knowing the difference between an Ethics of Law and an Ethics of Better, they complement standards about right and wrong with standards about better and worse. Knowing the power of affective conversion to instill hope, they add the narratives, myths, exemplars, and aesthetic expressions of the better ways we can live our lives.

Coordination

The previous specialty, *standards*, lays out moral objectives and attitudes rooted in the history of converted forebears and adapted to the present by converted ethicists. To put these into practice, there is a need for coordination along several fronts. There are the hermeneutical tasks of linking the ambiguous meanings of *incarnational* expressions to unambiguous expressions of principle and policy. There is the intellectual task of organizing the *principles* themselves into an intelligible, seamless whole, as well as the practical tasks of coordinating the *policies* issuing from these principles with policies of other institutions. Each of these tasks presents a unique set of challenges.

Narrative and aesthetic expressions of moral living are highly ambiguous. They can powerfully move our feelings but the values to which our feelings respond will differ according to our different moral horizons. As we saw, individuals can fall anywhere along a hierarchy of values ranging from mere personal pleasure to a fully detached and unrestricted desire for the better. So there is a need to select from among the various interpretations of particular incarnational expressions brought to light in dialectic. Ethicists working in standards look for those interpretations that best link their emotional impact to the transcending exigence experienced by those hearing the stories, listening to symphonies, seeing paintings, reading poetry, and so forth. Their task is not to promote certain works; they leave that to specialists in communication. Rather it is essentially to articulate, in categories grounded in the normative events of consciousness, the meanings and values of narrative and aesthetic forms that relate to people's innate desire to be fully open.

Many conceptual expressions of moral guidelines can seem unimpeachable as they stand, but are difficult to integrate with other principles. For example, it seems inconsistent to oppose abortion yet support capital punishment. These problems of harmonizing rely initially on *dialectic* to surface contradictions, and more basically on *foundations* to provide categories and structures with unambiguous and consistent meanings. When it comes to proposing positive principles, the effort is to harmonize them in language that is readily understood by people who have little understanding of ethics as a discipline. Similarly, the policies that derive from these principles need to be coordinated with policies proposed by other institutions. Treatment policies in medicine may need coordination with those in psychotherapy. Procedural rules in social work should dovetail with protocols in criminal justice. Research standards protocols in technology should connect to emission standards in industry.

One particularly important way of coordinating policies is *strategy*. We commonly think of a strategy is simply a plan to accomplish a goal, and of coordination as mainly the assignment of tasks. But concretely, plans always capture limited resources. So, realistically, a strategy is essentially a plan to deploy limited resources—time, space, material energy, and laborers. How we deploy our resources—for medical care, for wars, for education, for scientific research—are decisions that always pay some Paul at some Peter's expense. Directing money toward medical research to make life longer will divert money from social programs aimed to make life richer. The very effort to coordinate the deployment of resources often raises unnoticed questions about one's actual moral priorities. In this perspective, ethicists will think of a *strategic principle* as a statement that first identifies the gainers and losers in any deployment of resources, then prioritizes the allocation of resources, and finally develops convincing rationale for publication.

The field for these coordinating activities is enormous, complex, and constantly changing. We can expect that each culture will coordinate in its own way, selecting the incarnational and conceptual expressions which, through *dialectic*, seems best suited to meeting their respective moral issues. There are the macro-cultures of language groups and religions, the mezzo-cultures of nations and professional disciplines, and the mini-cultures of communities based on locale or special interests. Moreover, the task of coordination at any level is radically complicated by the fact that even when ethicists stand on conversion for their moral views, the people with whom they collaborate may stand on reputation or profit or loyalty to their constituencies. As we saw, here is where sharing descriptive views of history, and forging conceptual principles and policies inevitably overlaps with the dialectical process of a mutual exposure of horizons. Ideally, the dialectical process will draw the unconverted toward conversion, but this can take a long time. Still, one thing converted ethicists have in their favor is the expectation that asking collaborators to *amplify* by explaining more about the sources, motives and consequences of their positions may uncover bias and willfulness. One obvious lesson here is that the ethicist involved in these aspects of coordination had better be ready to spend time to ensure as full an engagement as feasible in the circumstances. It seems essential first to establish affective bonds of mutual trust.

Communications

Finally, there is the specialty of communicating moral wisdom effectively. Here is where the work of all converted ethicists bears fruit. I trust it is not absurdly obvious to say that the work of many ethicists has come to naught because their moral wisdom was never tested in the field. This often happens because ethics has specializations, and specialists typically forget that their work is demanded by problems originating in historical situations. For their work to be effective, they need to make room for adaptations needed in newly emerging historical circumstances.

Still, *communications* bears fruit all over the place. Recipients of moral guidance range from individuals to global communities. Moral guidance is sought by a dying woman who wants to end her pain. It is sought by all sorts of pairs seeking agreement on mutual expectations—parent-child, teacher-student, employer-employee, and professional-client. In all cases, there need to be adaptations to differences in culture and language as well as to media differences, seizing the opportunities inherent in some media and taking caution with the inherent limitations of others.

A far more fundamental problem involves adaptations to differences in horizons. Essentially, these are the differences in the set of questions people regard as important. Talk as much as you like to someone who does not understand your question and you may as well talk to a post. Effective talking needs to take into account the several ways horizons can differ from one another. In this respect, ethicists will simultaneously engage in both *communications* and *dialectic.*

In *communications,* they convey moral views in terms rooted in conversion. That is, to promote behaviors or policies, they invite their hearers to notice people's actual experience, to make intelligent connections to other policies and social systems, to verify the reasonableness of moral views in light of actual historical movement, to pay attention to their conscience, and to feel the noble desires they share with others and inherited from honored forebears.

In *dialectic*, they address differences as they arise. With perspectival differences, your life experiences are different from mine, so we do not have the same questions. Here, one ethicist aims to enlarge another's horizon by sharing questions on moral issues so that a merely perspectival difference might be recognized as also complementary to one's own views. With developmental differences, the most familiar issue is what to tell the kids. Knowing that the young rely heavily on notions of right and wrong prior to the discovery of their autonomous responsibility, wise ethicists will adjust their language accordingly. Then there are the radical oppositions about what learning is, how choosing should occur, and whether or not to let love lead. We saw how these oppositions are overcome only through intellectual, moral, and affective conversions. Here, experience suggests that *communications* will generally be more effective by aiming first at affective engagement. By engaging the hearer on the level of mutual trust, defenses against disturbing questions are lowered.

Communications clearly must adapt to the egocentric and reward/punishment moral world of the child, and to the teenager's world of social conventions and personal roles, before moving into the adult's world of rule-making, the autonomy of conscience, and a fully open horizon. Equally common, but often overlooked, are differences in the levels of bias in hearers. An adult neurotic does well to learn that all "shoulds" originate in people, some of them neurotic in their own way. The egotist does not need to be convinced about the *idea* of a common good as much as being *invited* to share the burden of pursuing it with others. Loyalists do well to trust their own moral judgments rather than the conventions of their communities as the final arbiters of what the better may be. To justify moral opinions by appealing to history or ethical theory works only with minds already familiar with these deeper dimensions of morality.

There are also developmental differences regarding entire realms of moral reflection. Everyone has some measure of common sense, but only some are familiar with moral issues in the theoretical realms explored by science, philosophy, and theology. Only some are familiar with moral issues in historical studies, in the arts, and in worship. And only those familiar with at least one of these

additional realms will be capable of thinking in the realm of a
generalized empirical method that compares the different manners
of moral reflection in two or more realms. Here, it is important not
to scare hearers who have little notion of the kinds of questions
that distinguish these different realms. Rather, some communications should introduce them to some basic issues in a realm that is
new to them.

The overall aim in *communications* is not just to tell people what to
do. What is communicated is not just moral opinion. Nor is it only
to join forces with others in pressing for change. It is also to invite
people to discover how their deepest desire for authenticity is met
by joining forces for making life better in specific ways. This
demands the full engagement of ethicists—not only what they
think but also what next steps they deeply desire on account of a
shared and unrestricted love. It demands a presence that will
enlighten practitioners and administrators about the importance of
noticing their inner exigences for authenticity. It demands a
witness of collaboration, in an air of open exploration, by men and
women seriously engaged, humbled by the burden, and joyful in the
enterprise of improving life on our planet.

11. CONCLUSION

THE STRATEGY

I have been extending the invitation of Bernard Lonergan to discover the methods natural to our minds and hearts. For over 50 years now, his work in philosophy, theology and economics has generated international discussion. But the enterprise is not concerned with winning debates or convincing people to try a new formula. Rather, Lonergan invites us to notice within ourselves the common normative drives on which all learning, choosing, and loving are based, and to consider where we stand regarding these horizons. So, expanding Lonergan's invitation into the field of ethics, I bid you to engage in a revolutionary, horizon-sharing program that tests all moral opinions against those normative drives.

Like any revolution, outcomes seldom rise to the level of hopes. Still, we have one good reason to be optimistic. The strategy aligns quite well with standard scientific method. It requires noticing the experiential data of our own transcendent movements; formulating hypotheses on how these movements produce learning, choosing, and loving; and verifying for ourselves that these hypotheses make sense of all the relevant experiential data. It is a self-correcting strategy. Even as we identify new elements in our self-transcending nature, or revise our hypotheses about those we already identified, the strategy remains the same: What sort of inner normative drives guide our learning, choosing and loving? Indeed, do these three categories of learning, choosing, and loving adequately represent what it means to be fully human? And how firmly are public moral opinions on concrete issues grounded in the normative drives that we in fact experience?

A REVOLUTION IN HUMAN STUDIES

This strategy for grounding moral views in our personal commitment to cooperate with our transcendent nature widens the field of ethics to encompass whatever concerns humans. And by "concerns humans," I mean anything about which we humans are actually concerned. More than rules, laws, codes, and exemplars, the strategy encompasses any effort to improve human well-being and any surrender to movements of love we call divine. And it promotes an affective openness that knows the power of symbols to instill hope. For we are also concerned about beauty. We cannot help it. It symbolizes for us our ultimate hope that the universe is not pointless, fruitless, or loveless.

More specifically, the next revolution in ethics will be a revolution in the human studies as we know them today. Currently, investigators in both the human sciences and in the humanities disagree among themselves on their respective methods, and practitioners disagree on how to improve situations in their fields. This is the problem that practically defines the next revolution in ethics: What method can we agree on for improving human life? To eliminate alternatives, we noted the shortcomings in ethical positivism, ethical naïveté, ethical optimism, and ethical relativism. We approached agreement by invitations to verify the workings of norms of consciousness, the several distinct realms of meaning available to consciousness, the dysfunctions of bias and willfulness, the healing power of love, and the need for intellectual, moral, and affective conversions. The next revolution in ethics is based on a personal discovery and verification of these ways we transcend ourselves.

Like most paradigm shifts, the revolution will likely occur along lines of affectivity and respect among scholars, scientists, and practitioners. These ethicists will not drive out old ideas; they probably will go about their business in the new, more invitational manner that invites a mutual exposure of horizons. Advances will occur in small pockets, but if attention to method produces better living, notice will be taken. We may also expect (perhaps *hope* is the better word) that the title "ethicist" will be transitional, since all human studies will deal with moral issues explicitly.

What might this incorporation of ethical concerns in human studies look like in the various professional disciplines?

Historiography: Historians still describe the emerging trends of a particular group but also fill out the ramifications of these trends for other groups and for the future. Following this amplification, they will assess those trends, in the style of the specialty *dialectic*.

Exegesis: Scholars interpreting texts will still report on what their authors believe but also promote setting their interpretations in the context of history, particularly the evaluative type that names where moral progress and moral decline took place.

Philosophy: Philosophers will still convey the wisdom of the past to the needs of the present but also articulate their theories in terms that are clearly linked to normative events in consciousness.

Theology: Theologians will still give historical and philosophical explanations of the meanings of religious doctrines but also collaborate with philosophers in grounding all views in the experience of an unrestricted normative drive toward all truth, the ever better, and the total engagement with transcendent mystery.

Psychology: Therapists will still use *analytical* techniques for identifying causes of neuroses but also use *healing* techniques for reversing neuroses, egotism, loyalism, commonsensism and willfulness.

Cultural anthropology: Investigators will still describe and classify cultural symbols, but also regard these symbols as carriers of the transcending exigence as experienced by specific communities. They will still study religions as phenomena, but will also identify which beliefs and practices need enrichment, and which are downright decadent.

Economics: Policy experts will still report on how money is flowing but also propose moral principles that specify where money *should* flow. They will recommend that the measure of a successful economic system is not profits but the improvement of people's well-being. Using ongoing analyses of current conditions, they will continually recommend rebalancing the flow—now toward capital investments, now toward higher wages, now toward strengthening infrastructures through taxes, now toward ensuring the basic well-being of the marginalized through charities.

Sociology: Sociologists will still study the patterns of a community's social arrangements but also make critical judgments on the quality of life among its members and propose policies for better living.

Political science: Experts will still analyze various political models shaping a nation's government but also publish moral critiques of the political, philosophical and religious commitments of political leaders and their constituencies.

Law: Experts in constitutional law will still interpret the intentions of the authors of a nation's founding documents but also take a stand on the adequacy of intellectual, moral, and affective horizons of these founding authors.

Art criticism: Critics will still spell out the effects of artistic products on people but also assess how deeply artists are wonder-struck by the mystery of self-transcendence in human affairs and analyze how effectively they elicit that wonder in their publics.

In each of these disciplines, personal horizons become public matters. Neurotic obsessions matter because they skew the deliberation needed for individuals making responsible choices that affect others. Self-centeredness and careerism matter because they skew the deliberation needed to reach reasonable compromises for the good of the group. Group interests matter, and although the "special interest group" has always been a public subject, its driving dynamic of a narrowed intelligence has yet to be the focus of moral criticism. And historical forgetfulness, myth and naïveté matter, since all moral opinions emerge from mindsets shaped by history, by symbolic narratives, and by the demanding concerns of an overrated common sense.

A REVOLUTION IN INTERNATIONAL RELATIONS

We may also look for a revolution in international relations. When group interests and historical forgetfulness infect the minds of politicians, the damage can be horrendous. Nations can be so obsessed with their "national self-interest" that they deliberately impede the social progress of other nations, thus breeding resentment, hatred, and retaliatory terrorist attacks. Combine this with historical forgetfulness of the judicious negotiating that was fruitfully carried out in previous eras by leaders on both sides, and we have a simple-minded populace. Citizens of underdog nations embrace myths of Victimhood, while those in the overdog nations assume a God-given destiny of superiority. Absent the controls of intelligence, reason, responsibility and love, social policy is driven by the feelings and images proper to the symbolic exigence but without the higher controls of the transcending exigence.

It is a rather straightforward matter to sketch the main types of problems in international relations from the perspective of a generalized empirical method. Citizens unfamiliar with the realms of science and scholarship will uncritically absorb a compromised moral heritage. Among the biases, egotism generates greed and power mongering; loyalism suppresses genuine concern for other nations; and commonsensism dismisses the value of in-depth analyses and historical-critical methods. Add our ubiquitous willfulness to the mix, and the downward spiral of decline grows steeper.

Effective therapy, however, is an altogether different matter. The healing of bias and willfulness is complicated beyond the easy generalizations of philosophers, theologians, scientists and historians. Certainly there is no easy fix. Indeed, since our creativity is wounded at its roots, no fix can be permanent. Still, some generalization may be helpful to bring into sharp relief where our international priorities ought to lie.

One is the priority of affective engagement. This is the familiar territory of the "friendly nations." They collaborate not only for mutual economic gains but also to have friends to count on in times of trouble. They trust one another to follow long-standing informal customs, as opposed to a mutual suspicion shored up with its industry of spies, counterspies, border patrols, and import/export regulatory agencies.

Another is the priority of the scientific and scholarly work needed to clarify problems and propose solutions. Much of this work will aim to demolish the simple-minded national myths such as "eminent domain" and "rights of redress." More constructively, economists will develop plans for increasing collaboration, while historians will make clear which national goals are driven by old resentments and therefore in need of healing.

Strategic Ideals

To promote further discussion, let me suggest four principles of international relations. A first is that a symbol for ideal international relations should be strategic. It is fine to speak of World Peace, but this defines a goal, not a strategy. It pictures life as serene and unchanging, which no one really expects. The symbol is essentially negative and static. It represents the absence of war, not the presence what might prevent wars. A positive and dynamic alternative might promote "World Talk" to represent the ongoing international activities we hope for. Talking symbolizes people who are genuinely interested in mutual understanding—the ongoing give-and-take involved in keeping any friendship alive. It pins hopes on authenticity in dialog rather than a utopian ideal order. The goal is still to achieve a common understanding, but prior to reaching that goal, and even when that goal seems terribly distant, talking springs from a mutual trust. We explore one another's horizons, hoping to find a common appreciation for wisdom and virtue. And where horizons are closed, talking is the ordinary way we notice that more openness is needed—sometimes in others and sometimes in ourselves.

As an ever present way of dealing with one another, a symbol such as World Talk also symbolizes an operational ideal at every sort of level below the international. We can see this if we take "world" to include the many "worlds" of shared concerns—the academic world, the parenthood world, the Hindu world, the astronomy world, the art world. In all these worlds, when as enmities rise, talking falls, resentments fester, and subworlds split off. Obviously, talking through problems would go a long way to forestall these breakdowns. But even when mutual opposition stiffens, one side can still talk to those people whom its opposition trusts. We befriend the friend of our enemy. The talk is mediated, but the concerns and aspirations can still be conveyed.

Economic Development

A second principle is that international economic agencies are responsible for coordinating the economic development of all countries, where "development" is measured by rising standards of living. The strategy includes noble, ongoing diplomatic negotiations to propose how best to deploy economic resources to keep abreast with undulations in capital investments and consumer buying power. It requires phasing in rising wages among underdeveloped countries in ways that increase their participation as consumers *and investors*, even when the effort drives up prices for goods and services in developed countries.

No doubt, there will always be greed, personal and corporate. And we cannot underestimate how creatively greed can duck notice and hide revenues from regulators. But between the very greedy and the very noble, there stands The Economic System. Neither extreme can pursue its aims without it, and, truth be told, neither understands much about how it works. As a result, self-preservation kicks in. The greedy grab for themselves, but in the face of an incomprehensible system even the noble will secure what they can for love of their families and countries.

This is why all efforts will be useless without an underlying macroeconomic analysis that (a) defines the purpose of an economy as improving human living, as opposed to maximizing profits, and (b) explains how money actually works to improve life. Unfortunately, we have no such analysis. Macroeconomic specialists are still searching for a theory whose value is recognized by everyone. Currently, leading economists are largely unconvinced that objectively better initiatives can result from in-depth analyses by people for whom *better* means more than *better for us*. In the meantime, absurdities in the global economy slide deeper in that spiral by which rich nations grow more militantly self-protective while poor nations grow more militantly terrorizing.

Historical-Critical Research

A third principle is that historical-critical research is needed to improve international relations. It is no overstatement to say that every adversarial relation between nations is fed by historical myths on both sides. Each side thinks it understands the other, when in reality it only imagines. The symbolizing exigence can affect our sense of national pride so powerfully that we do not bother with questions about what really happened in our history. But some account of the complex history of relations between nations is absolutely necessary to overcome this bias of common sense toward picture thinking. Such historical accounts must meet the requirements of the specialties *history* and *dialectic.* That is, they should aim first at clarifying what actually was going forward in the relationships between certain nations. This alone would expose some of the myths that enthrall a national self-consciousness. They amplify these accounts by commentaries on today's attitudes and tomorrow's challenges. They add an assessment of what elements were truly better or truly worse. The gain is that at least the educated members of different nations will be exposed to in-depth explanations of the interactions between their respective countries. They, in turn, through their writing and teaching, will provide the public with historical understanding to replace naïve pictures about "those others." The ideal is that this historical-critical research is carried out through a collaborative initiative by historians from the very nations that suffer mutual alienation The collaboration itself is a core element in World Talking.

Ethics of Intelligent Forgiveness

This leads to a fourth principle of international relations, namely, the priority of intelligent forgiveness. Besides exposing national myths, historical-critical research will also make evident to the world the specific ways that events driven by bias and willfulness distort the ways estranged nations regard each other. Commonly, misunderstanding between nations hunkers down to a long winter of blame. Mutual blame easily justifies economic or military harassment, which only increases the likelihood of retaliation. The more accurately historians identify the underlying bias and willfulness as wounds in need of healing, going beyond simple blame, the more likely all sides will see what needs to be done. Today, this issue is quickly growing more urgent. The technology of bomb-making has effectively eliminated the expectation that wars must have "fronts." Retaliation can occur in our city's water reservoir or on our children's school bus.

The biases of power-mongering egotism, of uncritical loyalism, and of simple-minded commonsensism, along with the willful hatreds they foster, are easily condemned; but condemnations are fruitless. Moral and religious leaders may preach forgiveness, but, to be precise here, what we need is an *intelligent forgiveness.* An intelligent forgiveness understands, and understanding comes from historical-critical studies, from the social sciences, from philosophy and theology. Ideally, they should reveal, in study after study, the many ways our creativity is in need of some form of healing love. Forgiveness comes from an affective conversion that genuinely desires friendship as shown in a constant willingness to talk. An intelligent forgiveness, recognizing in "the other" the same wounded creativity as in oneself, envisions a shared concern to defeat a shared enemy in our wounded nature.

Philosophy plays an essential role in an ethics of intelligent forgiveness. In chapter 1, we noted that ancient Greek philosophers found universal moral norms in our common nature. Insofar as we recognize that our nature is wounded by bias and willfulness, then some form of mutual forgiveness of failings seems essential to any moral philosophy. Such a philosophy could rely on scholarly studies and the social sciences to demonstrate the functional effectiveness of an ethics of forgiveness. Religion, of course, has played a leading role in an ethics of forgiveness. All major monotheistic religions find universal moral norms in a forgiving love that God bears toward all. Insofar as God invites all to a divine friendship, then God's friends would bear this forgiving love toward one another. Theologians can promote forgiveness buttressed by intelligence by integrating their work with any human studies that recognize the normative demands and dysfunctions of human consciousness.

A REVOLUTION IN EDUCATION

Besides these revolutions in human studies and in international relations, a revolution in education is needed to pass on a moral worldview to that unrelenting invasion of the uncivilized we call children. This means strategically leading them forward through the stages of moral development, respecting the criteria they use as appropriate to their age, but keeping alive the driving concerns and symbols that will carry their development along to higher stages. Likewise, we need to further the education of adults whose schooling has been restricted to job training. It means widening their perspectives on the workings of the human spirit and the lessons of human history so that they learn how to collaborate more effectively on doing what is truly better wherever they may work. It means a liberal education that actually liberates.

For adults, the history of ethics is essential. They might be led through the historical stages of ethics, beginning from one's natural focus on action, to the ethical principles needed to guide action, to the historical-mindedness needed to understand the origins of ethical principles, and finally to the dialectical-mindedness needed to validate moral opinions by appeal to the normative drives of consciousness. The payoff should be rewarding, as students see the wisdom born of experience behind time-honored moral standards. Still, the passage from one stage to the next is fraught with apprehension, as one discovers that some time-honored moral view is little more than a taboo, while newer moral views demand humble reassessments of one's own conduct and the conduct of others.

But because authenticity is an exigence experienced by everyone, we can hope that those who recognize their desires to learn about learning, to choose how they choose, and to let love take the lead will give a hearing to those educators who can lead them forward with grace and tact. Below are a few salient themes to consider as long threads to weave through the educational process.

Open Horizons.

One theme is the *experience* of openness. This is the pull on consciousness to the fuller truth, to the ever better, and to richer personal engagements. We all experience it whenever we wonder about anything. But experiencing the pull is one thing, and understanding it is quite another. Understanding requires noticing and giving distinct names to the different experiences of being self-transcending. Then again, understanding the meaning of the term *openness* is not the same thing as noticing where it occurs. To recognize it in others requires probing what they say and do. Even then, we can honor openness in others without yet committing ourselves to living the best we can. Commitment requires a personal moral judgment that this openness is the best way to live and a deliberate decision to live accordingly.

Of all the value judgments to be made about these pulls on our consciousness, perhaps the most important is this: *Our best selves are self-transcending selves.*

This value aligns well with the dynamics of a universe that leans toward the ever better. Each system, from subatomic soup, up through cellular proliferation, and on up to human wonder, is transcended-yet-incorporated when it is open to a higher integration. The topmost level is open to whatever may be more fully self-transcending. As an evolutionary process, it is real people being open through their questions to whatever is more beautiful, more harmonious, more transparent, more worthy, and more loving, without knowing ahead of time what exactly this openness will make of their lives. It includes a lifelong openness at least to the question of God and perhaps to a loving engagement.

Aside from the stresses rooted in our bodies—like being pregnant, ill, exhausted, or intoxicated—we are also stressed in our spirits. What we can explain to students is that spiritual stress is natural; it is our exigence to live in a self-transcending manner against the forces of a dysfunctional heritage, personal bias and perverse willfulness. Think about it: Outside of physical causes, is there any stress you feel that is *not* related to going beyond social pressures, neurotic obsession, excessive self-concern, the judgments of peers, the sneaking suspicion that you are making decisions out of ignorance, or the rationalizations you must devise when you act against your better judgment?

By making openness—or self-transcendence—a theme in education, we give students a way to think about what goes on in people when they say odd things, write peculiar opinions, and behave strangely. It also gives them a way to think about how they deal with the inspirations that come to their own minds about what to say, write and do, even when it runs against what everyone else expects.

Historical Mindedness

Another theme is how all situations have histories. Teenagers need to realize that rules have dates; in most cases, people made the rules to protect their loved ones. Adults need to realize that rightness and wrongness are lessons drawn from the past. They express value judgments of real people, some living and some dead. Any discussions about what is right and wrong should acknowledge that these judgments always come from people whose horizons may be more or less open, and are therefore more or less reliable, and therefore subject to scrutiny.

Collective Responsibility

Connected to historical mindedness is the notion of a collective responsibility. We each have our individual responsibilities, and we also have responsibilities that dovetail with those of others. We may follow common moral standards and coordinate our efforts for common goals. But when outcomes are worse than expected, as they often are, a common reaction is to find out who is to blame. Blaming has its merits: we identify who needs to be trained or excluded from deliberations; we teach society what behaviors undermine the common good, including the often covert behaviors that spawn and nourish oppressive social structures. But blame becomes scapegoating if everyone else feels exonerated. What historical mindedness brings is the realization that bad outcomes also present exigences to everyone's responsibility for improving the situation. No individual may be blameworthy; no individual may be "held responsible;" but every capable individual is nonetheless responsible for doing better.

Training

There are several other areas where specific kinds of training will help implement a generalized empirical method in ethics.

Feeling

We saw how feelings are our first response to what may be better or worse. They also solidify our value judgments by forming inner symbols of better and worse, which enable us to respond quickly to new threats and opportunities. We then noted that in normal moral growth, a person's priorities evolve. There is an upward movement from the self-absorption of vital values, through the social values of cooperation, through the cultural values that distinguish real value from mere efficiency or habit, through the personal value of taking responsibility for one's life, to the fully transcendent value of an openness to whatever is truly better. At the same time, this upward development is made inviting from above downward by an environment of love, which fosters trusting one's autonomous instincts to be open, which encourages one to take a stand about what is really better in concrete situations, which triggers insight into how to collaborate, when puts the everyday care for vitality, health and safety into a most wholesome perspective.

At every step in this growth, we need to adapt our feelings to the higher notion of value. This adaptation requires taking charge of our feelings—wet bars of soap when it comes to getting a grip.

With neurotic fixations, for example, certain questions about feelings are repressed, thereby distorting our moral orientation. Minor distortions may be reoriented through the natural engagements with good friends, but major distortions need the expertise of a therapist. Still, while neurosis feeds on repression, moral health can actually be nourished by suppression—the responsible suppression of those habitual feelings that may have been appropriate for an earlier stage but now need reorienting. In cultures that promote indulging every feeling without discrimination, moral education does well to challenge this advice.

One pedagogical technique for training one's feelings involves the discernment of inspirations. (Here, I am following Ignatius Loyola in his "Rules for Understanding Movements," found in any edition of his *Spiritual Exercises*.) Ultimately most, if not all, human choices are between options that arise from inspirations. If we understand how inspirations work, it can help us tell the difference between those that are reliable and those that are not.

First, notice that our "inspirations" may come either as vivid and powerful images or as the results of careful reasoning. Which kind is more reliable? Should we prefer affect-laden images of the heart or cool reasoning processes of the head? According to Ignatius, the answer depends on the kind of person we are. One kind should trust the heart more than the head; the other should trust the head more than the heart. Why is this? Here is a basic rule about how inspirations function: *Inspirations driven by our emotions and imagination ("heart") normally reinforce our stance in life, while inspirations driven by reasoning and calculation ("mind") tend to change it.*

So, in self-absorbed people, imagination and emotions tend to reinforce their self-regarding attitudes, withdrawing them even further from a fully open life. Delights and pleasures fill their memories and hopes while their thoughts tend to sting their consciousness. So they avoid serious analysis of the long-term consequences of their actions. On the other hand, in self-transcending people, imagination and emotions tend to open them ever wider to learning, to doing better, and to love without reserve. They joyfully remember good deeds and courageously hope the best for all concerned. When they become confused or anxious, it usually stems from fallacious reasoning about what that best might actually be.

This rule has very practical applications. People who are *open* can usually rely on their imagination and emotions without hesitation, but they need to be careful when their reasoning raises questions. Mental confusion can stifle genuine virtue in an open person. They do well to let the symbolic reasoning of heart take the lead. Likewise, open people who raise children, or teach, or manage employees, need to discern whether their child/student/employee is a basically "open" person. If so, then to propose changes, it will be more effective to use imagination and emotion than strict logic and if-then kinds of reasoning. But if not, they will do better to appeal to self-defeating outcomes and logic and hold back glowing visions of wonderful experiences.

Beauty

Closely related to feelings is the notion of beauty. In our analysis that links key moral categories to self-transcending events in consciousness, we explained how beauty symbolizes and promotes our openness. We noted that all beauty, both natural and artistic, symbolizes the mysterious objects of the transcending exigence. It represents to our imagination "the better" that we are impelled to pursue. It stimulates our emotions to support our innate drive to seek always more truth, more goodness, and more profound engagement with one another and with divine mystery. Even tragic operas, violent dances, and somber war memorials ignite our sense of beauty by their depiction of human failure to be self-transcending.

The next revolution in ethics will need the support of an education in beauty along these lines. A major theme in such an education is to teach that aesthetics are essentially *events* and only derivatively *objects*. The clearest example is music; it is the event of hearing that counts. If you ask someone, "*Where* is Beethoven's Fifth Symphony?" you will get a strange look because this work is no place. But this also applies to the plastic arts. A presumably "lost" Matisse asleep in the dust of a collector's attic is not functioning as art until it arouses a transcending desire in someone. When we are young, we may easily recognize Picasso's *Guernica* but be unmoved. But should we later be horrified to learn that it depicts the 1937 Nazi bombing of the Spanish village of Guernica, killing 1,600 people, then the art is an event of self-transcendence.

Good art functions as an invitation to be a more fully open person. Artists whose work "works," draw directly from a personal and specific experience of self-transcendence and aim to stimulate the same event in others. When, for whatever reason, a work of art no longer draws people out of their specific, everyday concerns and into its virtual, unrestrictedly *moral* space, it becomes just polite or fascinating. To draw people out into the open is a high achievement. Many artists never pull it off, and many others start with a keen sense of the alluring depths of ordinary experience, but they get seduced by thoughts of what will sell for a good price, or by a commission to stimulate some group's pride, or by the hope of being praised for their virtuosity.

I mean this as practical advice for the artist: It is quite difficult to remain in a self-transcending aesthetic frame of mind when painting, sculpting, designing dwellings and landscapes, or performing for others in poetry or song or drama or dance. Artists can be lured by the sirens of sensation to excite feelings for their own sake. Whether titillating or horrifying, bombastic or erotic, sentimental or indignant, sensational beauty affects just our nervous system—a far cry from lifting our spirits beyond ourselves. Or artists can think of themselves as masters of illusion, using beauty as propaganda, sometimes to portray themselves as possessing nearly magical powers and sometimes to trick people into buying a car or perfume.

Every person who hopes to live a genuinely better life absolutely must learn to distinguish between the demands of the heart to be fully open to life and the addiction to inner excitement of sensibilities and magical control over outer circumstances. If we do not learn, through ongoing personal experience, how the demand for genuine beauty feels like a movement to be more fully open, we will easily settle for living in the illusion of being capable and feeling the recurring need for more excitement of our senses. We lose our soul.

Religion

Training in religious awareness is particularly important for a moral education rooted in generalized empirical method. The key term here is *awareness*. Such training should lead students to notice that the experience of being drawn to beauty, order, truth, goodness, and shared living belongs to their nature as humans. The training should clarify how their openness to these transcendent values has no intrinsic limit and, as a result, validates that the *question* of God belongs to any authentic living, no matter what sort of answer—if any—they may embrace.

There are certainly pedagogical challenges to devise ways to elicit the question of God in students. The larger challenge is to bring religious questions back into those educational institutions that effectively ban anything smacking of religion. To bar the question of God from any humanities-based educational system is a refusal to deal with questions that belong to our nature. The typical cover story to justify this irrational prohibition is to depict all religious teaching as nothing but dogmatic propaganda. But the needed training in religious *awareness* promotes intelligent inquiry into our experiences of being drawn to unrestricted openness—a powerfully effective way to stave off dogmatism in the first place.

Religious awareness may focus on the commitments of others or one's own. Some colleges distinguish between religious studies and theology, where religious studies treat religion as a human phenomenon while theology aims to understand the significance of one's own faith for one's culture. Whatever the aim, whatever the name, attention to the experience of self-transcending movements is essential. In religious studies, all the creeds, codes, and cults of various religions have their origin in the historical experience of pulls toward self-transcendence experienced by their founders and subsequent leaders. The more a student of religious studies is aware of these inner pulls, the better questions he or she will ask about how external practices and beliefs may—or may not—be rooted in these self-transcendent movements. Likewise, the more students of theology are aware of these pulls, the more concerned they will be about how well their own beliefs, moral codes, and rituals express their personal experiences of the exigence toward a fully transcendent affective horizon. These concerns will be the pruning shears that keep a religion in bloom.

Dialog

By making openness a theme, we can help students realize that all opinions—intellectual, moral, or religious—are expressions of people wrestling with their own desires to be more open against the various forces that pull against these desires. As they grow wise about life, they realize that that there is not always a clear victory on either side. So they become more ready to sympathize with the efforts of people with whom they disagree.

It seems opportune to train the young in this readiness by teaching them how to talk "reasonably." Earlier we distinguished between between debate and dialog. In a debate, one side wins, often by undermining all the reasons given by the other side. Indeed, learning how to debate seems dangerously close to practice in being unreasonable. But in dialog, it is collaboration that wins and problems that are defeated. Different sides of a disagreement give their "reasons," and each side explores them "reasonably"—that is, sees if the evidence supports the opinion. A key element in learning productive dialog is how to express appreciation. Where a Jack widens the horizon of a Jill—whether by expressing a view that resolves a problem on Jill's mind or by raising a relevant question that had not occurred to Jill—she publicly thanks Jack for moving the discussion forward.

Diversity

Where dialog training teaches openness to the views of others, being critical-minded is important as well. As we saw earlier, an essential point about diversity is that there are different types and that each type requires a unique approach.

A perspectival diversity results from differences in people's experiences. The goal is to convert perspectival differences to the interlocking, complementary differences that form a larger and shared perspective. Training here aims to heal what we called loyalism—the assumption that other groups have little to offer.

A developmental diversity results from the simple fact that people grow up. Mature adults need more than simple rules about right and wrong, while children have yet to grasp the implications of being a responsible person. A major task in ethics is to tailor moral guidelines to the lower and higher stages of moral learning. Regarding bias, training in identifying the sorts of questions that certain literary or historical figures avoid, or the sorts of better judgments they refused to follow, can implant in students' minds the ever-relevant question, "What questions are avoided here?" Regarding willfulness, training in identifying literary or historical figures who acted against their better judgment can plant the question, "Are *we* doing what *we* know very well is better?"

Radical diversity results from opposed views on what learning is, opposed choices about how to choose, and/or opposed stands about letting love dominate one's life. Each radical opposition admits degrees of commitment and integration into one's entire life. So even when we recognize the issues about conversion, we need the help of teachers actually engaged in a mutual exposure of horizons to invite conversion in those who lack it and expand it in those who made the essential breakthrough.

Case Study Method

In chapter 10, we grouped the tasks of ethics into two phases: Engaging the Past and Engaging the Future. An effective case-study discussion can be similarly divided, allowing, however, that any question related to either phase may be raised at any time. The goal of Engaging the Past is not only to bring to light the experiences, the meanings, and the historical developments related to a case, but ultimately to expose operative horizons—as *dialectic* does regarding *research, interpretation,* and *history.*

When this discussion is free-floating, students will naturally share their views on whether things are better or worse, so it is important to keep in mind the double tactic of *dialectic.* The first is to *amplify* the viewpoints relevant to a case so that the root sources of differences may be more clearly evident. Perspectival differences lead to the question whether they can also be complementary: "Can your two views be combined?" When developmental differences along similar paths come to light, it becomes a "teaching moment" to explain how moral mindsets develop in stages. Radical differences will seem incomprehensible by those whose intellectual, moral or affective horizons are closed in any serious manner. Here is where the tactic of amplifying a viewpoint can be particularly effective. As a participant spells out in more detail his or her analyses of the meanings and trends in the case, relevant questions arise almost automatically—"Is that really what was going on? Is that really better? Do those people really like each other?"

The second tactic of *dialectic* is to *assess*. Initially, this regards the situation, but eventually it evolves into an *assessment* of the adequacy of one another's *assessments* of the situation. A facilitator needs to be as affectively open as possible here. I say "affectively" because maintaining an atmosphere of mutual respect is absolutely necessary to entice differences in priorities to venture into the open. As radical differences in horizon come to light, the facilitator can lead the group to spell out the differences as clearly as possible in the circumstances, both where horizons were widened and where they were not, but without trying to convince one another through argument or debate. The overall strategy, again, is not to prove or disprove anything but rather to tap latent desires for authenticity. It counts on this desire as the most effective force for fully opening one's learning, choosing, and loving. In practice, students may need the time and space to absorb the question, which may require a postponement of further discussion to another day.

Having clarified to some extent the nature of the differences, the facilitator will then move to the phase of Engaging the Future. (The strategy of *dialectic* is still on hand, as it were, because envisioning the future naturally amplifies intellectual, moral, and affective assumptions, which often calls for further assessment.) To engage the future is take a stand on *foundations* so as to carry out the tasks of *standards, coordination,* and *communication.* About *foundations*, one might ask, "What are the essentials to being fully human?" Student responses should be captured on a board or screen. Connections should be drawn between key elements and normative events in consciousness. Since questions like these are a far cry from the specifics of a case at hand, it may be advisable to cover *foundations* in a separate, introductory session. But at the same time, as discussions of a particular case focus around the familiar categories like *rights, principles, authority, ideals,* etc., it may be opportune to suspend discussion of the case and to define the category under discussion in the style of *foundations.* That is, aim to help students discover the events in consciousness that ground these categories, particularly as grounded in the inherent normativity of these events.

About *standards*, the question is what principles of ethics, what institutional policies, what historical exemplars, and what visions of best outcomes give basic guidance to the case under discussion. Students who are knowingly grounded in authenticity will be eager to see growth in authenticity as part of any "best outcome," while those for whom "best outcome" is restricted to social and material conditions—a rather stubborn restriction to overcome—will need some intervention to refocus their attention on the role of authenticity in ethics. *Coordination* involves organizing ethical principles into a coherent system, aligning the policies of any institutions that may be involved in a case, and gathering descriptive accounts of moral exemplars under ethical principles that are more explanatory. Obviously, there are many possible avenues to pursue here, so the facilitator's task is to help the group select which types of coordination are most important to discuss—ethical principles, institutional policies, historical exemplars, or visions of best outcomes. *Communication* in moral matters is most effective when the communicator engages the people in the situation as fully as possible. Here, a case study should address how fully involved the characters in the case will be in making a positive difference. For an orderly discussion, the facilitator might begin with what *learning* is needed for people in the situation, then what *choices* confront them, and finally, what *affective* engagements each might have.

Finally, while here I lay out distinct kinds of questions in an organized fashion, to avoid giving the impression that there is a recipe for moral reflection, it seems better to allow some measure of free-floating discussion. The facilitator lets his or her own intelligence raise whatever further relevant questions come to mind, understanding, of course, that this mind already understands the issues of method in ethics. Any more organized explanation of the issues and structures related to *method* in ethics would be better presented at a different time.

AN INVITATION

What I have presented is a set of hypotheses about what occurs in moral reflection, along with an invitation to verify them in your experience. The invitation is an extension into ethics of Lonergan's own invitation in *Insight* to discover what we do when we know anything. His invitation, in turn, is the product of his own years of struggling with philosophical problems about knowledge, objectivity, metaphysics, evolutionary process, historical process, economic process, as well as with theological problems about the nature of religion, grace, faith, charity, Christ Jesus, the development of religious doctrine, and the question of God. His struggle involved refuting many contrary positions on these topics, as well as tracing the actual developments of accepted positions in the ongoing history of ideas. But just as the structure of the DNA molecule is easier to explain than to discover, so I have taken the easier, pedagogical path and leave to others the more difficult, historical account of Lonergan's explorations that led to these discoveries, as well as the dialectal engagements with different, even opposed views of prominent ethicists.

Still, the point of the ethical specialty *dialectic* is precisely to leave the invitation open to amplify and assess these different views with the ultimate aim of actually doing better. Just as some proofs are in the recipe and others in the pudding, so some improvements in ethics will emerge from more comprehensive philosophical reflections on human nature and historicity, while others will emerge from the very experiment of history. The experiments of history, of course, are paid for dearly by people living their entire lives according to the directives of politicians, philosophers, and religious leaders who are hardly exempt from dysfunctions in their creativity. So to minimize the impacts of failed experiments on real people, it is imperative to conduct the collaborative process we describe here with a permanent sense of urgency.

It remains an open question whether the natural openness of our nature to learning, to doing better, and to loving will continue to be effective. Clearly, it will not be enough for people whose intellectual, moral and affective horizons are open to simply lay out their horizons for consideration by others. A fully open affective horizon will impel them to grab others by the throat, or should we say *heart*, to impress on them the urgency of dealing with moral issues at the level of method.

Collectively, do we ethicists experience this urgency directly? The invitation of this book extends beyond knowledge about a generalized empirical method in ethics. It asks you to yield to an inner demand to do better by choosing a better way of making choices. Again, the exigences of learning and choosing do not exhaust the exigences of our nature. We are also impelled by an affective exigence that opens us to become parts of larger unions based in love—in friendship, family, and society. Ethical collaboration, in other words, requires explicit attention to the demands of affective engagements. And because love, like learning and choosing, has no intrinsic limits, our very nature is open to the question whether the universe itself is essentially affective. This is the question whether our experience of urgency has a divine source, is also a present invitation, and moves us to a fully human life beyond death, and, if so, whether we will let this love lead our lives.

In light of the urgency of a methodological revolution ethics, dare we expect this revolution to be imminent? The very curiosity of people who take the empirical method of the natural sciences seriously will lead many to conduct empirical tests on their own conscious knowing, choosing, and loving. This field of consciousness opens human curiosity to identifying what we do when we know anything, select anything, commit ourselves to anything, and engage anyone in love. Moreover, attention to the data of consciousness gives us first-hand evidence of the criteria by which we distinguish between the beautiful and the ugly, the more and less cogent, the true and the false, the better and the worse, and between affective self-absorption and affective self-transcendence.

Just as Newton had little idea of the enormous difference scientific method would make on human life, so today we have only glimmerings of the differences to be made in ethics if empirical method were generalized to incorporate the data of consciousness—particularly the evidence of *normative* drives in consciousness. The entire range of human studies will be transformed. Understandably, scientists and scholars are reluctant to delve into the data of consciousness and fundamental method after having mastered the sense-data approaches of their disciplines. But is it not the case that you feel invited, perhaps by my words here, but, more importantly, by an urgency of your own heart? As ethicists like yourself accept the invitation, the next revolution in ethics will be upon us. Your personal acceptance of this invitation will also be an integral part of the universe doing better.

APPENDIX: FOUNDATIONAL ETHICAL CATEGORIES

CRITERIA FOR ETHICAL CATEGORIES

In ethics, we speak of justice, rights, authority, objectivity, duty, ideals, principles, virtues, and so on. But we can mean different things by these categories. These differences in their meanings will be as varied as the intellectual, moral, and affective developments in the ethicists who use them. The more variances, of course, the more difficult it will be for ethicists to converse in any convincing manner. What follows, then, are definitions of 31 key categories.

In our discussion of *foundations*, we outlined the criteria for developing categories for ethical reflection. They should be defined in ways that connect them clearly to the normative drives of consciousness to be attentive, intelligent, reasonable, responsible, and in love. The hope is that insofar as ethicists identify these drives in themselves as normative, they will agree that anyone's firsthand experience of these drives is the ground of any possible meanings of the word *should*. So there is the apriori possibility of assessing the validity of any ethical categories insofar as they are expressions of recognizable norms in consciousness itself.

In their discussions, ethicists are usually aware that they each bring a perspective that involves their whole persons. What the specialty *foundations* requires is the personal task of making explicit, in terms connected to the events of consciousness, what perspectives issue from their intellectual, moral, and affective conversions. The very effort to define categories in terms of the inherent norms of consciousness reveals further *shoulds* proper to the various field of ethics—politics, authority, medicine, business, economics, psychology, art, community, religion, stories, and so on. In this sense, the definitions that we propose below function as exercises that reveal normative dimensions. They not only fix the meaning of basic ethical categories; they also invite ethicists to accept, refine, or reject this or that definition as valid for expressing moral opinions. Among the global community of ethicists, such consciousness-grounded normative definitions are mutual invitations to open still further their intellectual, moral and affective horizons.

For example, in the discussion below on *authority* and *power*, you will see a distinction between physical power, social power, and moral power. This is followed by a definition of *authority* as "the moral power arising from authenticity." Does this meaning of *authority* encompass all the relevant questions about actual persons, groups, situations, and histories? Will this meaning provide verifiable explanations of any moral issue related to authority? Can this meaning be conveyed in any formulations of moral standards and opinions to society at large? The invitation is to find out for yourself. Whatever you answer, the exercise of finding out demands that you appropriate a meaning of authority that is consistent with how you personally learn and choose and love.

This is work indeed. As I hope is clear by now, to define any basic category in ethics, we go beyond the easy job of connecting concepts to one another. We also verify that the concepts used in definitions make better sense of our personal experience of the normativity of consciousness than any other concepts, and if they fall short, we formulate alternative definitions that might better explain our experience. Still, finding out *for* ourselves is seldom finding out *by* ourselves. The specialization *foundations* is a collaborative enterprise of building a model of the morality that serves as mutual invitations to ever wider horizons.

Each of the categories below is defined in relationship to at least one other category. That is, we understand the meaning of one category by understanding its relationship to associated categories. Then we seek to verify that these interrelationships explain our own self-transcending, normative operations and, through dialog with others, that they too come to the same conclusions. For fuller treatments of these and other categories, follow the leads in the Index.

31 ETHICAL CATEGORIES

Authority and Power

In ordinary conversation, we blend the meanings of authority and power as simply the ability to command compliance. Or we picture authority as the people having the power. But the relevant ethical question is whether or not this authority and power improve human living, and common sense finds it difficult to pin down exactly why they do or do not. This is because authority and power each has factors that beg distinctions outside the realm of common sense.

An initial meaning of power is physical, and physical power is multiplied by collaboration. Where collaboration is ongoing, a non-physical, *social* meaning of power emerges—the power produced by insights into how to work together in ways that vastly reduce the physical power needed while achieving vastly wider results. The social power of a community grows as it consolidates the gains of the past, restricts behaviors that would diminish the community's effectiveness, organizes labors for specific tasks, and spells out moral guidelines for the future. As social, the memories and commitments of this heritage constitute a community's "word of authority."

The community appoints "authorities" to assign tasks, pass laws, and arbitrate disputes. Authorities are the spokespersons, delegates, and caretakers of a community's spiritual and material assets. Winning the vote does not confer an authority upon them; it confers a responsibility upon them to speak and embody the community's word of authority, that is, its memories and commitments. The honor owed them by titles and ceremony derive from only two virtues—a respect for what is best in their community's history and the political skill to implement the common purpose with which they have been entrusted.

While the community's social power resides in its ways and means, not all its ways and means are morally justifiable. Its heritage is jumble of sense and nonsense. To the extent that authorities lack the authenticity of being attentive, intelligent, reasonable, responsible, and in love, their power to build up is diminished. Even if everyone does what they say, authorities will be blind to the higher viewpoints and better ideas needed to stave off chaos and seize opportunities for improving life together. Their power is justifiably called naked because it is stripped of the contributions that their authentic subjects are capable of making. Similarly, to the extent that the *subjects* lack authenticity, they will cripple their own creativity, which otherwise would foresee problems, overcome obstacles, and open new lines of development. The entire community, as the source of the "word of authority," falls short of authenticity. At the extremes, a noble leader of egotistical followers is no more effective in doing better than an egotistical leader of noble followers. Between these extremes, the typical dynamic is an ongoing dialectic between an incomplete authenticity of the community and an incomplete authenticity of its authorities.

Still, in communities whose heritage is largely rooted in authenticity, authority is effective for making life better. So besides physical power and social power, there is also a moral power. This is the power of people whose moral horizon is open to the truly better, as opposed to mere preference. It is indeed a power—the power of authenticity that invites others to moral openness and convinces others what it means to do better in concrete situations.

This analysis of power leads us directly to a normative definition of authority: *Authority is the moral power arising from authenticity.*

Authority is certainly more than physical power; indeed, it commands and organizes physical power. Authority is also more than social power: Where social power aims to be effective and efficient, authority decides whether or not social power actually contributes to doing better.

In this perspective, authority is that portion of a heritage produced by attention, intelligence, reason, responsibility, and love. It is a mistake to conceive of authority as any dictatorial iron law, or as any anarchical or libertarian social order, or as some natural, evolutionary dynasty. As only a portion of a heritage, authority is a dialectical reality; it is constantly worked out in mutual encounter.

This definition of authority as the moral power arising from authenticity supports the legitimacy of civil disobedience, civil war, and even some types of international war, on the grounds that some "authorities" may lack the genuine authority that stands on authenticity. It also offers historians defensible criteria for distinguishing between legitimate and illegitimate exercises of power in a historical period. And it offers policymakers the normative categories they need to explain to their constituents the reasons for proposed changes in the community's constitution, laws, and sanctions.

Autonomy and Self-Transcendence

There are several different meanings attached to *autonomy*. In fundamental ethical theory, Kant's *Critique of Practical Reason* (1788) brought the notion of autonomy front and center. In an attempt to establish a fundamental principle of morality, he proposed that while universal laws govern everything in nature, in humans, that governance depends on the will of the individual who conceptualizes those laws. So the principle of morality is found not in the duties imposed by common law but originally in the will of individuals who make the laws. Nor is it found in any so-called divine law, since that law derives from the wills of individuals who formulate it in human concepts. At the same time, this autonomy, or self-rule, is not a merely self-regarding. It is the nature of our wills, Kant proposed, to give laws that apply to everyone. Hence one formulation of his famous categorical imperative is that we should act on maxims that may serve as universal laws of nature.

A second meaning of autonomy emerged in medical ethics, where the principle of "patient autonomy" is about individual rights. It now takes priority over the classical criteria of nonmaleficence, beneficence, and distributive justice. Patients cannot be forced to accept any treatment, and providers are required to obtain an "informed consent" to treatments. A third meaning arises in developmental psychology, where autonomy refers to a stage of psycho-social growth. Erikson's *Childhood and Society* (1950) traces the emerging physical ability in infants to hold on and push away. Unless adults lead infants into the world of autonomous, free choices, infantile grabbing and pushing away become obsessions for their own sake. A fourth meaning of autonomy has been identified as a distinct achievement in moral development. Lawrence Kohlberg, in his *The Philosophy of Moral Development* (1981), identifies six stages, where the sixth is reached when one takes a stand on one's autonomous conscience and on a concern for universal justice. Carol Gilligan, in her *In a Different Voice: Psychological Theory and Women's Development* (1982), criticized Kohlberg's work as representing moral development only in males. She proposed that the autonomy of Kohlberg's sixth stage needs to be complemented by a concern generally found in females for affiliation with and care for others.

In an ethics based on a generalized empirical method, the *nomos* or "rule" in *auto-nomy* is an exigence for self-transcendence. It primarily represents a moral imperative incumbent on the self. As a result, the above disparate meanings of autonomy may be incorporated within the more comprehensive scheme of self-transcendence, specifically along the hierarchy of values from vital, to social, to cultural, to personal, to transcendent. By way of a preliminary sketch, then, we might consider Erikson's *autonomy* as rooted in a vital value, experienced in infancy as an imperative to survive and thrive. Yet to avoid the shame and doubt that accompany obsessive hanging on and pushing away, it requires the higher social value of freely deciding to cooperate with others. In medical ethics, the principle of *autonomy* is a social value that identifies the duties of healthcare providers to obtain an informed consent from patients. Yet to ensure that patients' decisions to consent to a specific treatment are genuinely better, cultural values are needed that give moral criteria to guide these decisions. The ethicists, pastors, and counselors who provide this moral guidance will be effective only to the extent that they recognize the *autonomy* of a personal value, recognized by Kant and amplified by Kohlberg that sees all laws and policies as originating from moral individuals. By the same token, the social values of distributive justice can be merely quantitative without the higher cultural values of interpersonal affiliation and care proposed by Gilligan. Those whose moral horizon includes this exigence to care must necessarily recognize an *autonomy* of a personal value that freely commits oneself to a *heteronomy* that shares responsibilities with others.

The full achievement of an *autonomy* equivalent to a commitment to personal value seems to rise necessarily to a yet higher value on the hierarchy by a personal acceptance of some form of self-transcendence without restriction. Concretely, this manifests itself in women and men engaged in a common enterprise to doing better. It brings them to the threshold of a moral conversion that is committed to what is truly better from every perspective rather than what seems better for oneself or one's community. It also brings them to the threshold of an affective conversion that relinquishes self-absorption in favor of an openness to loving and be loved. And because that openness has no intrinsic limits, it is

entirely compatible with the belief in a divine lover who is source
and hope of the moral order.

We should note, however, that these images of a hierarchy of
values and a journey over thresholds, while they may trigger
insights into the stages of growth, represent only the creative
movement of moral development. There is also, simultaneously, the
affective movement in which a child grows up feeling cared for and
challenged to let love lead. Here is where the values of affiliation
and care championed by Gilligan predominate. Indeed, the healing
function of the affective movement in children is typically the more
obvious and familiar. In compact, symbolic fashion, the child
experiences firsthand the values in the hierarchy, so that as
intellectual questions arise from below upward, as it were, answers
are forthcoming from their personal experience of being loved from
above downward.

In any case, as a category in ethics, *autonomy* should be subordi-
nated to the dynamics of self-transcendence. The "self-rule" of *autonomy*, which here we equate with personal value in the hierarchy of
values, can represent the exigence of the self to obey the "rule" that
self-fulfillment is found in self-transcendence. One faces the daily paradox
that the more one becomes a part of a true "we," the stronger grows
one's autonomy, and, conversely, one gains a true sense of oneself
only in giving up the self in love.

Consequences, Ideals, and Obligations

Three commonly used criteria for assessing moral problem are
consequences, ideals, and *specific obligations.* The criterion of *consequences*
includes both intended and the unintended outcomes, including
any changes in how people behave, in what resources will be
available to them, and in social expectations. They can also include
the internal changes in their habits, mindsets, and attitudes. We
examine consequences to compare the desired benefits against the
expected costs. We assume that some consideration of proportionality between benefits and costs affects the moral decision.

The criterion of *ideals* includes formal ideals such as "Treat others
as you would like to be treated" and "Act as though your actions
would be a model for everyone's actions." It also includes the
millions of informal ideals that constitute a culture's priorities, such
as the ideal place of women in society, the ideal way to care for

one's elders, and the sort of respect one ought to pay to religion. A consideration of ideals aims to apply those common moral guidelines that have stood the test of time.

The criterion of *specific obligations* covers the duties springing from one's roles and promises. To accept the role of parent means accepting commonly recognized duties. One's promises may be formal, as in contracts and treaties, or informal, as in our countless verbal promises. The reason for considering specific obligations is to identify any duties incumbent on specific individuals that fall outside the "natural" duties incumbent on everyone just for being human.

While these criteria serve well for surfacing various relevant questions in any moral discussion, some critical functions are missing. We can identify consequences and then set out to identify which are better and which are worse, but this kind of assessment depends on what the people mean by "better" and "worse." What a generalized empirical method adds is the further, dialectical step of distinguishing between the evaluations of consequences made by those who are morally closed and those who are morally open.

We can identify moral ideals, but it is quite another matter to understand them and use them appropriately. Many ethicists who focus on ideals rely exclusively on natural laws to deduce moral standards, overlooking the intrinsically historical dimension of all such standards. This neglect of the historical perspective limits the applicability of moral ideals in two ways: they do not convey all the qualifications that insight into historical origins would capture, and they are notoriously difficult to apply to new historical situations without qualification. Moreover, since values are concrete and ideals are abstractions from the concrete, it would be a mistake to overlook exemplary persons and communities as shaping a moral heritage.

Similarly, we can identify all sorts of specific obligations, but people whose moral horizons are limited to duties based on roles or promises will miss the many other specific obligations arising from personal inspirations. Personal inspirations may not feel as obligatory as the duties flowing from role or promise, but to people living in a world where every choice falls on a scale of better and worse, there is a quite specific duty to discern among their inspirations

and follow those that best align with one's exigence to live authentically.

Macroeconomics and Global Progress

Questions about the economy of a company or household fall
within the scope of *micro*economics. Here, the moral issues are
mainly about greed. And because the greedy are prompted by
egotism, the type of moral solution needed will be friendships based
on authenticity rather than on mere pleasure or usefulness.

Questions about the economy of the entire world fall within the
scope of *macro*economics. Preliminary questions are about exchanges of money for goods and services, and who the winners and
losers may be. Here too, ethicists can expect to find the greedy
doing their usual business, including entire nations that put their
own well-being above everyone else's. But a deeper question arises
because greed alone does not account for the global disparity
between rich and poor. Standards of living rise far beyond the basic
needs for some and sink far below for others, and it is not clear why.
This is a question for macroeconomic theory. The sort of understanding needed is like what is needed regarding ecological
systems: What poisons people downstream is seldom pure malice
but the dumping of toxic wastes by people who do not understand
chemistry and biology. The type of moral solution needed here is
similar: where an understanding of macroeconomics is absent, even
virtuous entrepreneurs and benefactor nations will oppress the
poor.

Who needs to understand macroeconomics? Certainly, ethicists
studying global poverty ought to. Leaders in business and government also should understand it, lest they continue to rely on
shallow ideas to make financial decisions that affect huge numbers
of people. And assuming that some form of participatory democracy
is the most effective means of raising relevant questions, ordinary
citizens also bear a responsibility to understand at least enough of
macroeconomics to make intelligent demands of their leaders.

Unfortunately, like other human sciences, macroeconomics is still
in the adolescent stage of trying on different outfits. Ethicists today
offer a variety of proposals about poverty without guidance from
any proven and commonly accepted criteria for identifying which
proposals are better. Economists disagree on what the fundamental

categories and inherent dynamics of macroeconomics ought to be. They typically accept as unavoidable the historical phenomena of the "trade cycle" of booms and slumps, but without any foundation in an analysis of macroeconomic process. The advice they give national and international monetary agencies is like the advice given by a psychiatrist who doesn't understand repression; the patient fails to improve and often gets sicker.

In his *Macroeconomic Dynamics: An Essay in Circulation Analysis*,[57] Bernard Lonergan offers to meet these difficulties. (1) He sets the meaning of the global economy in the context of the overall rhythms of human endeavors to improve living—including politics, wars, philosophy, religion, science, technology, art, law, medicine, and education. (2) He proposes *categories and models* of macroeconomic exchanges. (3) He *analyzes the flows* of money, goods and services. (4) He proposes *implicit moral precepts* that result from this analysis. And (5) he identifies how *misunderstanding* these exchanges results in worsening a people's well-being. Here, we can give some examples of each of these five efforts, but this is by no means a thorough summary. To understand the actual goings on in the global economy in this perspective requires an in-depth reading of Lonergan's work and a basic knowledge of the history and present workings of the global economy itself.

1. Economics and quality living

The goal of economic process is to provide the goods and services needed to support quality living. Its positive contribution includes ordinary products like food, clothing, shelter, communications, and roads. Its goal of quality living includes not only these material benefits but also the freedom from strictly material concerns to explore creative ideas and deepen one's wisdom through educational, legal, philosophical, artistic, religious and other cultural pursuits. It is from this free exploration that great advances are made in cultures. An economics that is not culturally liberating retards human development and degrades the living it proposes to improve.

2. Categories and models of macroeconomic exchanges

Regarding production, there are two fundamental categories relevant to a macroeconomic analysis:

Stages of Production: Basic and Surplus. The basic stage of production brings goods and services to the final market. The surplus stage is the infrastructure. At successive levels, it brings forth first the raw materials, then the refined materials, then a machinery-making industry, then the machinery and other products and processes needed to produce what will sell in the final markets at the basic stage. (Called "surplus" because capital investments come from the surplus of profits from the basic stage.) While the outputs of these two stages include both commodities and services, we ordinarily refer to them as *consumer goods* and *producer goods.*

Pure Surplus Income. At any level in the surplus stage, there is a "pure surplus income," beyond what is earmarked for purchasing goods and services, paying debts, paying interest on loans, ongoing maintenance, wages and salaries. It is income that is not owed to anyone. The existence of this entirely discretionary type of income raises the moral question about where better to spend it, and what should be done when this income drops.

3. An analysis of the flows of money, goods and services:

Here, Lonergan proposes a "pure case" of macroeconomic process. His strategy is to present what would happen if decision makers understood the underlying structure of the flows of money, goods and services, and made their decisions with the overall purpose of improving standards of living. This prepares the ground for identifying the precise ways in which certain "wounds" in our authenticity impede economic progress. As these "wounds" come to light, relevant questions arise about how to recover proper functioning.

In this pure case, basic and surplus stages each grow. But they do so in waves, not the ups and downs of of booms and slumps but of step-like waves of accelerating and steady flows of goods. In the surplus stage producer activity accelerates, owing mainly to scientific and technological advances, investments and loans. In meantime, the basic stage remains at a steady flow, both because the newer goods that the surplus expansion aims to provide have not yet reached the basic market and because sellers of basic goods are investing larger portions of profits toward the surplus expansion rather than giving the raises that would enable their workers to improve their standard of living as consumers.

Eventually, the surplus stage in any expanding major segment reaches full capacity as the new infrastructures supporting new processes and technologies are in place. (Think of the scientific revolution, then the industrial revolution, then the automotive industry in the mid 1900s and the computer industry beginning in the late 1900s and still expanding in telecommunications generally.) Their activity drops to a steady flow as the newer goods begin reaching the final market. Sellers of basic goods now redirect their profits from investments in surplus stage enterprises to higher wages in the basic stage, both because the demand for labor picks up and because opportunities for promising investments in surplus-stage firms have dried up. The higher wages and accelerating flow of basic goods results in a higher material standard of living and greater leisure for cultural pursuits.

4. Moral precepts implicit to macroeconomic process

This sketch of the pure case reveals certain moral precepts. During the surplus expansion stage, the moral precepts are "thrift and enterprise" (and, it may be added, "expand producer credit"), so that monies may be invested and producer goods may be purchased to support this expansion. As this stage is accelerating, labor's demand for steadily increasing wages cannot be justified solely on the fact that a producer company's profits are rising. As long as promising exploitation of a surplus expansion remains, it is better to invest monies in the surplus expansion because of the multiplier effect by which each new type of material or machine or process eventually produces *multiple* new types of goods destined for material improvements in the standard of living.

During the subsequent basic expansion stage, the moral precepts are "benevolence and enterprise" (and again, "expand consumer credit") aimed at raising wages and broadening employment for basic stage workers—including the least skilled—so they can improve their standard of living. As this stage is accelerating, demand for consumer goods and services rises, partly because of the current period of increased wages among basic-stage workers, and partly because the newly-available goods have reached the basic market. In this expansion, resistance to wage hikes among owners of basic stage firms cannot be justified solely on the fact that it cuts into their profits.

The problem now becomes clear when we look at not-so-pure reality. Entrepreneurs in the surplus stage tend to prolong their "pure surplus income" long after the natural period of acceleration of their sector has ended. This is commonly done through investments in uncertain enterprises, a variety of fixed-percent rents and royalties, investments in cheap labor in underdeveloped countries, favorable balances in foreign trade, and rash gambling on high-risk, high-yield loans. These are monies that in the pure case would have gone to wages that promote the acceleration of the basic stage and a rise in standards of living. The longer a significant aggregate of entrepreneurs in the surplus sector extends its efforts to continue raising their pure surplus income after the newly enhanced goods come to market, the slower the rise in the standard of living.

Overall, entrepreneurs of firms at both the basic and surplus stages have an obligation to see as their goal the "social dividend" of improving people's standard of living. To understand how to do this without going out of business, they must overcome the commonsense bias against in-depth study of macroeconomics. Of course the effects of this bias are exacerbated as greed among business individuals, investor groups, and nation-building constituencies cling to "maximize profits" as their absolute goal.

5. The problem of misunderstanding macroeconomics

Failure to understand such dynamics of macroeconomic process results in financial decisions that lead many politicians and business leaders to inadvertently eliminate the opportunities for improving standards of living among large sectors of their own country as well as among underdeveloped countries.

When proposals for economic progress fail to raise the standard of living of ordinary people and recession looms on the horizon, panic sets in for these surplus-stage entrepreneurs. Absent an understanding of macroeconomics (even despite an honest compassion for the poor), and even in the presence of genuine love for their families and countries, they resort to protecting and increasing their own assets in ways that unnecessarily delay the increase in incomes and expansions of consumer credit that would forestall recession and improve the standard of living for ordinary people.

Democracy itself is threatened insofar as economic decisions are made by the few. The economic base of civilization itself is threatened insofar as the few who make economic decisions never conceive of objective moral criteria that come to light when one understands macroeconomic dynamics. The ethical issue here is about the nature of economics itself. To many leaders of global enterprises, economics is a field of competition for maximizing profits. In Lonergan's perspective, economics is that dimension of human history in which people collaborate, through labor and loans, to improve the well-being of all. This explains why he also refers to his topic as a *political economy*: it is not restricted to material production and consumption. As such, economics is a part of the emerging, dialectical history of humans, in whom authenticity drives progress, unauthenticity drives decline, and love drives recovery. So the difference between the pure and actual cases of macroeconomic process lies in various forms of unauthenticity. The difference between absurd economic situations and their recovery lies in certain forms of conversion. An intellectual conversion is needed to understand macroeconomics; a moral conversion is needed where decision makers take to heart the goal of improving the material and cultural standards of living for society at large; and an affective conversion is needed that energizes nations and their peoples to expand their love to cover the earth.

Metaphysics and Self-Appropriation

In popular use, *metaphysics* suggests techniques for reaching higher forms of knowledge about the invisible dimensions of reality. Some aim toward a mystical contemplation of the oneness of the universe. Others promote psychic powers for seeing the future, reading minds, and communicating with the dead. What they have in common is a belief that the path to higher forms of knowing is through a disciplined and strongly focused imagination. Unfortunately, they also have in common a misunderstanding of what we do when we know anything.

In classical philosophies, *metaphysics* is the study of the underlying structures of any known reality. Materialist philosophers regard all reality as just matter in motion. Idealists regard reality as essentially spirit or ideas, of which we have no immediate experience, but only some experience of their physical manifestations. Philosophers in the Aristotelian-Thomist tradition regard reality as having intrinsic structures that shape our knowledge of them. They rely on distinctions between substance and accidents, matter and form, and essence and existence. Among the causes of anything real, they distinguish material, formal, efficient, instrumental, and final causes. They identify the proximate source of knowledge as the occurrence of a question in someone's mind. Their goal is a structured understanding of the entire set of questions anyone can ask about anything real.

The generalized empirical method proposed by Lonergan expands on this Aristotelian-Thomist context of knowers and knowns. But rather than first defining elements in the realities we know, Lonergan begins with a comprehensive *cognitional theory* of the operations of knowing, and follows this by an *epistemology* that demonstrates how these operations of knowing reach objective reality. *Metaphysics* then follows cognitional theory and epistemology as the science that correlates the structures of knowing with the structures of anything we can know. From the side of the knower, these structures are heuristic, meaning that they define certain features of what we hope to discover in any inquiry. By tying the known to people's actual knowing, the method gives immediately accessible data in the inquiring mind on what can be expected from any inquiry whatsoever. So this metaphysics is dynamic. It covers the operations of, first, *conceiving* a comprehensive heuristic structure of whatever can be known, then *validating* such a conception, and finally *implementing* it in concrete pursuits of knowledge. (Thus, the terms presented in chapter 9 on "Foundational Moral Elements" and in this present section may be called *metaphysical* or *foundational* categories since each is defined in terms of the operations of the subject.)

Underlying all these terms is the notion of an *exigence*. It corresponds to what Aristotle identified as *potency*—the inherent possibility that things and events may enter into higher organizations. He identified these higher organizations as *forms*. But, since Darwin, the attention of scientists and philosophers turned to the question of how earlier forms can evolve into increasingly ordered forms. One compelling answer lies in understanding the overall potency of the known universe as evolving in an upward manner. So, to the contemporary mind that seeks to understand the intrinsic intelligibility of things, the meaning of "upward" is a more intelligible organization; it is the emergence of forms whose intrinsic intelligibility is a higher integration of lower entities and functions. But to the heart that seeks to appreciate value, the meaning of "upward" is also something "better." Hence our use of the term *exigence*. It denotes not only the intrinsic intelligibility of the universe to produce higher forms but also an intrinsically moral dynamic or functional "demand" in the universe to improve.

The development of a comprehensive metaphysics is not a logical deduction from some apriori concepts about reality. It is certainly not founded on an imaginary drama played out by solemn forces in the cosmos. Rather it is a personal discovery of what is latent in one's own wonder. People who consistently tackle the right questions and sidestep the wrong ones already possess latent abilities to discern some structured features of the object of their inquiry. With moral questions, their heuristic anticipations show up as seemingly innate strategies: Do not chisel your moral principles in stone. Consider historical circumstances. Agreement does not necessarily mean better.

Eventually, should these canny men and women ask themselves how they ever learned to discern the difference between good thinking and bad thinking, they may probe behind the *objects* of their thoughts to wonder how their thinking works. They may realize that every philosophy stands on what one learns about learning, and when that learning about learning suffers from oversight, they build a philosophy on sand. So, to correctly understand their own cognitional activity, they may begin to make their latent metaphysics explicit. To the degree that they succeed, they understand their understanding, reasonably affirm their reason, and responsibly commit themselves to responsibility, and lovingly welcome being in love. This is the meaning of a *self-appropriation* that gives ethics its actual, functioning, *metaphysical* foundations.

Moral Right and Wrong

Our *ideas* of moral right and wrong are not the basis of our morality. They lie halfway between the dynamic orientation of consciousness toward what is better and the deeds we carry out that actually improve or worsen situations. As condensations of the moral wisdom of a tradition they are vital to the moral health of any community. Still, the scope of right and wrong is rather narrow. These terms typically represent an Ethics of Law, which functions mainly to remind us of the lessons learned by our forebears about certain outer limits of behaviors and internal requirements regarding our intentions. This leaves an Ethics of Better as an enormous field open to prudence, justice, creativity, risk, feedback, and lesson-learning.

The terms *good* and *bad* correspond to better and worse. They enjoy the advantage of making concrete a community's priorities, but they suffer several disadvantages. Because they assume an unchanging context, they lose their usefulness when situations change. They tend to indicate the value of observable behaviors while neglecting the actual questions of value that underlie behaviors. They tend to overlook any changes occurring in the individual making a choice, in the social or technical or economic orders, and in the cultural order where actual values are often reprioritized. Because of these shortcomings *good* and *bad* cannot rank among the basic explanatory categories in the foundations of ethics.

Natural Right and Human Rights

Classical Greek notions of morality began from questions on how people can live well together: On what grounds can we question authority? When we say something is "right," do we mean anything other than "legal" or "our custom"? To what might we appeal if we claim that our way of living together is better than anyone else's?

These questions may be reduced to asking, Is there some natural "right and wrong" that applies to all humans everywhere, or is "right and wrong" no more than social convention? Socrates, Plato, and Aristotle, the great founders of Western moral thought, clearly supported the notion of a human nature, common to all, that justifies criticism of authority, of existing laws, and of the conventions of any society. To recognize a natural moral order involves a conviction that "better" means more than just "better for us."

To this day, many philosophers appeal to human nature, or to natural law, or to natural rights to support their moral opinions. But appeals to human nature are not convincing to everyone. In some cases, they are so abstract that concrete deductions are impossible. Some will claim that it is natural to value human life above all, but without much difficulty find situations in which abortion or capital punishment are practically required. Similarly, it is one thing to support the abstract ideal of racial equality, but quite another to conclude that justice requires affirmative action to redress past inequalities.

At the opposite end, the notion of natural rights can be overly concrete, usually by being reduced to laws. The first legislators in the United States, following the philosophy of John Locke and the legal commentaries of William Blackstone, narrowly focused the meaning of natural rights on a right to own land—essentially a legal protection against trespass and government takeover. They seemed oblivious of the stark reality that the majority of U.S. citizens at that time, being female, enslaved, or aboriginal, would never own land. More recently, liberal social thought reduced the classical ideal of an objective "right and wrong" to practical, self-serving claims to social benefits and protections—now called "rights." No doubt, social welfare, international commerce, and suffrage are benefits indeed. And protections against invasion of privacy, libel, and coercion of religion are valuable for living well together. Still, we tend to justify specific laws and court decisions solely by an appeal to legal "rights," which most people understand as nothing more than entitlements protected by laws. This is a far cry from the classical notions of "right and wrong" that involve moral duties that are "natural" to the human spirit.

Today, liberal philosophers recognize several such natural rights—the right to life and bodily integrity, to political self-determination, to travel and migration, to association, to a fair wage and adequate working conditions, to freely choose one's state of life, to worship, and to free speech. Some regard these as no more than freedom to do what we please, without interference. But their historical sources regarded them as the conditions necessary for us to carry out what our nature requires. And our nature is a far cry from doing just what we please. Our nature is an exigence: we notice; we wonder; we discriminate between true and false, and between better and worse; we seek company in life's struggle. So the basic notion of "natural right" is a quest for the naturally right way to be, while the conditions we name "natural rights" are meant to facilitate this self-transcending quest.

Objectivity and Subjectivity

To understand objectivity and subjectivity in moral knowledge, we should first note there are two quite distinct modes of any knowing. In a commonsense mode, we want to know about things that relate to us personally, such as electing officials and getting along with neighbors. In a theoretical mode, we aim to know the relationships between things themselves, which we express in laws, correlations, and frequencies that under the same conditions hold anytime, anyplace. Because knowing occurs in these distinct modes, there are correspondingly distinct meanings of objectivity and subjectivity.[58] In the commonsense mode, objectivity concerns what is "out there" while subjectivity concerns what is "in here." In the theoretical mode, both objectivity and subjectivity concern a relationship between knowers and knowns within the universe of anything that can be known.

Images play an important role in understanding objectivity. Where the commonsense mode imagines the individual knower as standing over and against the known, the theoretical mode imagines all knowers as a subset of everything that could possibly be known. They are a subset because knowers can also know themselves knowing. From this image, there arises the question of the relationship between knowers and knowns within the field of everything knowable. So we may say that knowers and knowns are related through the exigences to be authentic—that is, through the knowers being attentive, intelligent, reasonable, and responsible. These are the subjective events by which humans notice salient aspects of experience, understand these aspects, verify that their understanding is probably or certainly valid, and appreciate the value of the realities in question. The resultant multi-leveled objectivity is the ongoing fruit of the authentic subjectivity in the set of humans who attend, understand, verify, and appreciate.

Accusations of "subjectivity" in moral judgments are essentially accusations of an *unauthentic* subjectivity, resulting from bias or willfulness.

Note that objectivity, the fruit of authentic subjectivity, is not some property inherent in objects. A property is a feature we abstract from the concreteness of realities, while existence and value are affirmations we make about realities in their concreteness. To reach objectivity in our affirmations is a subjective, ongoing, and collaborative process. To the degree that any ethical theory relies on logical deduction from abstract principles, objectivity is typically validated by how incontrovertible these abstract principles are and how rigorously they are applied. But in an ethics that relies also on creative inductions from concrete experience, particularly the experience of the exigences to self-transcendence, objectivity is a goal of a collaborative process that is approached asymptotically. Just as newer scientific theories replace the older to the extent that they provide more compelling explanations of data, so too, newer moral views replace the older to the extent that they provide more convincing assessments of historical outcomes. Here, moral objectivity is an ongoing, self-correcting process: We understand situations, assess their operative priorities, propose policies that feed the healthy roots and starve the unhealthy, implement these revised policies, and then, in the light that converted horizons shine on outcomes, we discard, revise, or confirm our moral judgments. In this fashion the cycle of moral experimentation continues toward objective moral truth.

Still, not all moral judgments are revisable. In the first place, there are the judgments of responsible subjects on the criteria for making moral judgments: It is unquestionably better to ask what is really better, to live in reality, to think, to notice. Then there is the set of moral judgments made throughout history that responsible women and men no longer question because the answers reached by their forebears keep on settling any questions that pop up: A human being is of higher value than an animal. Exploitation of humans for money or sex is wrong. Social orders that foster cooperation are better than those that foster isolation. As moral judgments like these become more unquestionable, the set of all unquestionable moral judgments grows. Indeed, this growth in moral objectivity is exactly the life and goal of the universal exigence to do better. And while it is the absence of relevant questions that secures objective judgments, the gains are maintained by the symbolizing exigence, as it focuses feelings to extol some acts and deplore others.

Praxis and Practicality

An ethics that is not practical is worthless. Practicality, in turn, occurs in humans—people who are universally prone to bias and willfulness and whose horizons may be closed in a variety of ways. Where these endemic wounds of our practicality affect our decisions, outcomes are at least short-sighted and commonly make matters worse.

The term *praxis*[59] was recently brought into philosophy by Karl Marx, who identified it with certain realizations about one's socio-economic situation and taking revolutionary action to improve it. This definition has been used by philosophers and theologians committed to the liberation of oppressed peoples. However, it was Aristotle who originally gave the term a definition based not on *what* one realizes but on *how*. He identified praxis with *conduct*, as opposed to *product*. This definition seems better than Marx's because it puts the focus directly on how we *conduct* our minds and hearts without assuming that the *product* must be some specific solution to a problem—such as communism, capitalism, feminism, or liberalism. For any political order, the concrete difference between progress and decline lies ultimately in how we *conduct* our minds and hearts.

To implement praxis in this sense, ethicists need to make the revolutionary turn to the methods of mind and heart. From an ethics already characterized by (1) universal moral standards and (2) experimental moral guidelines, praxis as conduct moves forward to (3a) the dialectics where minds and hearts are mutually exposed and (3b) the foundations that formulate basic ethical categories in terms of the operations of mind and heart.

Principles and People

A familiar use of "moral principle" means any expressed rule, like, "The punishment should fit the crime." However, when ethicists consider how moral principles should be used, disagreement arises. Some scorn them because principles are only abstract generalizations that do not easily apply in concrete situations. Disputes break out about the meaning of terms like "punishment" and "crime." Particular cases always require further moral judgments on the relative importance of mitigating factors, which generalizations necessarily omit.

Unimpressed by the value of moral principles, some ethicists focus on a thorough assessment of the concrete situation, followed by a choice motivated by genuine care. Others ethicists reject such situation-based ethics because even among people who genuinely care there are different intuitions about what should be done in particular situations. What is needed is a general principle that guides our intuitions about what really should be done. Moreover, history proves that formulated principles are good things. Because they represent wisdom gained by others who met threats to their well-being, to neglect them is to unknowingly expose oneself to the same threats. So we codify principles in our laws, appeal to them in our deliberations, and teach them to our children. For children in particular, and for adults whose moral intelligence has not matured, moral principles are firm anchors in a stormy sea.

A generalized empirical method links such principles to their origins in the methods innate to consciousness. It regards principles as concepts that survived the test of time. They are not really principles in the sense of *starting points*. That is, they are not the *source* of normative demands. The actual sources of normative demands are *people* being attentive, intelligent, reasonable, responsible and in love. Formulated *principles* are the products of people in historical situations, shaped by an ambiguous heritage, exposed to a dialectic of opinions, and directed by personal commitments within intellectual, moral and affective horizons. These horizons may complement each other; they may represent growth from earlier stages; or they may be dialectically opposed, as when people who mouth the same principles attach opposite meanings to them, or when people espouse the principle but act otherwise.

So in ethics we may distinguish *core* principles and *historical* principles. Core principles are men and women being authentic. Historical principles are formulated rules for living whose meanings are intrinsically related to their historical origins and to the emerging history in the situations at hand.

Moral principles proposed by religions are no exception. Generalized empirical method considers religious revelation as neither a delivery from the sky of inscribed tablets nor a dictation heard from unseen divinities. In the perspective of the data of consciousness, divine revelation is the historical occurrence of moral judgments in a holy person regarding known proposals, whether inscribed or spoken or imagined. Its religious sanction is based on this person's claim that the judgment is prompted by transcendent love from a transcendent source at the core of his or her heart.

Rights and Duties

David Hume, Ludwig Wittgenstein, J.L.Mackie, and Richard Rorty criticized the idea of natural human rights because they see it as indefensible by reason. In its place as a moral criterion, they point to an underlying sympathy for potentially injured parties. In contrast, a generalized empirical method looks to the intellectual, moral and affective contexts of our reason that identifies this or that expectation as a right.

We may ground the notion of rights in ethics in empirical consciousness by reflecting first on duties. The elemental meaning of duty is found in the originating set of "shoulds" in our normative drives to be attentive, intelligent, reasonable, responsible, and in love, plus the overriding inner demand for consistency between what we know, how we act, and our way of being ourselves. These "shoulds" not only produce all the norms expressed in written rules; they also issue far more commands and prohibitions than parents, police, and public policy ever could. It is this inner duty that enables us to break from a minor authenticity that obeys the written rule and to exercise a major authenticity that replaces illegitimate rules with legitimate alternatives.

At first glance, this view of morality may appear sympathetic to Kantian deontological theories that look to duty rather than consequences as the base of moral obligation. While it is true that all specific obligations may be traced to some sort of underlying duty, a generalized empirical method goes deeper than the typical "inner laws" in the style of Newtonian laws that characterize deontological theories; it rather anticipates the emergence of normative inspirations in the style of Darwinian evolutionary probability by identifying the dynamic, originating duty in every person to be authentic. By tracing the source of any maxims about duty to their historical origins, the possibility is left open that new historical circumstances may require new maxims.

As adults juggle their customary duties to social norms and their originating duty to be authentic, many discover that the best parts of these social norms arose from the authenticity of forebears. With this discovery comes the recognition of a present duty to *preserve* those portions of their heritage based on authenticity, to *critique* those portions based on bias, and to *create* the social and economic institutions that facilitate authenticity. Such preservation, critique, and creation of social norms are vital to the ongoing experiment of history. The success of the race, and of any particular peoples, depends on collaborative efforts to take charge of this experiment rather than becoming history's guinea pigs by ignoring this duty to one's heritage. Collaboration, in turn, requires authenticity of all collaborators.

This brings us to the actual context of rights. Any collaboration that successfully makes life more intelligible will require a freedom to speak one's mind, to gather with others, to maintain one's health, to travel, to participate in government, to worship, to be educated, and to work for a living. We call these *rights*. But while rights usually appear as one-way demands by one party upon others, their essential meaning is that they are expressions of the mutual demands intrinsic to any collaborative process aimed at improving life—a meaning derived from the nature of historical process itself.

So a right may be defined as *a mutual demand for authenticity*. I experience the exigence for authenticity in myself, and I assume others experience it in themselves. I have a duty to myself, and they have a duty to themselves. As each of us carries out our duties to be authentic, we both know and value such duties in each other. So your duty to respect my rights is, at its core, your duty to yourself. Any individual's claim in the name of rights is essentially a demand that others honor their duties to contribute to the experiment of improving a common heritage.

For example, Does society have a right to kill someone as punishment for a crime? Some say Yes and others say No. But let us rephrase the question: "Do the demands of being authentic persons require that we put this person to death?" Again, one might answer

Yes or No, but putting the question this way brings our own authenticity into the picture. The danger of a total prohibition such as "Society has no right to kill for reasons of punishment," is that it reads like an abstraction falling into the "bad" category. Certainly, blanket prohibitions are effective in passing on valuable history lessons to the young, but a defense of any prohibition will be more compelling when tied to the living authenticity of people rather than to abstract formulations that can seem like just social convention.

A similar analysis clarifies what occurs when rights-based claims seem to conflict. Conflicts of rights are often the ordinary conflicts involved in any compromise. More seriously, they may be differences between realms of moral reflection among a community's members. Minds focused strictly on action will think of rights as the behaviors and entitlements that lawmakers allow to citizens. Many will conclude that they have a right to do wrong. In contrast, minds aware of method will view lawmakers as responsible for protecting and promoting the liberty of citizens to live authentically. Thus, while the law lets every dog have a free bite, attention to method repudiates the conclusion that anyone has a right to do wrong.

Legislative bodies, in fact, do not grant rights. At best they protect the exercise of our demand for mutual authenticity by establishing certain sanctions by way of social rewards and punishments. So it would be inaccurate to say that the Soviet Union did not grant its citizens the right to free speech. The reality is that it prevented its citizens from fulfilling their duty to refine their heritage effectively through free speech.

Most discussions about rights stall when someone says that no right is absolute because every right is restricted by the rights of others. This view relies on the liberal imagination that sees rights as properties inherent in individuals. However, from the perspective of method, we can recover elements in the ancient notion of *natural right*[60] that include personal authenticity. There we find the elemental duties to care for one another and to build a harmonious society together.

So rights may be considered as historically conditioned means for authentic ends. As historically conditioned means, rights may take any number of legal and social forms. The historical expansion from civil rights (speech, assembly, suffrage) to social rights (work, education, health care), to group rights (women, homosexuals, ethnic groups) is evidence of the ongoing emergence of new kinds of claims on each other's duty to replenish a heritage. As oriented toward authentic ends, the validity of any rights claim depends on how well it enables authentic living, a question addressed through the mutual exposures that occur in the functional specialty *dialectic*. We may expect that ethicists familiar with a generalized empirical method would rely less on the language of rights and more on the language of dialog and encounter.

Stories and Moral Imagination

The ethical specialty *standards* identifies not only abstract moral principles but also those concrete, engaging stories that portray to moral imagination the struggle to do better. These stories may be legends, popularized histories, biographies, poems, operas, songs, dances. Every good story is about an effort to do better, following some circumstance considered worse. Characters appear with their priorities; their priorities conflict; there's trouble; someone's priorities will have to change. So we watch for some redemption from the trouble. In comedies, the redemption always comes, while in tragedies, the redemption is sought but not found.

What makes imagination moral is the way images evoke or represent our feelings about better and worse. It is our feelings that initially respond to possible values, and it is our feelings that finally confirm the values we embrace. And if we define "inner symbols" as compounds of images and feelings, then we may ask what fundamental inner symbols of trouble-redemption there may be that make up the total range of moral imagination. By identifying a limited set of these fundamental symbols, we will have a valuable tool for comparing different authors, different artists, and different cultures. What might these fundamental moral symbols be?

Consider these four:[61] Chaos-Order, Constraint-Freedom, Sterility-Fertility, and Alienation-Engagement. In each kind, there is trouble because priorities are threatened, and our innate exigence to do better seeks some sort of redemption. The "redemption" may be a recovery of a previous, healthier state or an improvement from a moderately healthy to a more healthy state.

Chaos-Order. The sun and seasons give us an elemental sense of order. It gives us as children a symbol of what it means to be faithful and dependable. Our political vision is dominated by the symbol of *Community* while our self-image is dominated by the symbol of *Integrity*. Moral living is the product of ordered hearts and minds. Be faithful to your duties and all shall be well. Trouble is *The Broken Routine*—lawbreaking, disorder, cross-purposes.

Constraint-Freedom. At some time in our growing up, when we discover that we took too many of our parents' constraints to heart, we wriggle to be free. Political imagination is dominated by the symbol of *Freedom* and *Individuality*. Self-images are dominated by the symbols of *Autonomy* and *Creativity*. Try new things! Be daring! Trouble is *The Crushed Creativity*—overregulation, warnings against change, mocking risk.

Sterility-Fertility. Everyone notices growth—in flowers, pets, children, towns, wisdom. Political imagination is dominated by the symbols of *Progress* and *Education*. Self-images are dominated by the symbol of *Self-Determination*. Your moral fertility is up to you. Take advantage of every resource at hand, and provide these resources for your children. Trouble is *The Bad Seed*—children taught to hate, chaotic public schools, unrepentant criminals.

Alienation-Engagement. Today, we are more keenly aware of how growing things are determined not only by origins or seeds but through a continual exchange with their environments. Political visions are dominated by the symbols of *Negotiation*, and *Win-Win*. Self-images are dominated by the symbol of *Engagement* with others and the *Existential Struggle* of living genuine lives. Trouble is *The Alienated Self*—social outcasts, hoarders, the compulsively suspicious and resentful.

These four symbols form a closed set. At any point in time, *any two events* may be related by some law (Chaos-Order); or they may emerge as mere coincidences under probabilities (Constraint-Freedom); or may be a combination of both. Moving forward in time, *any chain* of events may be a development pre-coded by certain drivers (Sterility-Fertility); or the chain may code itself as its several drivers are mutually changed in their interactions (Alienation-Engagement); or it may be a combination of both.

Still, from the perspective of an ethics rooted in historicity, the pair Alienation-Engagement holds a priority. Certainly, there are troubles related to breaking laws, to constraining what should be free, and about poisoning resources. But the lesson of history is that our main trouble is being alienated from our natural environments, from one another, from our own best possibilities, and, according to religious teachings, from our divine origin and destiny. We hoard our energy and exclude energy from others. We prefer being self-absorbed rather than self-transcending. It is only as a consequence of this radical and alienating hoarding that we break laws, impose crippling constraints, and sow weeds among the neighbor's wheat. The great preventable disasters of war and most famines can be understood as consequences of someone hoarding what they have—their money, their food, their information, particularly their kindness. The pattern should be evident that the process of moral progress is dialectical, and its source is mutual engagement. Unfortunately, the insight that better living lies in being open to the dialectics of mutual engagement is not as imaginable and compelling as insights into order, freedom, and fertility. While all four of these moral themes appear regularly, any story meant to promote any moral standards will be more incisive and compelling the more it conveys the dialectical engagements that lie in the hearts of persons and at the heart of history. When you consider any fiction or history that left a deep and lasting impression on you, the reason may well be that the author's imagination of better and worse aligns with the symbol of Alienation-Engagement.

Transcendent Value and Religion

Transcendent values are those that rank at the top of a hierarchy of values. Such a hierarchy is not an abstract ideal. Rather, it is a set of relationships between distinct types of values evident in human behavior. We may call these relationships "vertical," where, moving upward, each higher value makes the concrete realization of the one below it more likely.

> **Transcendent Values:**
>   Beauty, Order, Truth, Goodness, Love
> **Personal Values:**
>   Authenticity, Integrity, Self-Transcendence
> **Cultural Values:**
>   Moral Standards and Guidelines
> **Social Values:**
>   Cooperation, Organization, Efficiency
> **Vital Values:**
>   Health, Security, Survival

Thus, the social value of cooperation makes it easier for members of a community to ensure the vital values of their health, security, and survival. Then the cultural value of promoting common moral standards helps ensure that the social value of cooperation is directed to ends that actually improve a community's common life. Next, among those who contribute to cultural institutions, the personal value of being self-transcending provides the ground and justification for any standards of better and worse they propose to the community. Finally, transcendent values open the horizons of these individuals to beauty, order, truth, goodness and love without restriction.

Religion

It is the experience of the open-endedness of transcendent values that validates the question of God. Specifically, the experience of the desire to seek the ever better is grounds for asking, "From what source comes our open-ended desire for ultimates? Toward what destiny? And why?" The question may be suppressed, but it cannot be dismissed on any aesthetic, intelligent, reasonable, or responsible grounds. For these grounds are precisely our personally experienced evidence of exigences that prompt the question.

Those who affirm that there is a divine source and destiny to human striving usually seek to engage the divine with others in religious congregations. They worship together and share what they learn about living in religious love. They rely on their faith, the eye of their love, to reveal values that would be overlooked without that love. A religious engagement with the divine reveals an ultimate value of every human person insofar as he or she emerged from this same divine source and is called to the same divine destiny for the same divine purpose.

This recognition of the divine dimensions of every human life is the ground of any moral pronouncement that may be called "religious." It includes teachings on human reproduction, on war, on human rights, and on end-of-life issues. It also includes the edifying stories of communities and individuals named "holy." So any appeal to "religious values" to justify a moral opinion will be effective to the degree that it touches the experience of a common, open-ended desire to take our ultimate meaning seriously. In contrast, when religious authorities, using religious language, quoting religious standards, promote moral views without connecting them to human existential desires, their message seldom sinks into hearts thirsty for ultimates.

Dialectic

Obviously, anyone can defend a value by claiming divine authorization. But the history of such claims reminds us that justifications based on religion need to be carefully scrutinized. The values proposed by religious believers are no less in need of the ethical specialty *dialectic* than values proposed by anyone else.

One particularly important task is to bring to light the horizons of those who propose certain values as "religious," because different people of faith can understand their engagement with the divine in different ways. A fundamental difference depends on what differentiations of consciousness have occurred in a person. Those whose knowing is by an undifferentiated common sense, even when their dedication to divine reality is deep and passionate, will not grasp the issues of philosophical systems and historiography that concern ethicists. The consciousness of mystics is differentiated to engage the divine in silent and loving welcome while that of artists is differentiated in the direction of aesthetic expression. Again, theoreticians may understand religious dimensions of ethical systems, while historians and biographers may understand how religious sensibilities mature to a richness and how they wither and die. Finally, the consciousness of those familiar with method is differentiated to explore these very differences in method appropriate to each unique type of differentiation.

By bringing people's horizons to light, the specialty *dialectic* aims toward an explicit criticism of any view—religious or not—that violates the normative demands of consciousness. It also opens the perspectives of those with less differentiated consciousness to issues familiar to those with more differentiated consciousness. In this respect, *dialectic* invites religious believers with less differentiated consciousness into the realms of system, scholarship, aesthetics, mysticism, and method itself. Conversely, any ethics that excludes or omits the question effectively impedes collaboration between religious and secular voices.

God's Will

There is one important question that religious believers often pose: "How do I know God's will?" The specialty *foundations* can clarify the sort of answer believers can expect.

First, we should note that by expressing the question as knowing God's will usually masks the real concern of the person asking: "How can I *be sure* what God wants?" To understand what level of confidence a person may reasonably expect, the specialty *foundations* looks at what occurs when one seeks to "know" the will of God. Basically, what occurs is that a person is moved by transcendent love to see value in some option. He or she reaches, not a judgment of fact about the state of God's mind, but a judgment of value motivated by being in love with God. It is not like a boy knowing for certain that his mother wants him home on time for dinner. It is rather like a man who is convinced that his wife wants him to explore, with her, creative ways to help out a neighbor. No doubt, we will always hear claims that so-and-so has a message from God. Here, the specialty *dialectic* engages the messenger in a mutual exposure of horizons.

We also converse with ourselves about what God wills. A popular expression for this is "discerning God's will," which is unfortunate because it sets one up for resentment against God when God is silent. This approach may be based on a misunderstanding of Ignatius Loyola's highly influential "Rules for Discernment." There, the goal is not to discover the will of God. It is to identify, through an interior *dialectic*, which of several thoughts and feelings spring from the love of God and to allow that love to move one forward. When well-discerned, that transcendent love reveals values where reason and self-absorption are blind.

Value and Consciousness

In ethics, the meaning of *value* is derived from its relation both to responsible consciousness and to concrete reality. Specifically, a value is what a morally self-transcending person intends when assessing a concrete object of choice. The notion that a *true value* or an *objective value* must be somehow "out there" may be inspired by an admirable desire to resolve disagreements over moral standards, but it springs from a mistaken assumption that knowing a value is like looking at what is plain to see. But objectivity is not anything like seeing things "out there." By understanding what we do when we say X is better than Y, we realize that all things valuable are valued by responsible consciousness and that all *true values* are essentially lessons learned by people being responsible. In this respect, to propose this or that *value* as true can divert us from understanding what makes our *judgments of value* true, namely, responsible self-transcendence. The resolution of disagreements here belongs to the specialty *dialectic*, where a mutual exposure of horizons reveals questions that may prove relevant to changing one's value judgment.

Prior to asking any moral question, we experience an intimation about value. This intimation is not anything we make happen; it is our experience of the exigence of responsible consciousness to move toward the better and away from the worse in a concrete situation. It is a prior notion[62] of value that prompts questions of value. The exigence occurs and demands our attention. This intimation is carried by a feeling, where feelings are understood as initial responses to possible values. As experienced, it occurs prior to any formulated question of value to which it leads because it serves as the driver that raises the question. Also, these intimations of value occur prior to any concepts such as justice or rights, since concepts are products of insights, insights are into experience, and the intimation of value is an experience of an exigence.

As conscious anticipations of value in concrete reality, these prior intimations are highly conditioned by certain differentiations of consciousness[63] that may or may not have occurred in the person. Just as biological cells differentiate, making new kinds of organisms possible, so intelligent consciousness differentiates, making new kinds of questions possible. An initially undifferentiated common sense can differentiate into other realms of moral reflection. One can learn scientific theory, artistic expression, religious prayer, historical scholarship, and the philosophic interiority that grounds reflection on methods in human studies. Any individual may be more or less familiar with newly differentiated realms and more or less successful in distinguishing the methods proper to each. A child will not ask questions about theories; Aristotle asked no questions about historical process. So ethicists expect a pluralism in moral perspectives. But to successfully clarify the values inherent in any moral opinion and optimize mutual encounter of horizons, the more familiar they are with the full range of possible realms of moral reflection, the more likely a full encounter will occur.

Virtues and Values

It is easy to speak of virtues: We praise kindness, forgiveness, and patience. Ethicists explain how the virtues of understanding and compassion are essential to marriage, to parenting, to business, to civic awareness, to social participation, and so on. Yet these virtues do not easily translate into strategies, policies, plans, and action. A major reason for this is that virtues are neither languages that need only translation nor abstract concepts that give clear direction to people's lives. Virtues are always and everywhere actual habits in real people dealing with life. And no matter how long our list of virtues gets, it never captures all that is good about someone's life and person. Why? Because all values are originally incarnate. This is true of Abraham, Mohammed, Lincoln, and everyone else. It is true of *you*. If I say you are *fair-minded* and *kind-hearted*, I point to certain features that you share with others. These features are abstractions. I abstracted from what is concrete about you alone. There are no general words for what is special about you. What makes you unique is a wealth of *incarnate* values. You manifest "in the flesh" values never before seen, never before named.

This explains why an essential part of a community's moral heritage includes narratives. The adage among fiction writers is "Show. Don't Tell." For example, compare these two introductions to the same story:

> This is a story about a secure, gregarious, and healthy youth who turned into a poor, lonely old man.
>
> Jake reached into the V of his old red football sweater for a cigarette, waiting on the steps of his 3-floor walk-up for no one in particular.

The first tells; the second shows. The first is abstract, the second concrete. The first does not stir any questions in us while the second makes us wonder, "What's Jake feeling?" This is because incarnate values grab our moral attention. We see characters whose lives touch our sense of better and worse without our even thinking such abstract thoughts as, "This guy is lonely." And it is not only the saintly that touch us morally; even the scoundrels grab us by the *absence* of incarnate values.

Also, good stories grab different people differently. ("Honey, did you and I see the same movie?") Children are developmentally different from their parents. Men have a different perspective than women. Egotists see opportunities that openhearted people reject. It is for the sake of discussion that we use abstract words for virtues and vices to say things like "Javert is vengeful" and "Jean is courageous," but for the sake of convincing others of our opinion, we *describe* what these characters did.

Virtues we call "religious" are even more resistant to abstraction and more powerfully conveyed in concrete narratives. A good story opens even the non-religious to the mystery of values beyond human reckoning. Any atheist who lets a good story get into the heart cannot help but feel there is far, far more to life than words can capture. At the same time, good stories can point religious-minded people toward the *experience* of being always moved beyond themselves—a healthy reminder that the richer, original meanings of "holiness" or "wickedness" are not found in any dictionary but in the lives of people like Dorothy Day or Adolf Hitler.

In an ethics where progress depends on a mutual exposure of horizons, there will certainly be discussions about virtues. But the purpose of a mutual dialectic encounter is to expose *incarnate* values to one another. For whenever we see incarnate value—see with the eye of the heart—we want it. And to the extent that we pursue it, we become incarnate values ourselves—"in the flesh" invitations to moral greatness for all comers.

NOTES

In the usual fashion, these notes give you further sources on specific topics in this book. But to provide a list of key categories that Lonergan proposes, each note begins with the name of the topic it deals with. Some references are to works that, as of this writing, have already appeared in the *Collected Works of Bernard Lonergan*. In these, page numbers in parentheses will refer to pre-Collected Works editions.

To keep the notes uncluttered, here is the full bibliographical information on the works cited:

Insight: A Study of Human Understanding, The Collected Works of Bernard Lonergan, v. 3. Toronto: University of Toronto Press, 1997. It originally appeared in 1957 (London: Longmans, Green & Todd). Hereafter: *Insight.*

Collection. Montreal: Palm Publishers, 1967.

Method in Theology. New York: Herder & Herder, 1972.

A Second Collection. London: Darton, Longman & Todd. 1974.

A Third Collection. New York: Paulist Press. 1985.

Topics in Education. Collected Works v. 10. Toronto: University of Toronto Press, 1993. (Lectures Lonergan delivered in 1959 at Xavier University, Cincinnati)

For a New Political Economy. Collected Works v. 21. Toronto: University of Toronto Press, 1998.

Macroeconomic Dynamics: An Essay in Circulation Analysis. Collected Works v. 15. Toronto: University of Toronto Press, 1999.

Phenomenology and Logic: The Boston College Lectures on Mathematical Logic and Existentialism. Collected Works v. 8. Toronto: University of Toronto Press, 2001. (Lectures Lonergan delivered in 1957 at Boston College)

Philosophical and Theological Papers 1965-1980. Collected Works v. 17. Toronto: University of Toronto Press, 2004.

¹   **Human Studies.** Lonergan generally reserves "human studies" to scholarly studies (hermeneutics, history, etc.), relegating "human sciences" (psychology, anthropology, sociology, etc.) to an instrumental role in the study of humanity. (See *Method in Theology*, 212, 233-34; *Philosophical and Theological* the *Papers 1965-1980*, 370-72; *A Third Collection*, 63-65, 429.) In this work, "human studies" includes not only scholarly studies but also the human sciences, mainly because current works on "human studies" generally include human sciences, and at least some investigators in the human sciences incorporate meanings and values in their work.

²   **Generalized empirical method.** See "Generalized Empirical Method," sec. 5 of "Religious Knowledge" in *A Third Collection* (140-44). See also "Foundations," sec. 2 of "The Ongoing Genesis of Methods," also in *A Third Collection* (149-52).

³   **Realms of moral reflection.** These realms correspond in the field of morality to what Lonergan calls "realms of meaning" in the field of knowledge. See "Realms of Meaning" and "Pluralism in Expression," ch. 3, sec. 9 and ch. 11, sec. 3 in *Method in Theology* (81-85, 271-76).

⁴   **Stages of ethics.** These stages correspond in the field of morality to what Lonergan calls "stages of meaning" in the field of knowledge. See "Stages of Meaning," ch 3, sec. 10 in *Method in Theology* (85-99).

⁵   **Evolution.** Lonergan discusses the properties of an evolving world order under the term "emergent probability." See *Insight*, 144-61 (121-39).

⁶   **Duality of knowing.** See "Introduction" in *Insight*, 11 and 14-15 (xvii, xx-xxi), as well as "Bodies" 276-79 (250-54). The discovery of this duality in oneself is a *sine qua non* for understanding Lonergan's work on method. He refers to the "discovery—and one has not made it yet if one has no clear memory of its startling strangeness—that there are two quite different realisms." See "Introduction" in *Insight*, 22 (xxviii).

⁷   **Exigence, vertical finality.** I refer to the upward dynamic of world process as driven by "exigences." Lonergan deals with the same

dynamic under the category of "vertical finality." See the section
entitled "Vertical Finality" in "Finality, Love, Marriage," in *Collection*
(18-22). See also "Vertical Finality," sec. 1 in his "Mission and the
Spirit," *A Third Collection* (24). Lonergan's use of *finality* provides
continuity from Aristotelian-Thomist philosophy of ends to the
scientific view of evolution.

[8]   **Emergent probability.** Lonergan sets the notion of a vertical
finality within a framework of world design he names "emergent
probability." See *Insight*, 144-51 (121-28). The very idea that the universe
has an unfolding, upwardly-directed design is what prompted me to
select "exigence" as a category for tracing the emergence of specifically
moral patterns within the universal order.

[9]   **Sublation.** To denote how higher systems integrate otherwise
random elements in lower systems, Lonergan uses the term *sublation*.
This relationship between higher and lower systems appears across the
sciences, covering all orders of events, from the subatomic to the
humanly affective. For a basic treatment see the subhead "The Existential Subject," in "The Subject," in *A Second Collection* (79-84).

[10]   **Conscious.** For Lonergan's explanation of this definition of
"conscious," see "Introduction," sec. 1 of "Prolegomena to the Study of
the Emerging Religious Consciousness of Our Time" in *A Third
Collection* (55-60).

[11]   **Freely-formed images.** See *Understanding and Being*, vol. 5 of the
Collected Works, pages 313-15. For empirical evidence that for
experimental knowledge, apes are incapable of freely forming images
while humans are, Lonergan cites Wolfgang Kohler's classic work, *The
Mentality of Apes* (Penguin, 1925, 1957), originally appearing in German
in 1917.

[12]   **Symbol.** See "Symbols," ch. 3, sec. 4 in *Method in Theology* (64-69).

[13]   **Self-transcendence.** See "Self-Transcendence," sec. 1 of "Religious
Knowledge" in *A Third Collection* (131-34).

[14]   **Subject.** See "The Subject," *A Second Collection* (69-86). This article
explains the normative drives in the subject that ground the objectivity
of truth and of value.

¹⁵   **Norms of consciousness.** The notion that consciousness has norms appears throughout Lonergan's works. For example, see "Generalized Empirical Method," sec. 5 of "Religious Knowledge" in *A Third Collection* (140-45). I have devised these exercises to help my students discover these norms. I take the idea of exercises from Lonergan's invitation to his readers of *Insight* to notice what happens when they wonder, think, reflect, and come to know.

¹⁶   **Belief.** For material on belief as the source of most of our knowledge see "Beliefs," ch. 2, sec. 5 in *Method in Theology* (41-47). See also "Belief: Today's Issue" in *A Second Collection* (87-99).

¹⁷   **Affective movement.** See "Healing and Creating in History" in *A Third Collection* (100-09), and "The Dialectic of History," sec. 3 of "Natural Right and Historical Mindedness," also in *A Third Collection* (176-82).

¹⁸   **Authenticity.** This theme may be found throughout Lonergan's post-*Insight* works. A summary treatment may be found in "Self-Transcendence," ch. 4, sec. 2 in *Method in Theology* (104-05).

¹⁹   **Conscience.** For the methodological context of a definition of conscience, see "Foundational Reality," ch. 11, sec. 1 in *Method in Theology* (267-69).

²⁰   **The known known.** Lonergan discusses three parcels in the context of a person's horizon: the (1) known known, (2) known unknown, and (3) unknown unknown. See "Horizon," ch. 4, sec. 2.2 in *Topics in Education*, 88-91.

²¹   **Bias and scotoma.** The analogy between an intellectual bias and a physical blind spot is developed at length in "Dramatic Bias," ch. 6, sec. 2.7 in *Insight*, 214-27 (191-203). While Lonergan restricts the metaphor of a *scotoma* to the dramatic bias, where *repression* of images occurs without our realizing it, I expand the metaphor to include the deliberate *suppression* of questions that occurs in egotism, loyalism, and commonsensism.

²²   **Biases.** Material on four biases appear throughout Lonergan's works. A comprehensive presentation can be found in "Dramatic Bias,"

ch. 6, sec. 2.7, in "Individual Bias," "Group Bias," and in "General Bias," ch. 7, secs. 6-8 in *Insight*, 214-27, 244-57 (191-203, 218-28). In later works, he refers to them variously as (1) "the neurotic," (2) "the individual egotist," (3) "group egoism," and (4) "the overconfident shortsightedness of common sense." See "Healing and Creating in History," and "Mission and the Spirit," in *A Third Collection*, (100-09, 23-34). For brevity, I have named them neurosis, egotism, loyalism, and commonsensism, respectively. Lonergan identifies these as an illustration of how fruitful insight into insight can be, presumably leaving open the field to identifying further blind spots.

[23] **Evil.** Lonergan treats this under three headings: basic sin, moral evils, and physical evils. See "The Notion of God," ch. 19, sec. 9 in *Insight*, 689-92 (657-79). Basic sin corresponds to what I refer to as "acting against our better judgment," "willfulness," or "sin," depending on the context. Moral evils correspond to the distortions of situations that result from this basic sin. Physical evils correspond to the shortcomings inherent in a world that is evolving, in the sense that even such "evils" demand responsible action to overcome them through promoting development, as far as possible. See also Lonergan's discussion of typical escapes from moral responsibility (avoiding self-consciousness, rationalization, and moral renunciation) in "The Notion of Will," ch. 18, sec. 1.2 in *Insight*, 622-24 (598-600).

[24] **Progress, decline, redemption.** This procedure of successively treating the creative, wounded, and healing factors in morality relies on the method of successive approximations. Lonergan treats essentially the same issues under the headings of "progress, decline, and redemption." See "Progress and Decline" and "Faith," ch. 2, sec. 7, and ch. 3, sec. 7 in *Method in Theology* (52-55, 115-18). For a summary treatment, see "The People of God in the World of Today," sec. 4 of "The Transition from a Classicist World-View to Historical-Mindedness" in *A Second Collection* (1-9, at 7-8).

[25] **Healing and creating.** See "Healing and Creating in History" in *A Third Collection* (100-09). See also "The Dialectic of History," sec. 3 of "Natural Right and Historical Mindedness," also in *A Third Collection* (176-82). I have used the term "doing better" as the outcome of these two movements in the perspective of ethics.

²⁶ **Openness.** Material on openness in a religious context may be found in "Openness and Religious Experience" in *Collection* (198-201). I use the term to refer also to the fuller context of intellectual, moral, and affective self-transcendence. Material on this fuller context may be found under the terms horizon and conversion (in the following note).

²⁷ **Horizon and conversion.** See "Horizons" and "Conversions and Breakdowns," ch. 10, secs. 1-2 in *Method in Theology* (235-44).

²⁸ **Religious/affective conversion.** Lonergan generally uses *religious* conversion to discuss theological issues and *affective* conversion to discuss philosophical issues. While religious conversion has the divine as an explicit reality, an affective conversion opens onto the divine by recognizing at least the question of God and includes the love of human friendships and loyalties. For religious conversion, see "Conversions and Breakdowns," ch. 10, sec. 2 in *Method in Theology* (237-44). For affective conversion, see "The Dialectic of History," sec. 3 of "Natural Right and Historical Mindedness" in *A Third Collection* (176-82). For the present discussion of ethics and morality I use the term affective conversion to engage ethicists of any or no explicit religious commitments.

²⁹ **Learning, choosing, loving.** For a thorough and compendious treatment of learning, choosing, and loving, see "Meaning," "The Human Good," and "Religion," chs. 3, 2, and 4, respectively, of *Method in Theology* (57-99, 27-55, 101-24).

³⁰ **Absence of relevant questions, virtually unconditioned.** This criterion for judgment may be found in "The Transformation of the Notion of Science: From the Certain to the Probable: Science, Judgment, and Wisdom," ch. 6, sec 2.1 in *Topics in Education*, pp 146-53. See also "A Clarification," ch. 7, sec. 7, and "Critical History" of ch. 8, sec. 3 in *Method in Theology* (165-67, 185-96). The absence of relevant questions is the experiential equivalent to Lonergan's more formal designation of this criterion as a "virtually unconditioned." See "The General Form of Reflective Insight," *Insight*, 305-06 (280-81), *et passim*.

---

[31] **Intellectual conversion.** See "Pluralism and Conversion," sec. 3 of "Unity and Plurality" in *A Third Collection* (247-49) and "Conversions and Breakdowns" in *Method in Theology* (237-40).

[32] **Realms of meaning.** See "Realms of Meaning," ch. 3, sec. 9 in *Method in Theology* (81-85).

[33] **Choices.** Materials on three kinds of choices as corresponding to the three analogous meanings of "good" are found throughout Lonergan's works. See "The Structure of the Human Good," ch. 2, sec. 6 in *Method in Theology* (47-52).

[34] **Feelings, value judgments.** Material on feelings and other elements that enter into judgments of value can be found in "Feelings" and "Judgments of Value," of ch. 2, secs. 2 and 4 in *Method in Theology* (30-34, 36-41).

[35] **Criteria for value judgments.** See "The Notion of Value" and "Judgments of Value," of ch. 2, secs. 3-4 in *Method in Theology* (34-41) and "What Are Judgments of Value" in *Philosophical and Theological Papers, 1965-1980,* 140-56. Formally, the criterion for a judgment of value is the same as for a judgment of fact or of reasonableness: the fulfillment of conditions on a proposition, or more succinctly, a virtually unconditioned. With both kinds of judgments we experience an absence of relevant questions. Still, on the level of judgments of value, the question of my own self-transcendence is far more prominently relevant because of the enlarged engagement of my entire self, an engagement that always occurs in the context of my affective horizon.

[36] **Mere preference.** Lonergan defines moral conversion as a change in the criterion of one's decisions and choices from satisfactions to values. See "Conversions and Breakdowns" ch. 10, sec. 2 of *Method in Theology* (p. 240). The term *satisfaction* can cause some confusion because there is satisfaction in becoming self-transcendent. So I suggest that "mere preference" gives a more accurate contrast to self-transcendence.

[37] **Ethics of Law, Ethics of Achievement.** Here, in line with an ethics of change (the theme of "doing better"), I have renamed what

Lonergan called an "Ethics of Achievement" as an "Ethics of Better." See *Topics in Education*, pp. 103, 106.

[38] **Question of God.** Material on experiencing the question of God may be found in "The Question of God," ch. 4, sec. 1 in *Method in Theology* (101-03) and in *Philosophical and Theological Papers 1965-1980*, pp. 205-08.

[39] **Existential ethics.** For Lonergan's overall description of how the conversions unfold into the multiple elements of an explicit existential ethics, see "Foundational Reality," ch. 11, sec. 1 in *Method in Theology* (267-69). See also "Philosophic Significance of the Theme [on 'being oneself']," ch. 10, sec. 7 in *Phenomenology and Logic*, 242-46. See also "Questionnaire on Philosophy, Response" in *Philosophical and Theological Papers, 1965-1980*, 357-59. There he lists "existential ethics" as a fourth step following upon cognitional theory, epistemology, and metaphysics. This step is founded on the discovery that we are responsible for the life we lead. It becomes established when we live in love. It becomes transformed when God's own love floods our hearts, a love without limits. It becomes thematized as a concern of a theology which can encompass the whole of human living only by "broadening its horizon by uniting itself with philosophy as the basic and total science" (359).

[40] **Mutual exposure of horizons.** This material is based on Lonergan's discussion of the theological specialty, *dialectic*. The strategy, Lonergan proposes, is neither to prove one's position nor refute the other's but rather "...to exhibit diversity and to point to the evidence for its roots. In this manner he will be attractive to those that appreciate full human authenticity and he will convince those that attain it. Indeed, the basic idea of the method we are trying to develop takes its stand on discovering what human authenticity is and showing how to appeal to it. It is not an infallible method, for men easily are unauthentic, but it is a powerful method, for man's deepest need and most prized achievement is authenticity." See "The Dialectic of Methods: Part One," ch. 10, sec. 7 in *Method in Theology* (253-57).

[41] **Method.** See "Method," ch. 1 in *Method in Theology* (3-25). It is essential to note that the "method" is not a recipe proposed by Lonergan. Rather it constitutes the innate methods of mind and heart

that Lonergan asks his readers to verify, adding, "...we cannot succeed without an exceptional amount of exertion and activity on the part of the reader" (7).

[42] **Second enlightenment.** See "The Second Enlightenment," sec. 3 of "Emerging Religious Consciousness of Our Time" in *A Third Collection* (63-65). Lonergan relies on Frederick Lawrence for this term.

[43] **Good as concrete history.** This view (as opposed to "good" as an abstract quality) is found throughout Lonergan's works. See the section, "The Existential Subject" of "The Subject" in *A Second Collection* (79-84). See also "The General Notion of the Human Good," Ch. 2, section 9 of *Topics in Education* (32-33).

[44] **Integral heuristic structure.** This corresponds to Lonergan's definition of metaphysics as "the conception, affirmation, and implementation of the integral heuristic structure of proportionate being" See *Insight* 416 (391).

[45] **Historical mindedness and human nature.** See "The Transition from a Classicist World-View to Historical-Mindedness" in *A Second Collection* (1-9). Also, "Natural Right and Historical Mindedness," ch. 11 in *A Third Collection* (169-83).

[46] **Hierarchy/scale of values.** See *Insight*, 624-25 (601-02). See also the material on scales of preference in "The Structure of the Human Good," ch. 2, sec. 6 and "Verstehen," ch. 9, sec. 4 in *Method in Theology* (47-52, 208-14). Material on the development of values and a corresponding reorientation of feelings along this scale from self-regarding to self-transcending may be found in "Natural Right in Historicity," sec. 2 of "Natural Right and Historical Mindedness" in *A Third Collection* (171-75).

[47] **Consistency** among the norms of consciousness. See *Insight*, 623 (600).

[48] **Structure of the human good.** See "The Structure of the Human Good," ch. 2, sec. 6 in *Method in Theology* (47-52).

[49] **Dialectic.** Materials on dialectic appear throughout Lonergan's works. Definitions may be found in *Insight*, 242-44, 268-69, 446-48

(217-18, 243-44, 421-23). For material on dialectic as one of four heuristic anticipations of scientific method (with classical, statistical, and genetic) see *Insight*, 507-11, 766-68 (483-87, 745-47). Applications of the notion may be found in "Dialectic," sec. 4 of "The Ongoing Genesis of Methods," and in "The Dialectic of History," sec. 3 of "Natural Right and Historical Mindedness," in *A Third Collection* (176-82).

[50]   **Dialectical Analysis.** Lonergan warns about the difficulty of an inquiry into the dialectics of authority in concrete situations, calling the effort "complex, lengthy, tedious, and often inconclusive." In its place he proposes a "synthetic" or integrated view that simultaneously incorporates elements for progress, elements for decline, and elements for redemption. See "Dialectic of Authority," in *A Third Collection* (at pages 8-10).

[51]   **Alienation and ideology.** Lonergan uses "alienation" to refer to unauthenticity, or the refusal of self-transcendence. He uses "ideology" to refer to the intellectual justifications of this alienation. See "Progress and Decline," ch. 2, sec. 7 (and the index) in *Method in Theology* (52-55). In a later work (1977-78), Lonergan identifies a socio-cultural "alienation" that occurs between persons at earlier and later expansions of horizons: from commonsense, to theoretical, to method. The alienation affects both our social systems and the cultural systems that justify and critique specific social systems. In proposals for social systems, the earlier find the later incomprehensible while the later find the earlier simplistic. Among cultural initiatives, the earlier feel little appreciation for the creations of the later, while the later regard the creations of the earlier as crude. See "Philosophy and the Religious Phenomenon," in *Philosophical and Theological Papers, 1965-1980*, 391-08, particularly 404-08.

[52]   **Hermeneutics of suspicion and recovery.** See "Dialectic," sec. 4 of "The Ongoing Genesis of Methods" in *A Third Collection* (155-59). Lonergan relies on Paul Ricoeur for these terms.

[53]   **Double process of historical investigation.** See "Critical History," ch. 8, sec. 3 in *Method in Theology* (185-96).

[54]   **Categories.** See "Categories," ch. 11 sec. 5 in *Method in Theology* (281-85).

[55] **Functional specialties.** This material is drawn from the entire work, *Method in Theology*. An overview is presented in ch. 5 (125-45). While Lonergan's focus is on theology, some brief material on how the scope of his discussion covers all human studies can be found in "Society, State, Church" and "The Christian Church and its Contemporary Situation," ch. 14, secs. 3 and 4 in *Method in Theology* (358-67).

[56] **Positions and counterpositions.** Lonergan uses these terms to discuss how amplification and assessments result in developing statements compatible with conversion (which he calls "positions") and reversing statements that are not compatible ("counterpositions"). I have amplified this discussion by clarifying that it is not just positions and counterpositions as statements that are "developed" or "reversed." It is horizons. And not just intellectual horizons, but moral and affective horizons as well. In other words, the specialty *dialectic* is, as far as possible, a mutual enlargement of one's whole person. See "Dialectic: The Structure," ch. 10 sec. 5, "The Sufficiency of the Foundational Reality," ch. 11 sec. 2, and "Mystery and Problem," ch. 13 sec. 4, in *Method in Theology* (249-50, 269-71, 344-47).

[57] **Macroeconomics.** For Lonergan's early but clear introduction to the basic issues and the model he proposes, see *For A New Political Economy*, pp. 3-75. For an overview of the macroeconomic issues in general and Lonergan's proposed solutions, see, in *Macroeconomic Dynamics: An Essay in Circulation Analysis*, the "Editors' Introduction" by Frederick G. Lawrence, pp. xxv-lxxii. Lonergan's later and more complete analysis appears in Part One. Part Two, "Healing and Creating in History" gives the wider moral and religious context. Part Three gives earlier texts that provide more detail and more mathematical analyses.

[58] **Objectivity.** For Lonergan's compendious treatment of cognitive objectivity, see "The Notion of Objectivity," ch. 13 of *Insight*. For his treatment in the context of specific questions, see "Generalized Empirical Method," sec. 5 of "Religious Knowledge" and "Differentiations of Consciousness," sec. 1 of "Unity and Plurality: The Coherence of Christian Truth," both in *A Third Collection* (140-44, 239-43).

[59] **Praxis.** Lonergan describes the effort to reveal the level of personal development in investigators as a *praxis.* Where *practice* refers to what is done or produced, *praxis* refers to the doing and producing. Praxis employs a hermeneutic of suspicion regarding the horizons of investigators and a hermeneutic of recovery that acknowledges where genuine personal development occurred. His definition of *praxis* is aimed to give it explanatory status, as opposed to post-Marxist liberation philosophies which, he holds, do not sufficiently attend to the horizons of individuals. See "Theology and Praxis," and "Praxis," sec. 5 of "The Ongoing Genesis of Method," both in *A Third Collection* (184-201, 159-61).

[60] **Natural Right.** See "Natural Right and Historical Mindedness," ch. 11 in *A Third Collection* (169-83).

[61] **Fourfold battery of methods.** This analysis of four basic kinds of trouble is based on Lonergan's analysis of four basic methods of science—classical, statistical, genetic, and dialectical. As each method relies on a unique sort of insight, and insights are always into images, we can anticipate four basic images. See *Insight* pp. 630, 57-58, 76-81, 476-504, 242-44, 718-25 (607, 33-46, 53-69, 451-79, 217-18, and 696-703)—particularly in this order.

[62] **Notion of Value.** See "The Notion of Value," sec. 3, ch. 2 in *Method in Theology* (34-36). I prefer the term "intimation" because "notion" is too easily identified with "idea" or "concept," while Lonergan's meaning is the prior drive toward knowledge or values. He acknowledges that his own use is not uniformly technical. See "The Notion of Value," in *Philosophical and Theological Papers 1965-1980,* p. 337.

[63] **Differentiations of consciousness.** See "Pluralism in Expression," and "Pluralism in Religious Language," secs. 3 and 4 of ch. 11 in *Method in Theology* (271-81).

INDEX